GACE
ENGLISH 020, 021

By: Sharon Wynne, M.S.

XAMonline, INC.
Boston

To obtain permission(s) to use the material from this work for any purpose including workshops or seminars, please submit a written request to:

XAMonline, Inc.
25 First Street, Suite 106
Cambridge, MA 02141
Toll Free 1-800-509-4128
Email: info@xamonline.com
Web: www.xamonline.com
Fax: 1-617-583-5552

Library of Congress Cataloging-in-Publication Data

Wynne, Sharon A.
    GACE English 020, 021 / Sharon A. Wynne. 3rd ed
    ISBN 978-1-60787-062-3
    1. English 020,021
    2. Study Guides
    3. GACE
    4. Teachers' Certification & Licensure
    5. Careers

Disclaimer:

Printed in the United States of America   œ-1

GACE English 020, 021
ISBN: 978-1-60787-062-3

Table of Contents

DOMAIN II
READING SKILLS AND STRATEGIES

COMPETENCY 6
UNDERSTAND STRATEGIES FOR THE COMPREHENSION AND INTERPRETATION OF TEXTS

COMPETENCY 7
UNDERSTAND STRATEGIES FOR THE CRITICAL ANALYSIS AND EVALUATION OF TEXTS

COMPETENCY 8
UNDERSTAND SKILLS FOR EFFECTIVE READING ACROSS THE CURRICULUM

DOMAIN III
WRITING CONVENTIONS AND THE WRITING PROCESS 139

DOMAIN IV

COMPETENCY 12

COMPETENCY 13

COMPETENCY 14

COMPETENCY 15

DOMAIN V
ORAL AND VISUAL COMMUNICATIONS 265

COMPETENCY 16
UNDERSTAND PRINCIPLES AND TECHNIQUES FOR PREPARING AND DELIVERING ORAL AND VISUAL COMMUNICATION.. 267

COMPETENCY 17
UNDERSTAND TECHNIQUES FOR THE CRITICAL ANALYSIS OF ORAL AND VISUAL MESSAGES DELIVERED THROUGH VARIOUS MEDIA.. 280

SAMPLE TEST

GACE
ENGLISH 020, 021

SECTION 1
ABOUT XAMONLINE

XAMonline—A Specialty Teacher Certification Company

Created in 1996, XAMonline was the first company to publish study guides for state-specific teacher certification examinations. Founder Sharon Wynne found it frustrating that materials were not available for teacher certification preparation and decided to create the first single, state-specific guide. XAMonline has grown into a company of over 1800 contributors and writers and offers over 300 titles for the entire PRAXIS series and every state examination. No matter what state you plan on teaching in, XAMonline has a unique teacher certification study guide just for you.

XAMonline—Value and Innovation

We are committed to providing value and innovation. Our print-on-demand technology allows us to be the first in the market to reflect changes in test standards and user feedback as they occur. Our guides are written by experienced teachers who are experts in their fields. And, our content reflects the highest standards of quality. Comprehensive practice tests with varied levels of rigor means that your study experience will closely match the actual in-test experience.

To date, XAMonline has helped nearly 600,000 teachers pass their certification or licensing exams. Our commitment to preparation exceeds simply providing the proper material for study—it extends to helping teachers **gain mastery** of the subject matter, giving them the **tools** to become the most effective classroom leaders possible, and ushering today's students toward a **successful future.**

SECTION 2
ABOUT THIS STUDY GUIDE

Purpose of this Guide

Is there a little voice inside of you saying, "Am I ready?" Our goal is to replace that little voice and remove all doubt with a new voice that says, "I AM READY. **Bring it on!**" by offering the highest quality of teacher certification study guides.

Organization of Content

You will see that while every test may start with overlapping general topics, each are very unique in the skills they wish to test. Only XAMonline presents custom content that analyzes deeper than a title, a subarea, or an objective. Only XAMonline presents content and sample test assessments along with **focus statements**, the deepest-level rationale and interpretation of the skills that are unique to the exam.

Title and field number of test

→Each exam has its own name and number. XAMonline's guides are written to give you the content you need to know for the <u>specific</u> exam you are taking. You can be confident when you buy our guide that it contains the information you need to study for the specific test you are taking.

Subareas

→These are the major content categories found on the exam. XAMonline's guides are written to cover all of the subareas found in the test frameworks developed for the exam.

Objectives

→These are standards that are unique to the exam and represent the main subcategories of the subareas/content categories. XAMonline's guides are written to address every specific objective required to pass the exam.

Focus statements

→These are examples and interpretations of the objectives. You find them in parenthesis directly following the objective. They provide detailed examples of the range, type, and level of content that appear on the test questions. **Only XAMonline's guides drill down to this level.**

How Do We Compare with Our Competitors?

XAMonline—drills down to the focus statement level.
CliffsNotes and REA—organized at the objective level
Kaplan—provides only links to content
MoMedia—content not specific to the state test

Each subarea is divided into manageable sections that cover the specific skill areas. Explanations are easy to understand and thorough. You'll find that every test answer contains a rejoinder so if you need a refresher or further review after taking the test, you'll know exactly to which section you must return.

How to Use This Book

Our informal polls show that most people begin studying up to eight weeks prior to the test date, so start early. Then ask yourself some questions: How much do you really know? Are you coming to the test straight from your teacher-education program or are you having to review subjects you haven't considered in ten years? Either way, take a **diagnostic or assessment test** first. Also, spend time on sample tests so that you become accustomed to the way the actual test will appear.

This guide comes with an online diagnostic test of 30 questions found online at *www.XAMonline.com*. It is a little boot camp to get you up for the task and reveal things about your compendium of knowledge in general. Although this guide is structured to follow the order of the test, you are not required to study in that order. By finding a time-management and study plan that fits your life you will be more effective. The results of your diagnostic or self-assessment test can be a guide for how to manage your time and point you toward an area that needs more attention.

After taking the diagnostic exam, fill out the **Personalized Study Plan** page at the beginning of each chapter. Review the competencies and skills covered in that chapter and check the boxes that apply to your study needs. If there are sections you already know you can skip, check the "skip it" box. Taking this step will give you a study plan for each chapter.

Week	Activity
8 weeks prior to test	Take a diagnostic test found at www.XAMonline.com
7 weeks prior to test	Build your Personalized Study Plan for each chapter. Check the "skip it" box for sections you feel you are already strong in. ✗ SKIP IT ☐
6-3 weeks prior to test	For each of these four weeks, choose a content area to study. You don't have to go in the order of the book. It may be that you start with the content that needs the most review. Alternately, you may want to ease yourself into plan by starting with the most familiar material.
2 weeks prior to test	Take the sample test, score it, and create a review plan for the final week before the test.
1 week prior to test	Following your plan (which will likely be aligned with the areas that need the most review) go back and study the sections that align with the questions you may have gotten wrong. Then go back and study the sections related to the questions you answered correctly. If need be, create flashcards and drill yourself on any area that makes you anxious.

SECTION 3
ABOUT THE GACE EXAMS

What Is GACE?

GACE (Georgia Assessments for the Certification of Educators) tests measure the knowledge of specific content areas in K-12 education. The tests are a way of insuring that educators are prepared to not only teach in a particular subject area, but also have the necessary teaching skills to be effective. The Evaluation Systems group of Pearson Education, Inc. administers the tests and has worked with the Georgia Professional Standards Commission to develop the material so that it is appropriate for Georgia standards.

The most reliable source of information regarding GACE tests is either the Georgia state Department of Education or *www.gace.nesinc.com*. Either resource should also have a complete list of testing centers and dates. Test dates vary by subject area and not all test dates necessarily include your particular test, so be sure to check carefully.

If you are in a teacher-education program, check with the Education Department or the Certification Officer for specific information for testing and testing time-lines. The Certification Office should have most of the information you need.

If you choose an alternative route to certification you can either rely on our website at *www.XAMonline.com* or on the resources provided by an alternative certification program. Many states now have specific agencies devoted to alternative certification and there are some national organizations as well:

National Center for Education Information

http://www.ncei.com/Alt-Teacher-Cert.htm

National Associate for Alternative Certification

http://www.alt-teachercert.org/index.asp

Interpreting Test Results

The results of all GACE tests are reported as scaled scores rather than raw scores. The number of scorable questions that are answered correctly in the selected-response section are combined with the scores from the constructed-response section and the total is converted to a scale of 100-300 with 220 representing a passing score. Follow the guidelines provided by Pearson for interpreting your score.

What's on the Test?

GACE tests vary from subject to subject and sometimes even within subject area. For GACE English (020, 021), the assessment consists of two tests with a combined total of approximately 120 multiple-choice questions and 4 constructed-response questions. The breakdown of the questions is as follows:

Category	Approximate Number of Selected-Response Questions	Approximate Number of Constructed-Response Questions
020:		
I: Comprehension of Literary and Informational Texts	38	1
II: Reading Skills and Strategies	22	1
021:		
III: Writing Conventions and the Writing Process	20	1
IV: Writing for Various Purposes	27	1
V: Oral and Visual Communications	13	0

Question Types

You're probably thinking, enough already, I want to study! Indulge us a little longer while we explain that there is actually more than one type of multiple-choice question. You can thank us later after you realize how well prepared you are for your exam.

1. Complete the Statement. The name says it all. In this question type you'll be asked to choose the correct completion of a given statement. For example:

> The Dolch Basic Sight Words consist of a relatively short list of words that children should be able to:
>
> A. Sound out
>
> B. Know the meaning of
>
> C. Recognize on sight
>
> D. Use in a sentence

The correct answer is A. In order to check your answer, test out the statement by adding the choices to the end of it.

2. **Which of the Following.** One way to test your answer choice for this type of question is to replace the phrase "which of the following" with your selection. Use this example:

> **Which of the following words is one of the twelve most frequently used in children's reading texts:**
>
> A. There
>
> B. This
>
> C. The
>
> D. An

Don't look! Test your answer. _____ is one of the twelve most frequently used in children's reading texts. Did you guess C? Then you guessed correctly.

3. **Roman Numeral Choices.** This question type is used when there is more than one possible correct answer. For example:

> **Which of the following two arguments accurately supports the use of cooperative learning as an effective method of instruction?**
> I.   Cooperative learning groups facilitate healthy competition between individuals in the group.
> II.   Cooperative learning groups allow academic achievers to carry or cover for academic underachievers.
> III. Cooperative learning groups make each student in the group accountable for the success of the group.
> IV.   Cooperative learning groups make it possible for students to reward other group members for achieving.
>
> A. I and II
>
> B. II and III
>
> C. I and III
>
> D. III and IV

Notice that the question states there are **two** possible answers. It's best to read all the possibilities first before looking at the answer choices. In this case, the correct answer is D.

4. Negative Questions. This type of question contains words such as "not," "least," and "except." Each correct answer will be the statement that does **not** fit the situation described in the question. Such as:

> **Multicultural education is not**
>
> A. An idea or concept
>
> B. A "tack-on" to the school curriculum
>
> C. An educational reform movement
>
> D. A process

Think to yourself that the statement could be anything but the correct answer. This question form is more open to interpretation than other types, so read carefully and don't forget that you're answering a negative statement.

5. Questions that Include Graphs, Tables, or Reading Passages. As always, read the question carefully. It likely asks for a very specific answer and not a broad interpretation of the visual. Here is a simple (though not statistically accurate) example of a graph question:

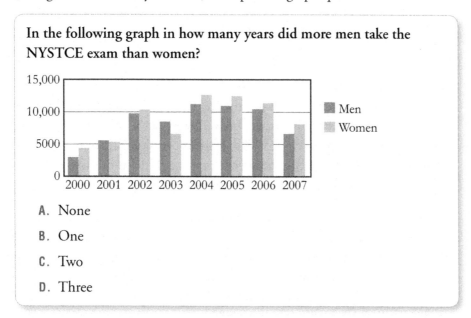

> **In the following graph in how many years did more men take the NYSTCE exam than women?**
>
> A. None
>
> B. One
>
> C. Two
>
> D. Three

It may help you to simply circle the two years that answer the question. Make sure you've read the question thoroughly and once you've made your determination, double check your work. The correct answer is C.

SECTION 4
HELPFUL HINTS

Study Tips

1. You are what you eat. Certain foods aid the learning process by releasing natural memory enhancers called CCKs (cholecystokinin) composed of tryptophan, choline, and phenylalanine. All of these chemicals enhance the neurotransmitters associated with memory and certain foods release memory enhancing chemicals. A light meal or snacks of one of the following foods fall into this category:

   - Milk
   - Rice
   - Eggs
   - Fish
   - Nuts and seeds
   - Oats
   - Turkey

   The better the connections, the more you comprehend!

2. See the forest for the trees. In other words, get the concept before you look at the details. One way to do this is to take notes as you read, paraphrasing or summarizing in your own words. Putting the concept in terms that are comfortable and familiar may increase retention.

3. Question authority. Ask why, why, why? Pull apart written material paragraph by paragraph and don't forget the captions under the illustrations. For example, if a heading reads *Stream Erosion* put it in the form of a question (Why do streams erode? What is stream erosion?) then find the answer within the material. If you train your mind to think in this manner you will learn more and prepare yourself for answering test questions.

4. Play mind games. Using your brain for reading or puzzles keeps it flexible. Even with a limited amount of time your brain can take in data (much like a computer) and store it for later use. In ten minutes you can: read two paragraphs (at least), quiz yourself with flash cards, or review notes. Even if you don't fully understand something on the first pass, your mind stores it for recall, which is why frequent reading or review increases chances of retention and comprehension.

5. **The pen is mightier than the sword.** Learn to take great notes. A by-product of our modern culture is that we have grown accustomed to getting our information in short doses. We've subconsciously trained ourselves to assimilate information into neat little packages. Messy notes fragment the flow of information. Your notes can be much clearer with proper formatting. ***The Cornell Method*** is one such format. This method was popularized in *How to Study in College*, Ninth Edition, by Walter Pauk. You can benefit from the method without purchasing an additional book by simply looking up the method online. Below is a sample of how *The Cornell Method* can be adapted for use with this guide.

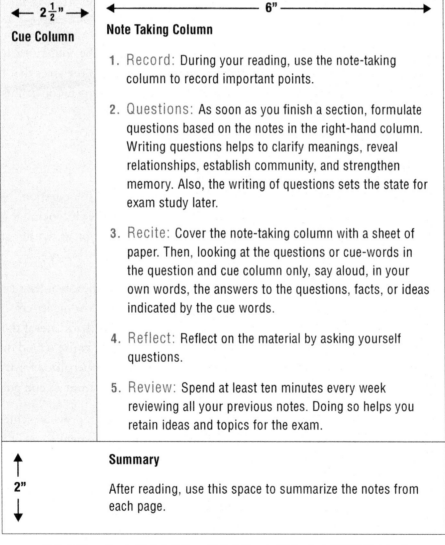

← 2½" → **Cue Column**	← 6" → **Note Taking Column** 1. Record: During your reading, use the note-taking column to record important points. 2. Questions: As soon as you finish a section, formulate questions based on the notes in the right-hand column. Writing questions helps to clarify meanings, reveal relationships, establish community, and strengthen memory. Also, the writing of questions sets the state for exam study later. 3. Recite: Cover the note-taking column with a sheet of paper. Then, looking at the questions or cue-words in the question and cue column only, say aloud, in your own words, the answers to the questions, facts, or ideas indicated by the cue words. 4. Reflect: Reflect on the material by asking yourself questions. 5. Review: Spend at least ten minutes every week reviewing all your previous notes. Doing so helps you retain ideas and topics for the exam.
↑ 2" ↓	**Summary** After reading, use this space to summarize the notes from each page.

Adapted from How to Study in College, Ninth Edition, by Walter Pauk, ©2008 Wadsworth

6. Place yourself in exile and set the mood. Set aside a particular place and time to study that best suits your personal needs and biorhythms. If you're a night person, burn the midnight oil. If you're a morning person set yourself up with some coffee and get to it. Make your study time and place as free from distraction as possible and surround yourself with what you need, be it silence or music. Studies have shown that music can aid in concentration, absorption, and retrieval of information. Not all music, though. Classical music is said to work best

7. Get pointed in the right direction. Use arrows to point to important passages or pieces of information. It's easier to read than a page full of yellow highlights. Highlighting can be used sparingly, but add an arrow to the margin to call attention to it.

8. Check your budget. You should at least review all the content material before your test, but allocate the most amount of time to the areas that need the most refreshing. It sounds obvious, but it's easy to forget. You can use the study rubric above to balance your study budget.

> *The proctor will write the start time where it can be seen and then, later, provide the time remaining, typically fifteen minutes before the end of the test.*

Testing Tips

1. Get smart, play dumb. Sometimes a question is just a question. No one is out to trick you, so don't assume that the test writer is looking for something other than what was asked. Stick to the question as written and don't overanalyze.

2. Do a double take. Read test questions and answer choices at least twice because it's easy to miss something, to transpose a word or some letters. If you have no idea what the correct answer is, skip it and come back later if there's time. If you're still clueless, it's okay to guess. Remember, you're scored on the number of questions you answer correctly and you're not penalized for wrong answers. The worst case scenario is that you miss a point from a good guess.

3. Turn it on its ear. The syntax of a question can often provide a clue, so make things interesting and turn the question into a statement to see if it changes the meaning or relates better (or worse) to the answer choices.

4. Get out your magnifying glass. Look for hidden clues in the questions because it's difficult to write a multiple-choice question without giving away part of the answer in the options presented. In most questions you can readily eliminate one or two potential answers, increasing your chances of answering correctly to 50/50, which will help out if you've skipped a question and gone back to it (see tip #2).

5. Call it intuition. Often your first instinct is correct. If you've been study-ing the content you've likely absorbed something and have subconsciously retained the knowledge. On questions you're not sure about trust your instincts because a first impression is usually correct.

6. Graffiti. Sometimes it's a good idea to mark your answers directly on the test booklet and go back to fill in the optical scan sheet later. You don't get extra points for perfectly blackened ovals. If you choose to manage your test this way, be sure not to mismark your answers when you transcribe to the scan sheet.

7. Become a clock-watcher. You have a set amount of time to answer the questions. Don't get bogged down laboring over a question you're not sure about when there are ten others you could answer more readily. If you choose to follow the advice of tip #6, be sure you leave time near the end to go back and fill in the scan sheet.

Do the Drill

No matter how prepared you feel it's sometimes a good idea to apply Murphy's Law. So the following tips might seem silly, mundane, or obvious, but we're including them anyway.

1. Remember, you are what you eat, so bring a snack. Choose from the list of energizing foods that appear earlier in the introduction.

2. You're not too sexy for your test. Wear comfortable clothes. You'll be distracted if your belt is too tight or if you're too cold or too hot.

3. Lie to yourself. Even if you think you're a prompt person, pretend you're not and leave plenty of time to get to the testing center. Map it out ahead of time and do a dry run if you have to. There's no need to add road rage to your list of anxieties.

4. Bring sharp, number 2 pencils. It may seem impossible to forget this need from your school days, but you might. And make sure the erasers are intact, too.

5. No ticket, no test. Bring your admission ticket as well as **two** forms of identification, including one with a picture and signature. You will not be admitted to the test without these things.

6. You can't take it with you. Leave any study aids, dictionaries, note-books, computers, and the like at home. Certain tests **do** allow a scientific or four-function calculator, so check ahead of time to see if your test does.

7. **Prepare for the desert.** Any time spent on a bathroom break **cannot** be made up later, so use your judgment on the amount you eat or drink.

8. **Quiet, Please!** Keeping your own time is a good idea, but not with a timepiece that has a loud ticker. If you use a watch, take it off and place it nearby but not so that it distracts you. And **silence your cell phone**.

To the best of our ability, we have compiled the content you need to know in this book and in the accompanying online resources. The rest is up to you. You can use the study and testing tips or you can follow your own methods. Either way, you can be confident that there aren't any missing pieces of information and there shouldn't be any surprises in the content on the test.

If you have questions about test fees, registration, electronic testing, or other content verification issues please visit *www.gace.nesinc.com*.

Good luck!

Sharon Wynne
Founder, XAMonline

DOMAIN I
COMPREHENSION OF LITERARY AND INFORMATIONAL TEXTS

PERSONALIZED STUDY PLAN

PAGE	COMPETENCY AND SKILL	KNOWN MATERIAL/ SKIP IT
5	**1: Understand various genres and identify the use and purpose of literary elements, themes, styles, and structures in works of literature**	☐
	1.1: Recognizing characteristic features of various genres of prose, poetry, and drama	☐
	1.2: Analyzing a variety of works to identify types of discourse	☐
	1.3: Demonstrating knowledge of characteristics of literature in various genres	☐
	1.4: Identifying and analyzing the use of literary elements	☐
	1.5: Analyzing a writer's purpose	☐
	1.6: Analyzing the use of theme and thematic elements	☐
	1.7: Comparing the treatment of a theme in different literary genres and across cultures and periods	☐
	1.8: Recognizing and analyzing organizational structures in works of literature	☐
33	**2: Understand the purposes, structures, elements, and meanings of U.S. prose, poetry, and drama of different movements and periods**	☐
	2.1: Analyzing prose, poetry, and drama characteristic of particular U.S. cultures, regions, or historical periods	☐
	2.2: Recognizing the relationship of U.S. works to the historical period or literary movement of which it is a part	☐
	2.3: Comparing themes in literary works from the same U.S. culture or period	☐
	2.4: Recognizing historical elements, references, and antecedents in U.S. prose, poetry, and drama	☐
	2.5: Analyzing the influence of mythic, traditional, or earlier literature on U.S. prose, poetry, and drama	☐
	2.6: Demonstrating familiarity with the historical development of U.S. prose, poetry, and drama	☐
55	**3: Understand the purposes, structures, elements, and meanings of British and Commonwealth prose, poetry, and drama of different movements and periods**	☐
	3.1: Analyzing prose, poetry, and drama that are characteristic of particular British and Commonwealth cultures, regions, or historical periods	☐
	3.2: Recognizing the relationship of British or Commonwealth works to the historical period or literary movement of which it is a part	☐
	3.3: Comparing themes in literary works from the same British or Commonwealth culture or period	☐
	3.4: Recognizing historical elements, references, and antecedents in British and Commonwealth prose, poetry, and drama	☐
	3.5: Analyzing the influence of mythic, traditional, or earlier literature on British and Commonwealth prose, poetry, and dramaa	☐
	3.6:Demonstrating familiarity with the historical development of British and Commonwealth prose, poetry, and drama	☐

PERSONALIZED STUDY PLAN

KNOWN MATERIAL/ SKIP IT

PAGE	COMPETENCY AND SKILL	
70	**4: Understand the purposes, structures, elements, and meanings of world prose, poetry, and drama of different movements and periods**	☐
	4.1: Analyzing prose, poetry, and drama characteristic of particular world cultures, regions, or historical periods	☐
	4.2: Recognizing the relationship of a work of world prose, poetry, or drama to the historical period or literary movement of which it is a part	☐
	4.3: Comparing themes in literary works from the same world culture or period	☐
	4.4: Recognizing historical elements, references, and antecedents in world prose, poetry, and drama	☐
	4.5: Analyzing the influence of mythic, traditional, or earlier literature in world prose, poetry, and drama	☐
	4.6: Demonstrating familiarity with the historical development of U.S. prose, poetry, and drama	☐
86	**5: Understand the purposes, structures, elements, and meanings of informational and technical texts**	☐
	5.1: Recognizing various types of informational and technical texts	☐
	5.2: Distinguishing different purposes for informational and technical writing	☐
	5.3: Identifying a writer's purpose, main ideas, and supporting details in a given informational or technical text	☐
	5.4: Applying knowledge of common textual features	☐
	5.5: Applying knowledge of common graphic features	☐
	5.6: Applying knowledge of common organizational structures and patterns	☐

COMPETENCY 1

UNDERSTAND VARIOUS GENRES (I.E., PROSE, POETRY, AND DRAMA) AND IDENTIFY THE USE AND PURPOSE OF LITERARY ELEMENTS, THEMES, STYLES, AND STRUCTURES IN WORKS OF LITERATURE

SKILL 1.1 Recognizing characteristic features of various genres of prose, poetry, and drama

Prose is divided into two main genres: nonfiction and fiction. Nonfiction is based on factual information, and fiction is based on an author's imagination.

The major literary genres include those listed below.

Nonfiction

Nonfiction has many subgenres. Students should be introduced to these as writings that can be informative as well as enjoyable.

Biography

A **BIOGRAPHY** is a portrait of the life of an individual other than oneself. Biographical prose is a subcategory of nonfiction. The earliest biographical writings were probably funeral speeches and inscriptions, usually praising the life and example of the deceased. Early biographies evolved from this and were almost invariably uncritical, even distorted, and always laudatory.

> **BIOGRAPHY:** a portrait of the life of an individual other than oneself

Autobiography

An **AUTOBIOGRAPHY** is a form of the biography written by the subject himself or herself. Autobiographies can range from very formal works to intimate journals and diaries in the course of a life, without a conscious eye toward publication.

> **AUTOBIOGRAPHY:** a form of biography written by the subject himself or herself

Informational books and articles

INFORMATIONAL BOOKS AND ARTICLES make up much of the reading of modern Americans. Magazines began to be popular in the nineteenth century in this country, and although many of the contributors to those publications intended to influence the political/social/religious convictions of their readers, many also simply intended to pass on information. A book or article whose purpose is

> **INFORMATIONAL BOOKS AND ARTICLES:** writings, such as in books or magazine, that are meant to pursuade or to provide information

simply to be informative—that is, not to persuade—is called exposition. An example of an expository book is the MLA Style Manual. The writers do not intend to persuade their readers to use the recommended stylistic features in their writing; they simply make them available in case a reader needs such a guide.

Newspaper accounts of events

A newspaper account of events is expository in nature, of course—a reporting of a happening. That happening might be a school board meeting, an automobile accident that sent several people to a hospital and left one passenger dead, or the election of the mayor. Although presented within the mannerisms of the objective viewpoint, newspaper accounts invariably contain the biases of the reporter and of the periodical or newspaper in which they appear. Even news stories headline some facts and omit others; by so doing they slant their stories to emphasize certain aspects of the truth over others. Today, with digital photography and computer-generated graphics, the story in the pictorial layout also influences the audience and is the choice of the paper's editorial board. Reporters are expected to be unbiased in their coverage, and most of them defend their disinterest fiercely; but what a writer sees in an event is inevitably shaped to some extent by his or her beliefs and experiences.

Types of nonfiction (not all) include:

- Almanac
- Autobiography
- Biography
- Blueprint
- Book report
- Diary
- Dictionary
- Documentary film
- Encyclopedia
- Essay
- History
- Journal
- Letter
- Philosophy book
- Science book
- Textbook
- User manual

Learn more about writing fiction:

http://crofsblogs.typepad.com/fiction/2003/07/narrative_voice.html

Elements of fiction:
- *Protagonist*
- *Antagonist*
- *Conflicts*
- *Plot*
- *Characterization*

Types of fiction:
- *Novel*
- *Short story*
- *Drama*
- *Poetry*

Fiction

Fiction is the opposite of fact, and, simple as that may seem, it's the major distinction between fictional works and nonfictional works.

A work of fiction typically has a central character, called the protagonist, and a character that stands in opposition, called the antagonist. The antagonist might be something other than a person. In Stephen Crane's short story "The Open Boat," for example, the antagonist is a hostile environment—a stormy sea.

Conflicts between protagonist and antagonist are typical of a work of fiction, and climax is the turning point at which those conflicts are resolved. The plot is the sequence of events during which the conflicts occur as the characters and plot move toward resolution.

A fiction writer artistically uses devices labeled characterization to reveal character. Characterization can depend on dialogue, description, or the attitude or attitudes of one or more characters toward another.

Enjoying fiction depends upon the ability of the readers to suspend disbelief. Readers make a deal with the writer that, for the time the readers take to read the story, the readers will replace their own beliefs with the convictions expressed by the writer and will accept the reality created by the writer.

This is not true in nonfiction. The writer of nonfiction must stick to verifiable facts. Thus, a writer of nonfiction is not free to create a character from imagination, no matter how realistic the author makes that character seem. All nonfiction characters have actually lived. The writer of nonfiction declares in the choice of that genre that the work is reliably based upon reality.

Types of fiction include, but are not limited to:

- Action-adventure
- Crime
- Detective
- Fantasy
- Horror
- Mystery
- Romance
- Science fiction
- Thriller
- Western

A *bildungsroman* (from the German) means "novel of education" or "novel of formation" and is a novel that traces the spiritual, moral, psychological, or social development and growth of the main character from childhood to maturity.

Dickens' *David Copperfield* (1850) represents this genre, as does Thomas Wolfe's *Look Homeward, Angel* (1929).

Novel

A **NOVEL** is the longest form of fictional prose, containing a variety of characterizations, settings, local color, and regionalism. Most novels have complex plots, expanded description, and attention to detail. Some of the great novelists include Austen, Twain, Tolstoy, Hugo, Hardy, Dickens, Hawthorne, Forster, and Flaubert.

Short Story

A **SHORT STORY**, typically, is a terse narrative with less developmental background

Learn more about elements of the short story:

http://www.yale.edu/ynhti/ curriculum/units/ 1983/3/83.03.09.x.html

NOVEL: the longest form of fictional prose

SHORT STORY: a terse narrative with less developmental background about characters than a novel about characters. Short stories may include description, author's point of view, and tone. Poe emphasized that a successful short story should create one focused impact. Considered to be great short story writers are Hemingway, Faulkner, Twain, Joyce, Shirley Jackson, Flannery O'Connor, de Maupasssant, Saki, Poe, and Pushkin.

Drama

DRAMA: a play, typically in five acts

A **DRAMA** is a play—comedy, modern, or tragedy—typically in five acts. Traditionalists and neoclassicists adhere to Aristotle's unities of time, place, and action. Modern playwrights have taken the form and broken it up as they please. Plot development is advanced via dialogue. Common dramatic devices include asides, soliloquies, and a chorus representing public opinion. Among the greatest of all dramatists/playwrights is Shakespeare. Other greats include Ibsen, Williams, Miller, Shaw, Stoppard, Racine, Moliére, Sophocles, Aeschylus, Euripides, and Aristophanes.

Comedy

Comedy is a form of dramatic literature that is meant to amuse and often ends happily. It uses techniques such as satire or parody and can take many forms, from farce to burlesque.

Tragedy

Read more about Greek tragedy:

http://depthome.brooklyn.cuny.edu/classics/dunkle/studyguide/tragedy.htm

Tragedy is comedy's other half. It is defined as a work of drama written in either prose or poetry, telling the story of a brave, noble hero who, because of some tragic character flaw, brings ruin upon himself. It is characterized by serious, poetic language that evokes pity and fear. In modern times, dramatists have tried to update tragedy's image by drawing its main characters from the middle class and showing their nobility through their nature instead of their standing.

Dramatic monologue

Types of poetry:
- *Narrative*
- *Epic*
- *Ballad*
- *Sonnet*
- *Limerick*
- *Cinquain*
- *Haiku*

A dramatic monologue is a speech given by an actor, usually intended for himself or herself, but with the intended audience in mind. It reveals key aspects of the character's psyche and sheds insight on the situation at hand. The audience takes the part of the silent listener, passing judgment and giving sympathy at the same time. This form was invented and used predominantly by Victorian poet Robert Browning.

Poetry

POETRY: a type of fiction whose only requirement is rhythm

POETRY is a type of fiction whose only requirement is rhythm. Poetry evolved from oral literature and folk tale as a written form with set patterns, which in English literature include the sonnet, elegy, ode, pastoral, and villanelle. Unfixed variations on traditional forms have trickled through blank verse and the dramatic monologue. From Modernism to the modern day, poets have transversed experiments with typography—Imagism—and self-revelatory themes—confessional poetry.

Narrative

The greatest difficulty in analyzing narrative poetry is that it partakes of many genres. It can have all the features of poetry, such as meter, rhyme, verses, and stanzas, but it can have all the features of fiction and nonfiction prose. It can have a protagonist, characters, conflicts, action, plot, climax, theme, and tone. It can also be a persuasive discourse and have a thesis (real or derived) and supporting points. The arrangement of an analysis depends largely upon the peculiarities of the poem itself.

Narrative poetry has been very much a part of the output of modern American writers, totally apart from attempts to write epics. Many of Dickinson's poems are narrative in form and retain the features that we look for in the finest of American poetry.

The first two verses of "A Narrow Fellow in the Grass" illustrate the use of narrative in a poem:

> A narrow fellow in the grass
> Occasionally rides;
> You may have met him—did you not?
> His notice sudden is.
> The grass divides as with a comb,
>
> A spotted shaft is seen;
> And then it closes at your feet
> And opens further on. . . .

This is certainly narrative in nature and has many of the aspects of prose narrative. At the same time, it is a poem with rhyme, meter, verses, and stanzas and can be analyzed as such.

Epic

An epic is a long poem, usually of book length, reflecting values inherent in the generative culture. Devices include the invocation of a muse for inspiration, prologue expounding a purpose in writing, universal setting, protagonist and antagonist who possess supernatural strength and acumen, and interventions of a God or the gods. Understandably, there are very few epics: Homer's *Iliad* and *Odyssey*, Virgil's *Aeneid*, Milton's *Paradise Lost*, Spenser's *The Fairie Queene*, Barrett Browning's *Aurora Leigh*, and Pope's mock-epic, *The Rape of the Lock*, are some examples.

Ballad

A ballad is an *in medias res* story told or sung, usually in verse, and accompanied by music. Literary devices found in ballads include the refrain, or repeated section, and anaphora, or incremental repetition, for effect. The earliest forms were anonymous folk ballads.

Sonnet

The sonnet is a fixed-verse form of Italian origin, which consists of fourteen lines that are typically five-foot iambics rhyming according to a prescribed scheme. Popular since its creation in the thirteenth century in Sicily, the sonnet spread first to Tuscany, where it was adopted by Petrarch.

The Petrarchan sonnet generally has a two-part theme. The first eight lines, the octave, state a problem, ask a question, or express an emotional tension. The last six lines, the sestet, resolve the problem, answer the question, or relieve the tension. The rhyme scheme of the octave is abbaabba; that of the sestet varies.

> *Learn more about poetry's many forms:*
> http://poetry.suite101.com/article.cfm/lyric_poetry

Sir Thomas Wyatt and Henry Howard, Earl of Surrey, introduced this form into England in the sixteenth century. It played an important role in the development of Elizabethan lyric poetry, and a distinctive English sonnet developed, which was composed of three quatrains, each with an independent rhyme scheme, and it ended with a rhymed couplet.

A form of the English sonnet created by Edmund Spenser combines the English Italian forms. The Spenserian sonnet follows the English quatrain and couplet pattern but resembles the Italian in its rhyme scheme, which is linked: *abab bcbc cdcd ee.* Many poets wrote sonnet sequences where several sonnets were linked together, usually to tell a story. Considered the greatest of all sonnet sequences is one of Shakespeare's, which is addressed to a young man and a "dark lady" wherein the love story is overshadowed by the underlying reflections on time and art, growth and decay, and fame and fortune.

The sonnet continued to develop, more in theme than in form. After John Donne in the seventeenth century married the form with religious themes, some of which are almost sermons, or personal reflections ("When I consider how my light is spent"), there were no longer any boundaries on the themes the sonnet could encompass.

The flexibility of form is demonstrated by the wide range of themes and purposes the sonnet has been used for—from frivolous concerns to statements about time and death. Wordsworth, Keats, and Elizabeth Barrett Browning used the Petrarchan form of the sonnet. A well-known example is Wordsworth's "The World Is Too Much With Us." Rainer Maria Rilke's *Die Sonette an Orpheus* (1922) is a well-known twentieth-century sonnet cycle.

Analysis of a sonnet should focus on the form. Does it fit a traditional pattern or does it break from tradition? If it does, why did the poet choose to make that break? Does it reflect the purpose of the poem? What is the theme? What is the purpose? Is it narrative? If so, what story does it tell, and is there an underlying meaning? Is the sonnet appropriate for the subject matter?

Limerick

The limerick probably originated in County Limerick, Ireland, in the eighteenth century. It is a form of short, humorous verse, often nonsensical and often ribald. Its five lines rhyme aabba, with three feet in all lines except the third and fourth, which have only two. Rarely presented as serious poetry, this form is popular because almost anyone can write it.

In the nineteenth century, Edward Lear popularized the limerick in *A Book of Nonsense*. Here's an example:

> *There was an Old Man with a beard,*
> *Who said, "It is just as I feared!*
> *Two Owls and a Hen,*
> *Four Larks and a Wren,*
> *Have all built their nests in my beard!"*

Analysis of a limerick should focus on its form. Does it conform to a traditional pattern, or does it break from the tradition? If so, what impact does that have on the meaning? Is the poem serious or frivolous? Is it funny? Does it try to be funny but not achieve its purpose? Is there a serious meaning underlying the frivolity?

Cinquain

A cinquain is a poem with one five-line stanza. Adelaide Crapsey (1878–1914) called a five-line verse form a cinquain and invented a particular meter for it. Similar to the haiku, there is a fixed syllabic scheme: two syllables in the first and last lines and four, six, and eight in the middle three lines. It has a mostly iambic cadence. Crapsey's poem, "November Night," is an example:

> *Listen…*
> *Like steps of passing ghosts,*
> *the leaves, frost-crisp'd, break from the trees*
> *And fall.*

Haiku

Haiku is a popular unrhymed form that is limited to seventeen syllables arranged in three lines thus: five, seven, and five syllables. This verse form originated in Japan in the seventeenth century, where it is still the country's most popular form.

While haikus originally dealt with the seasons, the time of day, and the landscape, the form has come into more common use in that the subjects have become less restricted. The imagist poets and other English writers used the form or imitated it. It's a form frequently used in classrooms to introduce students to the writing of poetry.

Here's an example by Japanese poet Kobaayashi Issa, translated by American poet Robert Haas:

> New Year's morning—
> everything is in blossom!
> I feel about average.

Analysis of cinquain and haiku poems should focus on form first. For a cinquain, does it have only five lines? For a haiku, does it conform to the seventeen-syllable requirement, and are the lines arranged in a five, seven, and five pattern? Does the poem distill the words so as much meaning as possible can be conveyed? Does it treat a serious subject? Is the theme discernable? Short forms like these seem simple to dash off; however, they are not effective unless the words are chosen and pared so the intended meaning is conveyed. The impact should be forceful, and that often takes more effort, skill, and creativity than for longer forms. Students should consider all this in their analyses.

The form of poetry

When we speak of form with regard to poetry, we usually mean one of three things.

The pattern of the sound and rhythm

Knowing the background of these characteristics is helpful. History was passed down in oral form almost exclusively until the invention of the printing press and was often set to music. A rhymed story is much easier to commit to memory than one that is not rhymed. Adding a tune makes it even easier to remember, so many of the earliest pieces of literature and the like were rhymed and were probably sung.

When we speak of "the pattern of sound and rhythm," we are referring to verse form and stanza form. The verse form is the rhythmic pattern of a single verse. An example would be any meter: blank verse, for instance, is iambic pentameter. A stanza is a group of a certain number of verses, having a rhyme scheme. If the poem is written, there is usually white space between the verses, although a short poem may be only one stanza long. If the poem is spoken, there is a pause between stanzas.

The visible shape it takes

In the seventeenth century, some poets shaped their poems to reflect the theme, called concrete poetry. A good example is George Herbert's "Easter Wings." Since that time, poets have occasionally played with this device; it is, however, generally viewed as nothing more than a demonstration of ingenuity. The rhythm, effect, and meaning are often sacrificed to the forcing of the shape.

Rhyme and free verse

Poets also use devices to establish form that will underscore the meanings of their poems. A very common one is alliteration, which is the repetition of initial sounds. When the poem is read aloud (which poetry is usually intended to be), the repetition of a sound may not only underscore the meaning, but also add pleasure to the reading. Following a strict rhyming pattern can add intensity to the meaning of the poem in the hands of a skilled and creative poet. When not used effectively, though, the meaning can be drowned out by the steady beat-beat-beat of it.

Shakespeare very skillfully used the regularity of rhyme in his poetry, breaking the rhythm in certain places to underscore a point very effectively. For example, in Sonnet 130: "My mistress' eyes are nothing like the sun," the rhythm is primarily iambic pentameter. It lulls the reader (or listener) to accept that this poet is following the standard conventions for love poetry, which in that day reliably used rhyme and, more often, than not iambic pentameter to express feelings of romantic love along conventional lines. However, the last two lines of Sonnet 130 sharply break from the monotonous pattern, forcing the reader or speaker to pause:

> And yet, by heaven, I think my love as rare
> As any she belied with false compare.

Shakespeare's purpose is clear: He is not writing a conventional love poem; the object of his love is not the red-and-white conventional woman written about in other poems of the period. This is a good example of a poet using form to underscore meaning.

Poets eventually began to feel constricted by the rhyming conventions and began to break away and make new rules for poetry. When poetry was only rhymed, it was easy to define. When free verse, or poetry written in a flexible form, came upon the scene in France in the 1880s, it quickly began to influence English-language poets such as T. S. Eliot, whose memorable poem "The Wasteland" had an alarming and desolate message for the modern world. It's impossible to imagine that it could have been written in the soothing, lulling, rhymed verse of previous periods. Those who first began writing in free verse in English were responding to the influence of the French *vers libre*.

However, free verse could be applied loosely to the poetry of Walt Whitman written in the mid-nineteenth century, as can be seen in the first stanza of "Song of Myself":

> *I celebrate myself, and sing myself,*
> *And what I assume you shall assume,*
> *For every atom belonging to me as good belongs to you.*

When poetry was no longer defined as a piece of writing arranged in verses that had a rhyme scheme of some sort, distinguishing poetry from prose became a point of discussion. Merriam Webster's current edition of the Encyclopedia of Literature defines poetry as "writing that formulates a concentrated imaginative awareness of experience in language chosen and arranged to create a specific emotional response through its meaning, sound and rhythm."

A poet chooses the form of poetry deliberately, based upon the emotional response being evoked and the meaning being conveyed. Robert Frost, a twentieth-century poet who chose to use conventional rhyming verse to make his point, is a memorable and often-quoted modern poet. Who can forget his closing lines in "Stopping by Woods"?

> *And miles to go before I sleep,*
> *And miles to go before I sleep.*

Would they be as memorable if the poem had been written in free verse? This is an example of the type of questions that critics explore when dealing with poetry.

Sample Test Questions and Rationale

(Average)

1. **Which is the best definition of free verse, or *vers libre*?**

   A. Poetry that consists of an unaccented syllable followed by an unaccented sound

   B. Short lyrical poetry written to entertain but with an instructive purpose

   C. Poetry that does not have a uniform pattern of rhythm

   D. A poem that tells the story and has a plot

The answer is C.

Free verse has lines of irregular length (but it does not run on like prose).

Sample Test Questions and Rationale (cont.)

(Rigorous)

2. Which sonnet form describes the following?

> My galley charg'd
>   with forgetfulness,
> Through sharp seas, in
>   winter night doth pass
> 'Tween rock and rock; and
>   eke mine enemy, alas,
> That is my lord steereth with
>   cruelness.
> And every oar a thought with
>   readiness,
> As though that death were
>   light in such a case.
> An endless wind doth tear
>   the sail apace
> Or forc'ed sighs and trusty
>   fearfulness.
> A rain of tears, a cloud of dark
>   disdain,
> Hath done the wearied
>   cords great hinderance,
> Wreathed with error and eke
>   with ignorance.
> The stars be hid that led me
>   to this pain
> Drowned is reason that
>   should me consort,
> And I remain despairing
>   of the poet

A. Petrarchan or Italian sonnet

B. Shakespearian or Elizabethan sonnet

C. Romantic sonnet

D. Spenserian sonnet

The answer is A.

The Petrarchan sonnet, also known as the Italian sonnet, is named after the Italian poet Petrarch (1304–1374). It is divided into an octave rhyming abbaabba and a sestet normally rhyming cdecde.

(Rigorous)

3. Which poem is typified as a villanelle?

A. "Do not go gentle into that good night"

B. "Dover Beach"

C. *Sir Gawain and the Green Knight*

D. *The Pilgrim's Progress*

The answer is A.

This poem by Dylan Thomas typifies the villanelle because it was written as such. A villanelle is a form that was invented in France in the sixteenth century and was used mostly for pastoral songs. It has an uneven number (usually five) of tercets rhyming aba, with a final quatrain rhyming abaa. This poem is the most famous villanelle written in English. "Dover Beach," by Matthew Arnold, is not a villanelle, while *Sir Gawain and the Green Knight* was written in alliterative verse by an unknown author usually referred to as The Pearl Poet around 1370. *The Pilgrim's Progress* is a prose allegory by John Bunyan.

Sample Test Questions and Rationale (cont.)

(Rigorous)

4. Which term best describes the form of the following poetic excerpt?

> And more to lulle him in his
> slumber soft,
> A trickling streake from high rock
> tumbling downe,
> And ever-drizzling raine upon
> the loft.
> Mixt with a murmuring winde,
> much like a swowne
> No other noyse, nor peoples
> troubles cryes.
> As still we wont t'annoy the
> walle'd towne,
> Might there be heard: but
> careless Quiet lyes,
> Wrapt in eternall silence farre
> from enemyes.

A. Ballad

B. Elegy

C. Spenserian stanza

D. Ottava rima

The answer is D.

The ottava rima is a specific eight-line stanza whose rhyme scheme is *abababcc*.

(Rigorous)

5. In classic tragedy, a protagonist's defeat is brought about by a tragic flaw, which is called:

A. Hubris

B. Hamartia

C. Catharsis

D. The skene

The answer is B.

Hubris is excessive pride, a type of tragic flaw. Catharsis is an emotional purging the character feels. "Skene" is the Greek word for scene. In Sophocles's *Oedipus Rex*, Oedipus's tragic flaw was his excessive pride. By the end of the play—after epiphany, suicide, self-mutilation, ignominy, and exile—he feels a cleansing and is able to continue living.

Sample Test Questions and Rationale (cont.)

(Rigorous)

6. What is the salient literary feature of this excerpt from an epic?

Hither the heroes and the nymphs resorts,
To taste awhile the pleasures of a court;
In various talk th'instructive hours they passed,
Who gave the ball, or paid the visit last;
One speaks the glory of the English Queen,
And another describes a charming Indian screen;
A third interprets motion, looks and eyes;
At every word a reputation dies.

A. Sprung rhythm

B. Onomatopoeia

C. Heroic couplets

D. Motif

The answer is C.

A couplet is a pair of rhyming verse lines, usually of the same length. It is one of the most widely used verse forms in European poetry. Chaucer established the use of couplets in English, notably in the *Canterbury Tales*, using rhymed iambic pentameters (a metrical unit of verse having one unstressed syllable followed by one stressed syllable), later known as heroic couplets. Other authors who used heroic couplets include Ben Jonson, John Dryden, and especially Alexander Pope, who became the master of them.

SKILL 1.2 **Analyzing a variety of works to identify types of discourse** *(e.g., satire, parody, allegory, pastoral)* **that cross the lines of genre classifications**

The major literary genres include allegory, ballad, drama, epic, epistle, essay, fable, novel, poem, romance, and the short story.

> *Check out more than 180 allegories, fables, parables, and teaching tales:*
>
> *http://www.insight-books.com/ALLF*

Allegory

An **ALLEGORY** is a story in verse or prose with characters representing virtues and vices. Allegories may be read on either of two levels, the literal or the symbolic. John Bunyan's *The Pilgrim's Progress* is the most renowned of this genre.

> **ALLEGORY:** a story in verse or prose with characters representing virtues and vices

Epistle

An **EPISTLE** is a letter that is not always originally intended for public distribution, yet because of the fame of the sender or recipient, becomes part of the public domain. Saint Paul wrote epistles that were later placed in the Bible.

Essay

An **ESSAY** is typically a limited-length prose work focusing on a topic and propounding a definite point of view and authoritative tone. Great essayists include Carlyle, Lamb, DeQuincy, Emerson, and Montaigne, who is credited with defining this genre.

Fable

A **FABLE** is a terse tale offering a moral or exemplum. Chaucer's "The Nun's Priest's Tale" is a fine example of a *bête fabliau*, or beast fable, in which animals speak and act characteristically human, illustrating human foibles.

Legend

A **LEGEND** is a traditional narrative or collection of related narratives, popularly regarded as historically factual but actually a mixture of fact and fiction.

Myth

A **MYTH** is a story that is more or less universally shared within a culture to explain its history and traditions.

Romance

A **ROMANCE** is a highly imaginative tale set in a fantastical realm dealing with the conflicts between heroes, villains, and/or monsters. "The Knight's Tale" from Chaucer's *Canterbury Tales* and Keats' "The Eve of St. Agnes" are prime representatives.

Children's Literature

Children's literature emerged as a distinct and independent form in the second half of the eighteenth century. *The Visible World in Pictures* by John Amos Comenius, a Czech educator, was one of the first printed children's works and the first picture book. For the first time, educators acknowledged that children were different from adults in many respects. Modern educators acknowledge that

EPISTLE: a letter not intended for public distribution but that becomes part of the public domain

ESSAY: a limited-length prose work focusing on a topic and propounding a definite point of view and authoritative tone

FABLE: a terse tale offering a moral or exemplum

LEGEND: a traditional narrative or collection of narratives that is a mixture of fact and fiction

MYTH: a story more or less universally shared within a culture

ROMANCE: a highly imaginative tale set in a fantastical realm

Check out Sur La Lune fairy tales and folklore:

http://www. surlalunefairytales.com/ introduction/index.html

introducing elementary students to a wide range of reading experiences plays an important role in their mental, social, and psychological development.

COMMON FORMS OF CHILDREN'S LITERATURE	
Traditional Literature	Traditional literature opens up a world where right wins out over wrong, hard work and perseverance are rewarded, and helpless victims find vindication—all worthwhile values that children identify with, even as early as in kindergarten. In traditional literature, children are introduced to fanciful beings, humans with exaggerated powers, talking animals, and heroes that inspire them. For younger elementary children, traditional stories in Big Book format are ideal for providing predictable and repetitive elements that children can grasp.
Folktales/ Fairy Tales	Adventures of animals or humans and the supernatural characterize these stories. The hero is usually on a quest and is aided by other-worldly helpers. More often than not, the story focuses on good and evil and reward and punishment. Some examples are "The Three Bears," "Little Red Riding Hood," "Snow White," "Sleeping Beauty," "Puss-in-Boots," "Rapunzel", and "Rumpelstiltskin."
Tall Tales	These are purposely exaggerated accounts of individuals with superhuman strength. Examples include "Paul Bunyan," "John Henry," and "Pecos Bill."
Modern Fantasy	Many of the themes found in these stories are similar to those in traditional literature. The stories start out based in reality, enabling readers to suspend disbelief and enter worlds of unreality: Little people live in the walls in *The Borrowers*, for example; time travel is possible in *The Trolley to Yesterday*. Including some fantasy tales in the curriculum helps students develop their imaginations. These stories often appeal to ideals of justice and good and evil. Because students tend to identify with the characters, they are likely to retain the message.
Science Fiction	Robots, spacecraft, mystery, and civilizations from other ages often appear in these stories. Most anticipate advances in science on other planets or in a future time. Most children like these stories because of their interest in space and the "what if" aspect of the stories. Examples include *Outer Space and All That Junk* and *A Wrinkle in Time*.
Modern Realistic Fiction	These stories are about real problems that real children face. By finding that their hopes and fears are shared by others, student readers can find insight into their own problems. Young readers also tend to experience a broadening of interests as the result of this kind of reading. It's good for them to know that someone like them can be brave and intelligent and can solve difficult problems.
Historical Fiction	This type of fiction uses historical settings, events, and characters as a backdrop for storytelling. *Rifles for Watie* is an example of this kind of story. Presented in a historically accurate setting, it's about a young boy of sixteen who serves in the Union army. He experiences great hardship but discovers that his enemy is an admirable human being. It provides a good opportunity to study history in a beneficial way.
Informational Books	These provide ways to learn more about something interesting or to explore something very new. Encyclopedias are good resources, of course, but a book like *Polar Wildlife* shows pictures and facts that can capture the imaginations of young children.

Nonfiction versus Fiction

Students often misrepresent the differences between fiction and nonfiction. They mistakenly believe that stories are always examples of fiction. The truth is that stories are both fiction and nonfiction. The primary difference is that fiction is made up by the author and nonfiction is generally true (or an opinion). It is harder for students to understand that nonfiction entails an enormous range of material, from textbooks to true stories to newspaper articles to speeches. Fiction, on the other hand, is fairly simple to identify—made-up stories and novels. But students also need to understand that most of fiction throughout history has been based on true events. In other words, authors use their own life experiences to create works of fiction.

Appreciating the artistry in telling a story to convey a point is important for understanding fiction. When students see that an author's choice in a work of fiction is for the sole purpose of conveying a viewpoint, they can make better sense of the specific details in the work of fiction.

Distinguishing a fact from a perspective is important in understanding nonfiction. Often, a nonfiction writer will present an opinion, and that opinion is very different from a factual truth. Knowing the difference between the two is crucial.

In comparing fiction to nonfiction, students need to learn about the conventions of each. In fiction, students can generally expect to see plot, characters, setting, and themes. In nonfiction, students may see a plot, characters, settings, and themes, but they will also experience interpretations, opinions, theories, research, and other elements. Any characters in nonfiction will have actually been born.

Overall, students can begin to see patterns that distinguish fiction from nonfiction. For instance, the more fanciful or unrealistic a text or story is, the more likely the chance that it is fiction.

Sample Test Questions and Rationale

(Easy)

1. A traditional, anonymous story, ostensibly having a historical basis, usually explaining some phenomenon of nature or aspect of creation defines a/an:

   A. Proverb

   B. Idyll

   C. Myth

   D. Epic

The answer is C.

A myth is usually traditional and anonymous, and explains natural and supernatural phenomena. Myths are usually about creation, divinity, the significance of life and death, and natural phenomena.

Sample Test Questions and Rationale (cont.)

(Easy)

2. Which of the following is not a characteristic of a fable?

   A. Animals that feel and talk like humans

   B. Happy solutions to human dilemmas

   C. Teaches a moral or standard for behavior

   D. Illustrates specific people or groups without directly naming them

The answer is D.

A fable is a short tale with animals, humans, gods, or even inanimate objects as characters. Fables often conclude with a moral, delivered in the form of an epigram (a short, witty, and ingenious statement in verse). Fables are among the oldest forms of writing in human history: They appear in Egyptian papyri of c.1500 B.C.E. The most famous fables are those of Aesop, a Greek slave living in about 600 B.C.E. In India, the *Pantchatantra* appeared in the third century. The most famous modern fables are those of seventeenth century French poet Jean de La Fontaine.

(Average)

3. Children's literature became established in the:

   A. Seventeenth century

   B. Eighteenth century

   C. Nineteenth century

   D. Twentieth century

The answer is A.

In the seventeenth century, Jean de La Fontaine and his fables, Pierre Perreault's tales, Mme d'Aulnoye's novels based on old folktales, and Mme de Beaumont's *Beauty and the Beast* all created a children's literature genre. In England, Perreault was translated. and a work allegedly written by Oliver Smith, *The Renowned History of Little Goody Two Shoes*, also helped establish children's literature in England.

(Average)

4. Latin words that entered the English language during the Elizabethan age include:

   A. Allusion, education, and esteem

   B. Vogue and mustache

   C. Canoe and cannibal

   D. Alligator, cocoa, and armadillo

The answer is A.

These words reflect the Renaissance interest in the classical world and the study of ideas. The words in Answer B are of French derivation, and the words in Answers C and D have younger etymologies.

> ## SKILL 1.3 Demonstrating knowledge of characteristics of literature in various genres written for adolescents and young adults

Prior to twentieth-century research on child development and child/adolescent literature's relationship to that development, books for adolescents were primarily *didactic*. They were designed to address history, manners, and morals.

Middle Ages

As early as the eleventh century, Anselm, the Archbishop of Canterbury, wrote an encyclopedia designed to instill in children the beliefs and principles of conduct acceptable to adults in medieval society. Early monastic translations of the Bible and other religious writings were written in Latin for the edification of the upper class.

Fifteenth-century hornbooks were designed to teach reading and religious lessons. William Claxton printed English versions of *Aesop's Fables*, Malory's *Le Morte d'Arthur*, and stories from Greek and Roman mythology. Though printed for adults, tales of the adventures of Odysseus and the Arthurian knights were also popular with literate adolescents.

Renaissance

The Renaissance saw the introduction of inexpensive chapbooks, small in size and 16–64 pages in length. Chapbooks were condensed versions of mythology and fairy tales. Designed for the common people, chapbooks were imperfect grammatically but immensely popular because of their adventurous contents. Though most of the serious, educated adults frowned on the sometimes vulgar little books, chapbooks received praise from Richard Steele (of *Tattler* fame) for inspiring his grandson's interest in reading and in pursuing his other studies.

Meanwhile, the Puritans' most popular reads were the Bible, John Foe's *Book of Martyrs*, and John Bunyan's *The Pilgrim's Progress*. Though venerating religious martyrs and preaching the moral propriety that was to lead to eternal happiness, the stories of the *Book of Martyrs* were often lurid in their descriptions of the fate of the damned. In contrast, *The Pilgrim's Progress*, not written for children and difficult reading even for adults, was as attractive to adolescents for its adventurous plot as for its moral outcome.

In Puritan America, the *New England Primer* set forth the prayers, catechisms, Bible verses, and illustrations meant to instruct children in the Puritan ethic.

The seventeenth-century French used fables and fairy tales to entertain adults, but children found them enjoyable as well.

Late Seventeenth Century

The late seventeenth century brought the first concern with providing literature specifically targeting the young. Pierre Peril's *Fairy Tales*, Jean de la Fontaine's retellings of famous fables, Mme. d'Aulnoy's novels based on old folktales, and Mme de Beaumont's *Beauty and the Beast* were written to delight as well as instruct young people.

In England, publisher John Newbury was the first to publish a line of books for children. These included a translation of Perrault's *Tales of Mother Goose; A Little Pretty Pocket-Book*, "intended for instruction and amusement" but decidedly moralistic and bland in comparison to the previous century's chapbooks; and *The Renowned History of Little Goody Two Shoes*, allegedly written by Oliver Goldsmith for a juvenile audience.

Eighteenth Century

Largely, eighteenth-century adolescents were finding their reading pleasure in adult books: Daniel Defoe's *Robinson Crusoe*, Jonathan Swift's *Gulliver's Travels*, and Johann Wyss's *Swiss Family Robinson*. More books were being written for children, and moral didacticism, though less religious, was nevertheless present. The short stories of Maria Edgeworth, the four-volume *The History of Sandford and Merton* by Thomas Day, and Martha Farquharson's twenty-six volume *Elsie Dinsmore* series dealt with pious protagonists who learned restraint, repentance, and rehabilitation from sin.

Two bright spots in this period of didacticism were Jean Jacques Rousseau's *Emile* and *The Tales of Shakespeare*, and May and Charles Lamb's simplified versions of Shakespeare's plays. Rousseau believed that a child's abilities were enhanced by a free, happy life, and the Lambs subscribed to the notion that children were entitled to entertaining literature written in language comprehensible to them.

Nineteenth Century

Child/adolescent literature truly began its modern rise in nineteenth-century Europe. Hans Christian Andersen's *Fairy Tales* were fanciful adaptations of the Grimm brothers' somber revisions in the previous century. Andrew Lang's series of colorful fairy books contain the folklores of many nations and are still part of the collections of many modern libraries. Clement Moore's "A Visit from St. Nicholas" is a cheery, non-threatening child's view of the night before Christmas. The humor of Lewis Carroll's books about Alice's adventures, Edward Lear's poems with caricatures, and Lucretia Nole's stories of the Philadelphia Peterkin family are full of fancy and not a smidgen of morality.

For more information, read "Introductory lecture on children's & adolescent literature":

http://homepages. wmich.edu/~tarboxg/ Introductory_Lecture_on_ Children's_&_Adol_Lit. html

Other popular Victorian novels introduced the modern fantasy and science fiction genres: William Makepeace Thackeray's *The Rose and the Ring*, Charles Dickens' *The Magic Fishbone*, and Jules Verne's *Twenty Thousand Leagues Under the Sea*. Adventure to exotic places became a popular topic: Rudyard Kipling's *Jungle Books*, Jules Verne's *Around the World in Eighty Days*, and Robert Louis Stevenson's *Treasure Island* and *Kidnapped*. In 1884, the first English translation of Johanna Spyri's *Heidi* appeared.

North America was also finding its voices for adolescent readers. American Louisa May Alcott's *Little Women* and Canadian L. M. Montgomery's *Anne of Green Gables* ushered in the modern age of realistic fiction. American youth were enjoying the adventures of Mark Twain's mischievous heroes Tom Sawyer and Huckleberry Finn. For the first time, children were able to read books about real people just like themselves.

Twentieth Century

The literature of the twentieth century was extensive and diverse and, as in previous centuries, much influenced by the adults who wrote, edited, and selected books for youth consumption. In the first third of the century, suitable adolescent literature dealt with children from good homes with large families. These books projected an image of a peaceful, rural existence.

Though the characters and plots were more realistic, the stories maintained focused on topics that were considered emotionally and intellectually proper. Popular at this time were Laura Ingalls Wilder's *Little House on the Prairie* series and Carl Sandburg's biography *Abe Lincoln Grows Up*. English author J.R.R. Tolkein's fantasy, *The Hobbit*, prefaced modern adolescent readers' fascination with the works of Piers Antony, Madelaine L'Engle, and Anne McCaffery.

Sample Test Questions and Rationale

(Easy)

1. Among junior high school students of low-to-average readability levels, which work would most likely stir reading interest?

   A. *Elmer Gantry*, Sinclair Lewis

   B. *Smiley's People*, John Le Carre

   C. *The Outsiders*, S. E. Hinton

   D. *And Then There Were None*, Agatha Christie

   The answer is C.

   The students can easily identify with the characters and the gangs in the book. S. E. Hinton has actually said about this book: "*The Outsiders* is definitely my best-selling book; but what I like most about it is how it has taught a lot of kids to enjoy reading."

(Average)

2. Most children's literature prior to the development of popular literature was intended to be didactic. Which of the following would not be considered didactic?

   A. "A Visit from St. Nicholas" by Clement Moore

   B. McGuffy's Reader

   C. Any version of Cinderella

   D. Parables from the Bible

   The answer is A.

   "A Visit from St. Nicholas" is a cheery, non-threatening child's view of Christmas Eve. "Didactic" means intended to teach some lesson.

SKILL 1.4 **Identifying and analyzing the use of literary elements** *(e.g., character development, setting, mood, point of view, foreshadowing, irony, diction, imagery, symbolism, figurative language)*

Students will develop critical thinking skills by learning to identify literary elements and analyzing how they help authors develop themes in their works.

CHARACTER DEVELOPMENT is a commonly studied story element. In stories, we often find heroes, villains, comedic characters, dark characters, and the like. When we examine the characters of a story, we look at who they are and how their traits contribute to the story. Often, because of the characters' traits, plot elements become more interesting. For example, authors may pair unlikely characters together to create specific conflict.

The **SETTING** of a story is the place or location where the action occurs. Often, the specific place is not as important as some of the details about it. For example, the location of *The Great Gatsby*, New York, is not as significant as the fact that the story takes place amongst incredible wealth. Conversely, *The Grapes of Wrath*, although it takes place in Oklahoma and California, is set amidst extreme poverty. In fact, as the story takes place around other migrant workers, the setting is even

> **CHARACTER DEVELOPMENT:** a literary element, based on a work's characters, used in analyzing works of literature

> **SETTING:** a literary element based on the place a work is situated

MOOD: a literary element based on the atmosphere or attitude the writer conveys through descriptive language

POINT OF VIEW: a literary element based on who is narrating the story

FORESHADOWING: a literary element based on giving clues about future developments

DICTION: a literary element based on the distinctive vocabulary choices a writer makes

Learn more about teaching imagery:

http://students.ed.uiuc.edu/vallicel/Teaching_imagery.html

IMAGERY: a literary element based on use of a word or sequence of words to refer to a sensory experience

more significant. In a way, the setting serves as a reason for various conflicts to occur.

The **MOOD** of a story is the atmosphere or attitude the writer conveys through descriptive language. Often, mood fits nicely with theme and setting. For example, Edgar Allan Poe's stories often reveal a mood of horror and darkness. Mood helps readers better understand the writer's theme and intentions through descriptive, stylistic language, characterization, setting, and specific plot elements.

Stories are narrated from a particular **POINT OF VIEW**, or perspective. First-person narration means that the story is being told by a character in the story. Such a narrator uses first-person pronouns (I, me, we, us, our, my, mine, ours). Third person narration means that the story is being told by someone not in the story and uses third-person pronouns (such as he, she, it, they, theirs, them). This general distinction is further modified by third-person omniscient or third-person limited narration, meaning that the narrator seems to know everything that is going on inside every character's head or seems to know only about one character's perspective.

FORESHADOWING, giving clues about future developments, is a technique authors use to build cohesion into their stories and to promote readers' engagement with them. Readers' mindsets are guided in ways that promote subtle expectations about future events. A skillful writer rewards or otherwise manipulates those expectations for purposes of keeping the reader engaged in the narration.

DICTION pertains to the distinctive vocabulary choices a writer makes and to the characteristic ways a writer structures words and phrases. The hallmark of a great writer is precise, unusual, and memorable diction the use of the right word(s) in the right place for the right purpose.

IMAGERY can be described as a word or sequence of words that refers to any sensory experience—that is, anything that can be seen, tasted, smelled, heard, or felt on the skin or fingers. Although prose writers may also use these devices, they are most distinctive of poetry. The poet appeals to one of the senses in order to make an experience available to the reader. The poet deliberately paints a scene in such a way that the reader can visualize it.

However, the purpose is not simply to stir the visceral feeling but also to stir the emotions. A good example of imagery can be found in "The Piercing Chill" by Taniguchi Buson (1715–1783):

The piercing chill I feel:
My dead wife's comb, in our bedroom,
Under my heel . . .

In only a few short words, the reader can feel many things: the shock that might come from touching the comb, a literal sense of death, the contrast between her death and the memories he has of her when she was alive. Imagery might be defined as speaking of the abstract in concrete terms—a powerful device in the hands of a skillful poet.

SYMBOLISM is using an object or action that can be observed with the senses to suggest or represent something else. The lion is a symbol of courage; the cross is a symbol of Christianity; the swastika was a symbol of Nazi Germany.

Symbols used in literature are usually a different sort. Their significance is only evident in the context of the work where they are used. A good example is the huge pair of spectacles on a signboard in Fitzgerald's *The Great Gatsby*. It is interesting as a part of the landscape, but it also symbolizes divine myopia. A symbol can certainly have more than one meaning. Occasionally, the meaning may be as personal as the memories and experiences of the particular reader.

When analyzing a poem or a story, students should identify the symbols and their possible meanings. Looking for symbols is often challenging, especially for novice poetry readers. However, these suggestions may be useful:

1. First, pick out all the references to concrete objects such as a newspaper, black cats, or other nouns. Note any that the poet emphasizes by describing in detail, by repeating, or by placing at the very beginning or ending of a poem. Ask: what is the poem about? What does it add up to? Paraphrase the poem and determine whether the meaning depends upon certain concrete objects. Then ponder what the concrete object symbolizes in this particular poem.

2. Look for a character with the name of a prophet who does little but utter prophecy or a trio of women who resemble the Three Fates. A symbol may be a part of a person's body, such as the eye of the murder victim in Poe's story "The Tell-Tale Heart," or a look, a voice, or a mannerism.

3. A symbol is not an abstraction such as truth, death, and love; in narrative, a well-developed character who is not at all mysterious; or the second term in a metaphor. In Emily Dickenson's "The Lightning Is a Yellow Fork," the symbol is the lightning, not the fork.

FIGURATIVE LANGUAGE is also called figures of speech. If all figures of speech that have ever been identified were listed, the list would be very long. However, for purposes of analyzing literature, a handful will suffice.

Alliteration is the repetition of consonant sounds in two or more neighboring words or syllables. In its simplest form, it reinforces one or two consonant sounds.

> **SYMBOLISM:** a literary element based on using an object or action that can be observed with the senses to suggest or represent something else

> **FIGURATIVE LANGUAGE:** a literary element based on use of figures of speech

One example comes from Shakespeare's Sonnet 12:

> *When I do count the clock that tells the time*

Some poets have used more complex patterns of alliteration by creating consonants both at the beginning of words and at the beginning of stressed syllables within words. Shelley's "Stanzas Written in Dejection Near Naples" provides such an example:

> *The City's voice itself is soft like Solitude's*

Bathos is a ludicrous attempt to portray pathos (that is, to evoke pity, sympathy, or sorrow). It may result from inappropriately dignifying the commonplace, using elevated language to describe something trivial, or greatly exaggerated pathos.

The Climax is a number of phrases or sentences that are arranged in ascending order of rhetorical forcefulness. An example is from Melville's *Moby Dick*:

> *All that most maddens and torments; all that stirs up the lees of things; all truth with malice in it; all that cracks the sinews and cakes the brain; all the subtle demonisms of life and thought; all evil, to crazy Ahab, were visibly personified and made practically assailable in Moby Dick.*

Euphemism is the substitution of an agreeable or inoffensive term for one that might offend or suggest something unpleasant. For example, to avoid using the word "death," you might use a euphemism such as "passed away," "crossed over," or nowadays "passed."

Hyperbole is the deliberate exaggeration for effect or comic effect. An example is from Shakespeare's *The Merchant of Venice*:

> *Why, if two gods should play some heavenly match*
> *And on the wager lay two earthly women,*
> *And Portia one, there must be something else*
> *Pawned with the other, for the poor rude world*
> *Hath not her fellow.*

Irony is expressing something other than and particularly opposite to the literal meaning, such as words of praise when blame is intended. In poetry, irony is often used as a sophisticated or resigned awareness of contrast between what is and what ought to be and expresses a controlled pathos without sentimentality. It is a form of indirection that avoids overt praise or censure. An early example: the Greek comic character Eiron, a clever underdog who by his wit repeatedly triumphs over the boastful character Alazon.

Malapropism is a verbal blunder in which one word is replaced by another similar in sound but different in meaning. This derives from Sheridan's Mrs. Malaprop in *The Rivals* (1775). Thinking of the geography of contiguous countries, she speaks of the "geometry" of "contagious countries." Meaning the "pinnacle of perfection," she describes someone as "the pineapple of perfection."

Metaphor is indirect comparison between two things. It is the use of a word or phrase denoting one kind of object or action in place of another to suggest a comparison between them. While poets use metaphors extensively, they are also integral to everyday speech. For example, chairs are said to have "legs" and "arms" although we know that humans and other animals have these appendages.

Parallelism is the arrangement of ideas in phrases, sentences, and paragraphs that balance one element with another of equal importance and similar wording. An example is from Francis Bacon's *Of Studies*:

> *Reading maketh a full man, conference a ready man, and writing an exact man.*

Personification is when human characteristics are attributed to an inanimate object, an abstract quality, or an animal. For example, John Bunyan wrote characters named Death, Knowledge, Giant Despair, Sloth, and Piety in his *Pilgrim's Progress*. Carl Sandburg, in his poem "Fog," writes:

> *The fog comes*
> *on little cat feet.*
>
> *It sits looking*
> *over harbor and city*
> *on silent haunches*
> *and then moves on.*

Onomatopoeia is the naming of a thing or action by a vocal imitation of the sound associated with it, such as *buzz* or *hiss* or the use of words whose sound suggests the sense. A good example is from "The Brook" by Tennyson:

> *I chatter over stony ways,*
> *In little sharps and trebles,*
> *I bubble into eddying bays,*
> *I babble on the pebbles.*

Oxymoron is a contradiction in terms deliberately employed for effect. It is usually seen in a qualifying adjective whose meaning is contrary to that of the noun it modifies, such as "wise folly" or "jumbo shrimp."

Simile is a direct comparison between two things using "like," "as," or "such as." An example is Robert Burns's poem "My love is like a red, red rose."

Poets use figures of speech to sharpen the effect and meaning of their poems and to help readers see things in ways they have never seen them before. Marianne Moore observed that a fir tree has "an emerald turkey-foot at the top." Her poem makes us aware of something we probably had never noticed before. The sudden recognition of the likeness yields pleasure in the reading.

> *Figurative language allows for the statement of truths that more literal language cannot. Skillfully used, a figure of speech helps the reader better understand a text and focus upon particulars.*

Figures of speech add many dimensions of richness to our reading and understanding of a poem; they also allow many opportunities for worthwhile analysis. The approach to take in analyzing a poem on the basis of its figures of speech is to ask several questions: What does a particular figure of speech do for the poem? Does it underscore meaning? Does it aid understanding? Does it increase the intensity of my response?

Sample Test Questions and Rationale

(Easy)

1. The substitution of "went to his rest" for "died" is an example of a:

   A. Bowdlerism

   B. Jargon

   C. Euphemism

   D. Malapropism

   The answer is C.

   A euphemism replaces an unpleasant or offensive word or expression with a more agreeable one. It also alludes to distasteful things in a pleasant manner, and it can even paraphrase offensive texts.

(Average)

2. In literature, evoking feelings of pity or compassion is to create:

   A. Colloquy

   B. Irony

   C. Pathos

   D. Paradox

   The answer is C.

   A very well known example of pathos is Desdemona's death in *Othello*, but there are many other examples of pathos. In *King Lear*, Cordelia accepts defeat with this line: "We are not the first / Who with best meaning have incurred the worst."

(Average)

3. The literary device of personification is used in which example below?

   A. "Beg me no beggary by soul or parents, whining dog!"

   B. "Happiness sped through the halls, cajoling as it went."

   C. "O wind thy horn, thou proud fellow."

   D. "And that one talent which is death to hide."

   The answer is B.

   "Happiness," an abstract concept, is described as if it were a person.

> **SKILL Analyzing a writer's purpose in the use of a particular genre or**
> **1.5 particular literary elements, stylistic devices, and structures**

See Skills 5.2, 7.2, 8.2, 12.5, 15.4

> **SKILL Analyzing the use of theme and thematic elements in works**
> **1.6 of literature**

See Skill 1.4

> **SKILL Comparing the treatment of a theme in different literary genres**
> **1.7 and across cultures and periods**

See Skills 1.3, 2.1, 3.3, 4.3

> **SKILL Recognizing and analyzing the effects of various organizational**
> **1.8 structures** *(e.g., chronological, in medias res, flashback, frame narrative)* **in**
> **works of literature**

Literature typically uses narrative discourse—that is, it tells a story. At the same time, though, other types of discourse are an inevitable part of a good story. A writer may even stop the narrative and lapse into a persuasive section to bring the reader around to a particular point of view, or one character may attempt to persuade another one. Description and explanation are also used in many ways and places in a good story.

Chronological Structure

Stories are usually arranged in a CHRONOLOGICAL STRUCTURE, meaning in the actual order that events unfold. For that reason, a writer's control over and handling of the chronology in a story is very important. If the sequence of events is clouded or confusing to the reader, the story is not effective. Successful writers, however, use techniques, such as the ones discussed below, to handle the chronology of their stories creatively and effectively.

> **CHRONOLOGICAL STRUCTURE:** a type of discourse in which the story is arranged in the order that events unfold

In Medias Res

IN MEDIAS RES: a type of discourse in which the story opens somewhere in the middle

One device that has remained popular since the time of Homer is called **IN MEDIAS RES**. This tool enables a writer to open the story somewhere in the middle for the purpose of grabbing and holding the attention of the reader. The writer will, of course, go back and fill in the necessary details so the reader can eventually construct the overall narrative and chronology. In the *Iliad,* Homer begins his story with the quarrel between Achilles and Agamemnon. As we continue to read, we fit this quarrel into the context of the rest of the entire story.

Epistolary

EPISTOLARY: a type of discourse in which a series of letters or correspondences tell a story

A writer may use a series of letters or correspondences between two characters to tell a story. This technique is called **EPISTOLARY**. The letters generally are arranged according to the date on each one. *In medias res* can be used in this arrangement, such as when a story in the middle of the plot is presented early on via correspondence to pique the reader's curiosity and keep him or her reading to find out THE story's conclusion. An example of an epistolary novel is Bram Stoker's *Dracula*.

Flashback

FLASHBACK: a type of discourse in which a story is told in normal chronology with an episode from an earlier time inserted from time to time

Another tool a writer may use to manipulate the chronology in a story is the **FLASHBACK**. With this technique, the story moves along in a normal chronology. However, inserted from time to time is an episode from an earlier time. Flashbacks are usually used to fill in background information in an interesting way.

Frame Narrative

FRAME NARRATIVE: a type of discourse in which there is a main story within which one or more tales are related

In a **FRAME NARRATIVE**, there is a main story within which one or more tales are related. The main story accommodates a set of shorter stories-within-stories or surrounds a single story-within-a-story. An early example of a frame narrative is Chaucer's *Canterbury Tales*, in which the pilgrimage is the frame story that brings together all of the pilgrim/storytellers.

Sample Test Question and Rationale

(Rigorous)

1. The technique of starting a narrative at a significant point in the action and then developing the story through flashbacks is called

    A. *In medias res*

    B. Ottava rima

    C. Irony

    D. Suspension of willing disbelief

The answer is A.

As its Latin translation suggests: in the middle of things. An ottava rima is a specific eight-line stanza of poetry whose rhyme scheme is abababcc. Lord Byron's *Don Juan* is written in ottava rima. Irony is an unexpected disparity between what is stated and what is really implied by the author. Benjamin Franklin's "Rules by Which A Great Empire May be Reduced to a Small One" and Voltaire's tales are texts that are written using irony. Drama is what Coleridge calls "the willing suspension of disbelief for the moment, which constitutes poetic faith."

COMPETENCY 2

UNDERSTAND THE PURPOSES, STRUCTURES, ELEMENTS, AND MEANINGS OF U.S. PROSE, POETRY, AND DRAMA OF DIFFERENT MOVEMENTS AND PERIODS

SKILL **Analyzing structures, elements, and themes of U.S. prose, poetry**
2.1 **and drama that are characteristic of particular U.S. cultures, regions, or historical periods**

Although American literature does not have the long history of other countries, it is still rich and diverse. Students will discover the interconnectedness of writing as a reflection of the historical, social, ethnic, political, and economic environment of the time.

The Colonial Period

William Bradford's excerpts from *The Mayflower Compact* relate vividly the hardships of crossing the Atlantic Ocean in such a tiny vessel, the misery and suffering of the first winter, the approaches of the American Indians, the decimation of the pilgrims' ranks, and the establishment of the Bay Colony of Massachusetts. Anne Bradstreet's poetry relates colonial New England life. From her journals, modern readers learn of the everyday life of the early settlers, the hardships of travel, and the responsibilities of different groups and individuals in the community. Early American literature also reveals the commercial and political adventures of the Cavaliers who came to the New World with King George's blessing.

William Byrd's journal, *A History of the Dividing Line*, concerning his trek into the Dismal Swamp separating the Carolinian territories from Virginia and Maryland, makes quite lively reading. A privileged insider to the English Royal Court, Byrd, like other Southern Cavaliers, was given grants to pursue business ventures.

The Revolutionary Period

The Revolutionary period produced great orations such as Patrick Henry's "Speech to the Virginia House of Burgesses" (the "Give me liberty or give me death" speech) and George Washington's "Farewell to the Army of the Potomac." Less memorable are Washington's inaugural addresses, which strike modern readers as lacking sufficient focus.

The *Declaration of Independence*, the brainchild predominantly of Thomas Jefferson (along with some prudent editing by Benjamin Franklin), is a prime example of neoclassical writing—balanced, well crafted, and focused.

Epistles include the exquisitely written, moving correspondence between John Adams and Abigail Adams. The poignancy of their separation—she in Boston, he in Philadelphia—is palpable and real.

The Romantic Period

Early American folktales and the emergence of a distinctly American writing constitute the Romantic period.

Washington Irving's characters, Ichabod Crane and Rip Van Winkle, represent a uniquely American folklore devoid of English influences. These characters are indelibly marked by their environment and the superstitions of the New Englander.

The early American writings of James Fenimore Cooper, particularly his *Leatherstocking Tales*, provide readers a window into their American world through the stirring accounts of drums along the Mohawk, the French and Indian Wars, the futile British defense of Fort William Henry, and the brutalities of this period.

Natty Bumppo, Chingachgook, Uncas, and Magua are unforgettable characters who reflect the American spirit in thought and action.

The poetry of the Fireside Poets—James Russell Lowell, Oliver Wendell Holmes, Henry Wadsworth Longfellow, and John Greenleaf Whittier—was read and recited by American families during the long New England winters. In "The Courtin'," Lowell uses Yankee dialect to tell the story. Spellbinding epics by Longfellow (such as *Hiawatha, The Courtship of Miles Standish*, and *Evangeline*) tell of adversity, sorrow, and ultimate happiness in a distinctly American fashion.

"Snowbound" by Whittier relates the story of a captive family isolated by a blizzard, stressing family closeness.

Nathaniel Hawthorne and Herman Melville are the preeminent early American novelists, writing on subjects regional, specific, and American, yet sharing insights about human foibles, fears, loves, doubts, and triumphs.

Hawthorne's writings range from children's stories, like the *Cricket on the Hearth* series, to adult fare of dark, brooding short stories such as "Dr. Heidegger's Experiment," "The Devil and Tom Walker," and "Rapuccini's Daughter." *The House of the Seven Gables* deals with kept secrets, loneliness, societal pariahs, and love ultimately triumphing over horrible wrong. Hawthorne's masterpiece, *The Scarlet Letter*, takes on the society of Puritan New Englanders, who ostensibly left England to establish religious freedom but who have become entrenched in judgmental attitudes in the New World. They ostracize Hester and condemn her child, Pearl, as a child of Satan. Great love, sacrifice, loyalty, suffering, and related epiphanies add universality to this tale.

Herman Melville's magnum, *Moby Dick*, follows Captain Ahab on his Homeric odyssey to conquer the great white whale that has outwitted him and his whaling crews time and again. The whale has even taken Ahab's leg and, according to Ahab, wants all of him. Melville recreates in painstaking detail the harsh life of a whaler out of New Bedford by way of Nantucket.

Melville's comparatively succinct tale of *Billy Budd* describes the title character's Christ-like sacrifice to the black-and-white maritime laws on the high seas. An accident results in the death of one of the ship's officers, who had taken a dislike to the young, affable, shy Billy. Captain Vere must hang Billy for the death of Claggert. He knows that this is not right; however, an example must be given to the rest of the crew so that discipline can be maintained.

Edgar Allan Poe creates a distinctly American version of romanticism with his sixteen-syllable line in "The Raven," the classical "To Helen," and his Gothic "Annabelle Lee." The horror short story can be said to originate from Poe's pen,

Learn more about the life and works of Herman Melville:

http://www.melville.org/

too. "The Tell-Tale Heart," "The Cask of Amontillado," "The Fall of the House of Usher," and "The Masque of the Red Death" are exemplary short stories. In addition, the genre of detective story emerges with Poe's "Murders in the Rue Morgue."

American Romanticism has its own offshoot in the Transcendentalism of Ralph Waldo Emerson and Henry David Thoreau. The former wrote about transcending the complexities of life; the latter, who wanted to get to the marrow of life, immersed himself in nature at Walden Pond and wrote an inspiring autobiographical account of his sojourn, aptly titled *On Walden Pond*. Thoreau also wrote passionately regarding his objections to the interference of government imposed on the individual in "On the Duty of Civil Disobedience."

Emerson's elegantly crafted essays and war poetry still validate several important universal truths. Probably most remembered for his address to Thoreau's Harvard graduating class, entitled "The American Scholar," he defined the qualities of hard work and intellectual spirit required of Americans in their growing nation.

> Find more sites about American literature:
>
> http://www.wsu.edu/~campbelld/amlit/sites.htm

The Transition between Romanticism and Realism

The Civil War period ushered in the poignant poetry of Walt Whitman and his homage to all who suffer from the ripple effects of war and presidential assassination. His "Come Up from the Fields, Father" (about a Civil War soldier's death and his family's reaction) and "When Lilacs Last in the Courtyard Bloom'd" (about the effects of Abraham Lincoln's death on the poet and the nation) should be required readings in any American literature course. Further, his *Leaves of Grass* gave America its first poetry truly unique in form, structure, and subject matter.

Emily Dickinson, like Walt Whitman, left her literary fingerprints on a vast array of poems, all but three of which were never published in her lifetime. Her themes of introspection and attention to nature's details and wonders are, by any measurement, world-class works. Her posthumous recognition reveals the timeliness of her work.

During this period, such legendary figures as Paul Bunyan and Pecos Bill rose from the oral tradition. Anonymous storytellers around campfires told tales of a huge lumberman and his giant blue ox, Babe, whose adventures were explanations of natural phenomena like those of footprints filled with rainwater becoming the Great Lakes. The whirling-dervish speed of Pecos Bill explained the tornadoes of the Southwest. Like ancient peoples finding reasons for the happenings in their lives, these American pioneer storytellers created a mythology appropriate to the vast reaches of the unsettled frontier.

Mark Twain also made a literary impact with his unique blend of tall tale and fable. "The Celebrated Jumping Frog of Calaveras County" and "The Man who

Stole Hadleyburg" are epitomes of short-story writing. Twain again rises above others with his bold, oft-banned, still disputed *The Adventures of Huckleberry Finn*, which examines such taboo subjects as a white person's love of a slave, leaving children with abusive parents, and the outcomes of family feuds. Written partly in dialect, *The Adventures of Huckleberry Finn* is touted by some as the greatest American novel.

The Realistic Period

Realistic writers wrote of common, ordinary people and events using realistic detail to reveal the harsh realities of life. They broached taboos by creating protagonists whose environments often destroyed them. Romantic writers, by contrast, had only protagonists whose indomitable wills helped them rise above adversity.

The late nineteenth century saw a reaction against the tendency of romantic writers to look at the world idealistically. Writers like Frank Norris (*The Pit*) and Upton Sinclair (*The Jungle*) used their novels to decry conditions for workers in slaughterhouses and wheat mills. In *The Red Badge of Courage*, Stephen Crane wrote of the daily sufferings of the common soldier in the Civil War. Crane's *Maggie: A Girl of the Streets* deals with a young woman forced into prostitution to survive. In "The Occurrence at Owl Creek Bridge," Ambrose Bierce relates the hanging of a Confederate sympathizer who is caught trying to sabotage a Union stronghold.

Other short stories, like Bret Harte's "The Outcasts of Poker Flat" and Jack London's "To Build a Fire" deal with people whose luck in life has run out. Many writers of this period, subclassified as naturalists, believed that man was subject to a fate over which he had no control.

> *Learn more about Upton Sinclair:*
>
> http://www.online-literature.com/upton_sinclair/

The Modern Era

Twentieth-century American writing can be divided into the following three genres:

American drama

The greatest and most prolific of American playwrights include:

- Eugene O'Neill, *Long Day's Journey into Night, Mourning Becomes Electra,* and *Desire Under the Elms*
- Arthur Miller, *The Crucible, All My Sons,* and *Death of a Salesman*
- Tennessee Williams, *Cat on a Hot Tin Roof, The Glass Menagerie,* and *A Streetcar Named Desire*

- Edward Albee, *Who's Afraid of Virginia Woolf,? Three Tall Women,* and *A Delicate Balance*

American fiction

The renowned American novelists of this century include:

- Eudora Welty, *The Optimist's Daughter*
- John Updike, *Rabbit Run* and *Rabbit Redux*
- Sinclair Lewis, *Babbit* and *Elmer Gantry*
- F. Scott Fitzgerald, *The Great Gatsby* and *Tender Is the Night*
- Ernest Hemingway, *A Farewell to Arms* and *For Whom the Bell Tolls*
- William Faulkner, *The Sound and the Fury* and *Absalom, Absalom!*
- Bernard Malamud, *The Fixer* and *The Natural*

American poetry

The poetry of the twentieth century is multifaceted, as represented by Edna St. Vincent Millay, Marianne Moore, Richard Wilbur, Langston Hughes, Maya Angelou, and Rita Dove. Perhaps best known are the many-layered poems of Robert Frost. His New England motifs of snowy evenings, birches, apple picking, stone wall mending, hired hands, and detailed nature studies relate universal truths in exquisite diction, polysyllabic words, and rare allusions to either mythology or the Bible.

American Indian Literature

The foundation of American Indian writing is found in story telling, oratory, autobiographical and historical accounts of tribal village life, reverence for the environment, and the postulation that the earth was given in trust, to be cared for and passed on to future generations.

Early American Indian writers include:

- Hal Barland, *When the Legends Die*
- S. M. Barrett, Editor, *Geronimo: His Own Story (Apache)*
- C. Eastman and E. Eastman, *Wigwam Evenings: Sioux Folktales Retold*
- L. Riggs, *Cherokee Night* (drama)

Twentieth-century American Indian writers include:

- V. Deloria, *Custer Died for Your Sins* (Sioux)
- M. Dorris, *The Broken Cord* (Modoc)
- L. Hogan, *Mean Spirited* (Chickasaw)
- C. F. Taylor, *Native American Myths and Legends*

Female Writers

Willa Cather's work moves the reader to the prairies of Nebraska and the harsh existence eked out by the immigrant families who choose to stay there to farm. Her most acclaimed works include *My Antonia* and *Death Comes for the Archbishop.*

Kate Chopin's regionalism and local color takes her readers to the upper-crust Creole society of New Orleans and resort isles off the Louisiana coast. "The Story of an Hour" is lauded as one of the greatest of all short stories. Her feminist liberation novel *The Awakening* is still hotly debated.

Eudora Welty's regionalism and dialect shine in her short stories of rural Mississippi, especially in "The Worn Path."

Modern black female writers

Modern black female writers have explored the world of feminist/gender issues as well as class prohibitions. They include:

- Alice Walker, *The Color Purple*
- Zora Neale Hurston, *Their Eyes Were Watching God*
- Toni Morrison, *Beloved, Jazz,* and *Song of Solomon*

Feminists

- Louisa May Alcott, *Little Women*
- Betty Friedan, *The Feminine Mystique* and *The Second Stage*
- Elizabeth Janeway, *Man's World, Woman's Place: A Study in Social Mythology*
- Adrienne Rich, *Of Woman Born: Motherhood As Experience* and *Institution and Driving into the Wreck*

Sample Test Questions and Rationale

(Easy)

1. The tendency to emphasize and value the qualities and peculiarities of life in a particular geographic area exemplifies:

   A. Pragmatism

   B. Regionalism

   C. Pantheism

   D. None of the above

The answer is B.

Pragmatism is a philosophical doctrine according to which there is no absolute truth. All truths change their trueness as their practical utility increases or decreases. The main representative of this movement is William James, who in 1907 published *Pragmatism: A New Way for Some Old Ways of Thinking*. Pantheism is a philosophy according to which God is omnipresent in the world: Everything is God, and God is everything. The great representative of this sensibility is Baruch Spinoza. Also, the works of writers such as William Wordsworth, Percy Bysshe Shelley, and Ralph Waldo Emerson illustrate this doctrine.

(Easy)

2. Which poet was a major figure in the Harlem Renaissance?

   A. e. e. cummings

   B. Rita Dove

   C. Margaret Atwood

   D. Langston Hughes

The answer is D.

Hughes's collection of verse includes *The Weary Blues* (1926), *Shakespeare in Harlem* (1942), and *The Panther and the Lash* (1967). e. e. cummings preferred the lower case in the spelling of his name until the 1930s. He is also a celebrated poet, but he is not a part of the Harlem Renaissance. Rita Dove is a very famous African American poet, but she was born in 1952 and therefore is not a part of the Harlem Renaissance. Margaret Atwood is a Canadian novelist.

(Average)

3. Which of the writers below is a renowned African American poet?

   A. Maya Angelou

   B. Sandra Cisneros

   C. Richard Wilbur

   D. Richard Wright

The answer is A.

Among Angelou's most famous work are *I Know Why the Caged Bird Sings* (1970), *And Still I Rise* (1978), and *All God's Children Need Traveling Shoes* (1986). Richard Wilbur is a poet and a translator of French dramatists Racine and Molière, but he is not African American. Richard Wright was a very important African American author of novels such as *Native Son* and *Black Boy*. However, he was not a poet. Sandra Cisneros is a Latina author who is very important in developing Latina women's literature.

Sample Test Questions and Rationale (cont.)

(Average)

4. Which of the following titles is known for its scathingly condemning tone?

   A. Boris Pasternak's *Dr. Zhivago*

   B. Albert Camus' *The Stranger*

   C. Henry David Thoreau's "On the Duty of Civil Disobedience"

   D. Benjamin Franklin's "Rules by Which a Great Empire May Be Reduced to a Small One"

The answer is D.

In this work, Benjamin Franklin adopts a scathingly ironic tone to warn the British about the probable outcome in their colonies if they persist with their policies. These are discussed one by one in the text, and the absurdity of each is condemned.

(Average)

5. American colonial writers were primarily:

   A. Romanticists

   B. Naturalists

   C. Realists

   D. Neoclassicists

The answer is D.

The early colonists had been schooled in England, and even though their writing became quite American in content, their emphasis on clarity and balance in their language remained British. This literature reflects the lives of the early colonists, such as William Bradford's excerpts from "The Mayflower Compact," Anne Bradstreet's poetry, and William Byrd's *A History of the Dividing Line*.

(Average)

6. Which of the following writers did not win a Nobel Prize for literature?

   A. Gabriel Garcia-Marquez of Colombia

   B. Nadine Gordimer of South Africa

   C. Pablo Neruda of Chile

   D. Alice Walker of the United States

The answer is D.

Even though Alice Walker received the Pulitzer Prize and the American Book Award for her best-known novel, *The Color Purple*, and is the author of six novels and three collections of short stories that have received wide critical acclaim, she has not yet received the Nobel Prize.

(Rigorous)

7. What were two major characteristics of the first American literature?

   A. Vengefulness and arrogance

   B. Bellicosity and derision

   C. Oral delivery and reverence for the land

   D. Maudlin and self-pitying egocentricism

The answer is D.

This characteristic can be seen in Captain John Smith's work, as well as William Bradford's and Michael Wigglesworth's works.

> **SKILL 2.2** Recognizing the relationship of a U.S. work of prose, poetry, or drama to the historical period or literary movement of which it is a part

American literature is marked by a number of clearly identifiable periods. Although these stand alone, they can also be useful as histories across the curriculum.

Civil Rights

Many of the abolitionists were also early crusaders for civil rights. However, the 1960s civil rights movement focused attention on the plight of the people who had been "freed" by the Civil War in ways that brought about long-overdue changes in the opportunities and rights of African-Americans.

David Halberstam, who had been a reporter in Nashville at the time of the sit-ins by eight young African-American college students, wrote *The Children*, published in 1998 by Random House, for the purpose of reminding Americans of the courage, suffering, and achievements of those eight students. Congressman John Lewis, Fifth District, Georgia, who has gone on to a life of public service, was one of those eight young men. Halberstam records that when older African-American ministers tried to persuade these young people not to pursue their protest, John Lewis responded: "If not us, then who? If not now, then when?"

Examples of civil rights protest literature include:

- James Baldwin, *Blues for Mister Charlie*
- Martin Luther King, *Where Do We Go from Here?*
- Langston Hughes, *Fight for Freedom: The Story of the NAACP*
- Eldridge Cleaver, *Soul on Ice*
- Malcolm X, *The Autobiography of Malcolm X*
- Stokely Carmichael and Charles V. Hamilton, *Black Power*
- Leroi Jones, *Home*

Immigration

Immigration has been a popular topic for literature from the time of the Louisiana Purchase in 1804. The recent *Undaunted Courage* by Stephen E. Ambrose is ostensibly the autobiography of Meriwether Lewis but is actually a recounting of the Lewis and Clark expedition. Presented as a scientific expedition by President Jefferson, the expedition actually was intended to provide maps and information for the opening up of the West. A well-known novel about the settling of the

Check out the brief timeline of American literature:

http://www.wsu.edu/~campbelld/amlit/timefram.html

Learn more about civil rights literature of the 1960s:

http://www.lib.virginia.edu/small/exhibits/sixties/civil.html

Some clearly identifiable periods of U.S. history that have influenced literature:
- *Civil rights*
- *Immigration*

West by immigrants from other countries is *Giants in the Earth* by Ole Edvart Rolvaag, himself a descendant of immigrants.

John Steinbeck's *Cannery Row* and *Tortilla Flats* glorify the lives of Mexican migrants in California. Amy Tan's *The Joy Luck Club* deals with the problems faced by Chinese immigrants.

Leon Uris's *Exodus* deals with the social history that led to the founding of the modern state of Israel. It was published in 1958, only a short time after the Holocaust. It also deals with attempts of concentration camp survivors to get to the land that has become the new Israel. In many ways, it is the quintessential work on the causes and effects of immigration.

See also Skill 2.1

SKILL 2.3 Comparing themes shared in several literary works from the same U.S. culture or period

See Skill 2.1

SKILL 2.4 Recognizing historical elements, references, and antecedents in U.S. prose, poetry, and drama

Prose Writers

Herman Melville was born in 1819 and grew up in upper-class New York neighborhoods. His mother was a strict Calvinist Presbyterian and had strong views regarding proper behavior. Melville tended to be a rebellious sort, and to some extent his conflicts regarding his mother's viewpoints were never resolved. When Melville was eleven years old, his father's business failed, and he died shortly afterward. Melville tried working in business for a while but soon decided that he wanted to go to sea.

While working on ships and traveling, Melville began to write nonfiction pieces about his experiences. In July 1851, he wrote his most famous work, *Moby Dick*. Before he died, he wrote poems and another well-known novel, *Billy Budd*, which was not published until 1924. Just as he began to write *Moby Dick*, he became friends with Nathaniel Hawthorne, who happened to be his neighbor. Hawthorne's works and friendship became an important influence on his writing.

The style of *Moby Dick* is indicative of the reportorial writing of Melville's earlier period; however, it is far more than that. It is seen as a great American epic, even though the work is not poetry. Unfortunately, *Moby Dick* was not successful in Melville's lifetime. Its success came much later.

Some themes include:

- Man in conflict with the natural world
- Religion and God's role in the universe
- Good and evil
- Cause and effect
- Duty
- Conscience

Check out the Willa Cather Foundation:

http://www.willacather.org

Willa Cather grew up on the western plains in Nebraska, and much of her best fiction focuses on the pioneering period in that part of the country. She was born in Virginia in 1873 on her family's farm, but in 1884, the family moved to Nebraska where other relatives had settled. Much of the lore that is the basis of her stories came from her visits with immigrant farmwomen around Red Cloud, where the family eventually made their home.

When she was sixteen, Cather enrolled at the University of Nebraska in Lincoln. There, an essay she wrote for her English class was favorably accepted, and she began to support herself as a journalist.

Cather later moved to Pittsburgh and was working as a writer and editor when she decided that she wanted to teach school. Even so, she continued to develop her writing career. On a trip back to Nebraska, she witnessed a wheat harvest, which triggered her motive for writing about the pioneer period of American history.

Some themes include:

- The American dream
- Prejudice
- Coming of age
- Nostalgia

The Mississippi writers page—Richard Wright:

http://www.olemiss.edu/ depts/english/ms-writers/ dir/wright_richard/

Richard Wright was the grandson of slaves and grew up in a time when the lives of African-Americans tended to be very grim. His responses to living so close to those recently risen from bondage permeates his writing.

Wright's writing went through many changes, just as his response to the reality of life as a black person in a white-dominated world went through many changes.

To understand his work, the date of the writing—the stage he was undergoing at the time—is very important. He was influenced early on by Maxim Gorky, whose own life experience had similarities to Wright's own. Later, Dostoevsky heavily influenced him, and the Russian writer's themes can be identified in the work from his last period.

Many African-American communities felt that survival required conformity to whatever white people demanded, but Wright rejected that premise. He felt profoundly alienated and felt that his individuality had been wounded. He became a proletarian revolutionary artist in the earliest years of his career.

The American Communist Party considered Wright as their most illustrious recruit to the newly established literary standards of proletarian realism. He rejected the "conspicuous ornamentation" of institutions such as the Harlem Renaissance.

At the same time, he felt that consciousness must draw its strength from the lore of a great people, his own. He sought in the early years of the twentieth century to integrate the progressive aspects of African-American folk culture into a collective myth that would promote a revolutionary approach to reality.

Wright left the Communist Party in 1944, largely as a result of his own evolution. *Black Boy*, an autobiographical account of his childhood and young manhood, appeared in 1945. He settled in Paris as a permanent expatriate shortly after its publication.

His first stories—*Uncle Tom's Children*—are a reconception of Negro spirituals and black Christianity in which the hero chooses to risk martyrdom in progressively more elevated stages of class consciousness.

His technique and style are not as important as the impact his ideas and attitudes have had on American life. He set out to portray African-Americans to white readers in such a way that the myth of the uncomplaining, comic, obsequious black man might be replaced.

Some themes include:

- The inability of the South to nourish human beings, especially African-Americans

- Rejection of black pandering to white America

- Violent, battered childhood and victorious adulthood

- Suffocation of instinct and stifling of potential

- Mature reminiscences of a battered childhood

- Black mother's protective nurture and the trauma of an absent or impotent father

Maxine Hong Kingston's parents were Chinese immigrants who lived in Stockton, California. Her fiction is highly autobiographical, and she weaves Chinese myths and fictionalized history with the aim of exploring the conflicts between cultures faced by Chinese-Americans.

Her writing exposes the trials and tribulations of Chinese immigrants who were exploited by American companies, particularly in the railroad and agriculture industries. She also explores relationships within Chinese families, particularly between parents who were born in China and children who were born in America. In a 1980 *New York Times Book Review* interview, she said, "What I am doing in this new book [*China Men*] is churning America."

Some themes include:

- Discovery
- The American dream
- Male/female roles
- Metamorphosis
- Enforced muteness
- Vocal expression
- Family

Poets

Walt Whitman's poetry was inspired, primarily, by the Civil War. He is one of America's greatest romantic poets, and many of his poems relate to and stem from the conflict between the Northern and Southern states. The Civil War was not Whitman's only influence, though; he wrote many poems on topics that are not directly related to it. His major work, *Leaves of Grass*, was revised nine times before he died. He was an innovator, using sophisticated, previously unexplored linguistic devices. Even though he dealt with a vast, panoramic vision, his style has a personal and immediate effect on readers.

Learn more about Walt Whitman:

http://www. whitmanarchive.org

Whitman was born on Long Island in New York in 1819, a time of great patriotism for the new nation. His father was a carpenter and then a farmer. Whitman was the second-born of eight children, the first son. He had six years of public education before he went to work for Brooklyn lawyers and began to educate himself in the library.

He began his writing career as a journalist, and Whitman eventually wrote short stories that also were published in newspapers. His unconventional techniques were his own creation and, in *Leaves of Grass*, he intended to speak for all Americans.

Working as a volunteer in hospitals to help care for soldiers and the ensuing first-hand experience with the horrors of the Civil War deeply affected Whitman.

His poetry was considered indecent by some, and he was both praised and vilified during his lifetime. He died in 1892 of tuberculosis.

Some themes include:

- Imagination versus the scientific process

- Individualism

Emily Dickinson has been called the "myth of Amherst" because so little is known of her. She was born in 1830, the second child of Edward and Emily Dickinson. Her family was prominent in Massachusetts and played a major role in the founding of Amherst College. Her father's stern, puritanical control of his family played a pivotal role in the poetry that his daughter eventually wrote.

Learn more about Emily Dickinson:

http://www.emilydickinson. org

Although he was severe and controlling, Edward Dickinson saw that his daughters received a strong education. Dickinson attended Amherst Academy and then Mount Holyoke Female Seminary. She obtained a copy of Emerson's poems in 1850 and began to develop her own beliefs regarding religion and the severe God that her father represented.

Only a few of Dickinson's poems were published during her lifetime, and she was unknown until after her death. After withdrawing from school, she became more and more reclusive; after the death of her father in 1874, she never again left her home. Dickinson died of Bright's disease in 1886. Her sister Lavinia found roughly 2,000 poems on small pieces of paper, which were published in several editions. The first full three-volume edition was released in 1955. She has come to be known for her superb use of concrete language and imagery to express and evoke abstract issues. Most people have a favorite Dickinson poem.

Some themes include:

- Sanity/insanity
- Doubt
- Death

- Individuality
- Defiance
- Feminism

Gwendolyn Brooks was the first African-American to receive a Pulitzer Prize for poetry with her acute images of African-Americans in the cities of America. Born in 1917 to a schoolteacher and a janitor, she grew up in Chicago. She was named poet laureate of Illinois in 1978 and was the first black woman honorary fellow of the Modern Language Association.

Learn more about Gwendolyn Brooks:

http://www.english.uiuc. edu/maps/poets/a_f/ brooks/brooks.htm

Her family was close-knit, and Brooks tended to spend her time reading when she was a child. She began writing poems at a very young age. She also had a successful teaching career at several universities including City University of New York, where she was Distinguished Professor.

Brooks wrote about the experience of being African-American long before the concept became mainstream. She underwent an evolution in subject matter and thinking about being black because of the Civil Rights movement and its effects on the validity of African-Americans. She died of cancer in 2000.

Some themes include:

- Poverty and racism
- Self-respect
- Heritage
- Community
- Family
- Black unity
- Black solidarity
- The basic humanness in everyone
- Pride

Leslie Marmon Silko is a Laguna Indian of mixed ancestry that includes Cherokee, German, English, Mexican, and Pueblo. Several remarkable women in her life, among them grandmothers and aunts, taught her the traditions and stories of the Pueblo. At the same time, her father's role in his tribe also made her aware of the abuses her people had experienced at the hands of the government. Silko believed that she could change things by writing about them.

Some themes include:

- Evil
- Reciprocity
- Individual/community
- Native American traditions
- Native American religion
- Mixed breeds
- Scapegoats, racism, prejudice

Local Color

LOCAL COLOR:
the presenting of the peculiarities of a locality

LOCAL COLOR is defined as the presenting of the peculiarities of a locality and its inhabitants. Although there were precursors, such as Washington Irving and his depiction of life in the Catskill Mountains of New York, the local colorist movement is generally considered to have begun in 1865, when humor began to permeate the writing of those who were focusing on a particular region of the country.

The country had just emerged from its "long night of the soul," a time when death, despair, and disaster had preoccupied the nation for almost five years. It's no wonder that artists sought to relieve the grief and pain and lift spirits, nor is it surprising that their efforts brought such a strong response. **Samuel L. Clemens (Mark Twain)** is best known for his humorous works about the Southwest, such as "The Celebrated Jumping Frog of Calaveras County." Mark

Twain is generally considered to be not only one of America's funniest writers but also one who wrote great and enduring fiction.

Other examples of local colorists who used many of the same devices include:

- George Washington Cable
- Joel Chandler Harris
- Bret Harte
- Sarah Orne Jewett
- Harriet Beecher Stowe

> **Read more about regional realism:**
>
> *http://www.learner. org/amerpass/unit08/ usingvideo.html*

Slavery

The best known of the early writers who used fiction to move a political statement about slavery is Harriet Beecher Stowe, author of *Uncle Tom's Cabin*. Her first novel, it was published first as a serial in 1851 and then as a book in 1852. This antislavery book infuriated Southerners. However, Stowe herself had been angered by the 1850 Fugitive Slave Law that made it legal to indict those who assisted runaway slaves. The law also took away rights of both the runaways and of the free slaves. Stowe intended to generate a protest of the law and of slavery in general.

The novel is about three slaves, Tom, Eliza, and George, who are together in Kentucky. Eliza and George are married to each other but have different masters. They successfully escape with their little boy, but Tom does not. Although he has a wife and children, Tom is sold, ending up finally with the monstrous Simon Legree, where he dies at last. *Uncle Tom's Cabin* was the first effort to present the lives of slaves from their standpoint.

Stowe cleverly used depictions of motherhood and Christianity to stir her readers. When President Lincoln finally met her, he told her that her book started the Civil War.

Many other writers used the printed word to protest slavery, including:

- Frederick Douglass
- William Lloyd Garrison
- Benjamin Lay, a Quaker
- Jonathan Edwards, a Connecticut theologian
- Susan B. Anthony

Sample Test Questions and Rationale

(Average)

1. Arthur Miller wrote The Crucible as a parallel to what twentieth century event?

   A. Sen. McCarthy's House un-American Activities Committee hearing

   B. The Cold War

   C. The fall of the Berlin wall

   D. The Persian Gulf War

   The answer is A.

   The episode of the seventeenth century witch-hunt in Salem, Massachusetts, gave Miller a storyline that was very comparable to what was happening to persons suspected of Communist beliefs in the 1950s.

(Average)

2. Which of the following is not a theme of Native American writing?

   A. Emphasis on the hardiness of the human body and soul

   B. The strength of multicultural assimilation

   C. Contrition for the genocide of native peoples

   D. Remorse for the love of the Indian way of life

   The answer is B.

   Native American literature was first a vast body of oral traditions from as early as before the fifteenth century. The characteristics include reverence for and awe of nature and the interconnectedness of the elements in the life cycle. The themes often reflect the hardiness of body and soul, remorse for the destruction of the Native American way of life, and the genocide of many tribes by the encroaching settlements of European Americans. These themes are still present in today's contemporary Native American literature, such as in the works of Duane Niatum, Gunn Allen, Louise Erdrich and N. Scott Momaday.

Sample Test Questions and Rationale (cont.)

(Rigorous)

3. Mr. Phillips is creating a unit to study *To Kill a Mockingbird* and wants to familiarize his high school freshmen with the attitudes and issues of the historical period. Which activity would familiarize students with the attitudes and issues of the Depression-era South?

   A. Create a detailed timeline of 15–20 social, cultural, and political events that focus on race relations in the 1930s

   B. Research and report on the life of its author Harper Lee. Compare her background with the events in the book

   C. Watch the movie version and note language and dress

   D. Write a research report on the stock market crash of 1929 and its effects

The answer is A.

By identifying the social, cultural, and political events of the 1930s, students will better understand the attitudes and values of America during the time of the novel. Although researching the author's life could add depth to their understanding of the novel, it is unnecessary to the appreciation of the novel by itself. The movie version is an accurate depiction of the novel's setting, but it focuses on the events in the novel, not the external factors that fostered the conflict. The stock market crash and the subsequent Great Depression would be important to note on the timeline, but students would be distracted from themes of the book by narrowing their focus to only these two events.

SKILL 2.5 **Analyzing the influence of mythic, traditional, or earlier literature on U.S. prose, poetry, and drama**

Fables and Folktales

Fables and folktales were originally transmitted orally to the common populace to provide models of exemplary behavior or of deeds worthy of recognition and homage.

In **FABLES**, animals talk, feel, and behave like human beings. Fables always have a moral, and the animals represent specific people or groups. For example, the lion in Aesop's *Fables* represents the king, and the wolf represents the cruel, often

FABLE: a form of literature that has a moral and in which animals talk, feel, and behave like human beings

unfeeling, nobility. In *The Lion and the Mouse*, the moral is that "little friends may prove to be great friends." In *The Lion's Share*, though, it is "might makes right."

British **FOLKTALES** *(How Robin Became an Outlaw* and *St. George Slaying of the Dragon),* meanwhile, investigate the interplay between power and justice.

Classical Mythology

Much of the **MYTHOLOGY** alluded to in American literature is a product of ancient Greece and Rome because Greek and Roman myths have been widely translated. Some Norse myths are also well known.

Because ancient people sought explanations for what happened in their lives in a manner that is accessible and familiar to children, myths frequently appeal to young people. These stories provide insight into the order and ethics of life. In them, ancient heroes overcome the terrors of the unknown, and explanations are given for frightening natural phenomena like thunder and lightning, the changing seasons, and the origin and function of magical creatures of the forests and sea. There is often a childlike directness in the emotions of supernatural beings.

Many good translations of myths exist, but Edith Hamilton's *Mythology* is the definitive choice for adolescents.

Fairy Tales

FAIRY TALES are lively fictional stories involving animals or children who come into contact with supernatural beings via magic. They provide happy solutions to human dilemmas. The fairy tales of many nations are peopled by trolls, elves, dwarfs, and pixies—child-sized beings capable of fantastic accomplishments.

Among the most famous fairy tales are "Beauty and the Beast," "Cinderella," "Hansel and Gretel," "Snow White and the Seven Dwarfs," "Rumplestiltskin," and "Tom Thumb." In each tale, the protagonist survives some type of prejudice, imprisonment, ridicule, and even death to receive justice in an otherwise cruel world.

Older readers encounter a kind of fairy tale world in Shakespeare's *The Tempest* and *A Midsummer Night's Dream*, both of which use pixies and fairies as characters. Adolescent readers today are fascinated by the creations of fantasy realms in the works of Piers Anthony, Ursula LeGuin, and Anne McCaffrey. An extension of interest in the supernatural reveals itself the popularity of science fiction, which allows readers to use current knowledge to predict the possible course of the future.

FOLKTALE: a form of literature, similar to fables, that investigates the interplay between power and justice

MYTHOLOGY: ancient stories (many translated from Greek or Roman) that provide insight into the order and ethics of life

FAIRY TALE: a lively fictional story involving animals or children who come into contact with supernatural beings via magic

Angels (or sometimes fairy godmothers) play a role in some fairy tales, and John Milton in *Paradise Lost* and *Paradise Regained* also used angels and devils.

Biblical stories also generate many allusions. References to the treachery of Cain and the betrayal of Christ by Judas Iscariot are oft-cited examples. Parables, moralistic-like fables but with human characters, include the stories of the good Samaritan and the prodigal son.

American Folktales

American folktales are divided into two categories: tall tales and legends.

TALL TALES, also called imaginary tales, are humorous tales based on nonexistent, fictional characters developed through blatant exaggeration.

- John Henry is a two-fisted steel driver who beats out a steam drill in competition.

- Rip Van Winkle sleeps for twenty years in the Catskill Mountains and upon awakening cannot understand why no one recognizes him.

- Paul Bunyan, a giant lumberjack, owns a great blue ox named Babe and has extraordinary physical strength. He is said to have plowed the Mississippi River while the impression of Babe's hoofprints created the Great Lakes.

> **TALL TALE:** a category of folktale based on nonexistent fictional characters developed through blatant exaggeration

LEGENDS, also called real tales, are based on real persons who accomplished the feats that are attributed to them, even if they are slightly exaggerated.

- For more than forty years, Johnny Appleseed (John Chapman) roamed Ohio and Indiana planting apple seeds.

- Daniel Boone—scout, adventurer, and pioneer—blazed the Wilderness Trail and made Kentucky safe for settlers.

- Paul Revere, a colonial patriot, rode through the New England countryside warning of the approach of British troops.

- George Washington cut down a cherry tree, which he could not deny. Or did he?

> **LEGEND:** a category of folktale based on real persons who accomplish great feats, even if they are slightly exaggerated

Sample Test Questions and Rationale

(Average)

1. Which of the following definitions best describes a parable?

   A. A short entertaining account of some happening, usually using talking animals as characters

   B. A slow, sad song or poem, or prose work expressing lamentation

   C. An extensive narrative work expressing universal truths concerning domestic life

   D. A short, simple story of an occurrence of a familiar kind, from which a moral or religious lesson may be drawn

   The answer is D.

   A parable is usually brief and should be interpreted as an allegory teaching a moral lesson. Jesus' forty parables are the model of the genre, but modern, secular examples exist, such as Wilfred Owen's "The Parable of The Young Man" and "The Young" (1920) or John Steinbeck's prose work *The Pearl* (1948).

(Rigorous)

2. Which is not a biblical allusion?

   A. The patience of Job

   B. Thirty pieces of silver

   C. "Man proposes; God disposes"

   D. "Suffer not yourself to be betrayed by a kiss"

   The answer is C.

   This saying is attributed to Thomas à Kempis (1379–1471) in his Imitation of Christ, Book 1, chapter 19. Anyone who exhibits the patience of Job is being compared to the Old Testament biblical figure who retained his faith despite being beset by a series of misfortunes. "Thirty pieces of silver" refers to the amount of money paid to Judas to identify Jesus. Although used by Patrick Henry, the quote in Answer D is a biblical reference to Judas' betrayal of Jesus by a kiss.

SKILL 2.6 **Demonstrating familiarity with the historical development of U.S. prose, poetry, and drama**

See Skill 2.1

COMPETENCY 3

UNDERSTAND THE PURPOSES, STRUCTURES, ELEMENTS, AND MEANINGS OF BRITISH AND COMMONWEALTH PROSE, POETRY, AND DRAMA OF DIFFERENT MOVEMENTS AND PERIODS

SKILL 3.1 Analyzing structures, elements, and themes of British and Commonwealth prose, poetry, and drama that are characteristic of particular British and Commonwealth cultures, regions, or historical periods

---

In Western civilization, the British literary canon has had the strongest impact on American literature and is still one of the most prevalent taught in U.S. schools today. While educators are making efforts to expand the spectrum of literary studies, British literature remains a staple of secondary English education.

Anglo-Saxon

The Anglo-Saxon period spanned six centuries but produced only a smattering of literature. The first British epic is *Beowulf*, anonymously transcribed by Christian monks many years after the events in the narrative supposedly occurred. This Teutonic saga relates the three-time triumph of the title character over monsters. "The Seafarer," a shorter poem, some history, and some riddles comprise the rest of the Anglo-Saxon canon.

Check out this lesson plan—An introduction to Beowulf language and poetics:

http://www.readwritethink. org/lessons/lesson_view. asp?id=813

Medieval

The Medieval period introduces Geoffrey Chaucer, considered the father of English literature. His *Canterbury Tales* are written in the vernacular, or common language of England, not in Latin. Thus, the tales are said to be the first work of British literature.

Thomas Malory's *Le Morte d'Arthur* brings together the extant tales from continental Europe as well as England concerning the legendary King Arthur, Merlin, Guenevere, and the Knights of the Round Table. This work is the generative work that gave rise to the many Arthurian legends, nearly all of which stir the chivalric imagination.

Renaissance and Elizabethan Periods

The Renaissance, the most important literary period since it is synonymous with William Shakespeare, begins with importing the idea of the Petrarchan or Italian sonnet into England. Sir Thomas Wyatt and Sir Philip Sydney wrote English versions of the Petrarchan sonnet.

Examine links to Renaissance—the Elizabethan world-related sites:

http://elizabethan.org/sites.htm

Sir Edmund Spenser invented a variation on this Italian sonnet form, aptly called the Spenserian sonnet. His masterpiece, the epic *The Faerie Queene*, honors Queen Elizabeth I's reign. He also wrote books on the Red Cross Knight, St. George and the Dragon, and a series of Arthurian adventures. Spencer was dubbed the "Poet's Poet." He created a nine-line stanza, the Spenserian stanza, consisting of eight lines of iambic pentameter and an extra-footed ninth line called an alexandrine.

William Shakespeare, the Bard of Avon, wrote 154 sonnets, 39 plays, and 2 long narrative poems. The sonnets are justifiably called the greatest sonnet sequence in all literature. Shakespeare dispensed with the octave/sestet format of the Italian sonnet and invented his three quatrain/one heroic couplet format. His plays are divided into comedies, history plays, tragedies, and romances or "problem plays." Lines from these plays are more often quoted than from any other work. The "Big Four" tragedies—*Hamlet, Macbeth, Othello,* and *King Lear*—are acknowledged to be the most brilliant examples of this genre.

Seventeenth Century

John Milton's devout Puritanism was the wellspring of the creative genius that closes the remarkable productivity of the English Renaissance. His social commentary in such works as *Aereopagitica, Samson Agonistes*, and his elegant sonnets would be enough to solidify his stature as a great writer. However, a masterpiece based in part on the Book of Genesis places Milton among the most renowned of all writers. *Paradise Lost*, written in balanced, elegant neoclassic form, truly does "justify the ways of God to man."

The greatest allegory about man's journey to the Celestial City (heaven) was written at the end of the English Renaissance, as was John Bunyan's *The Pilgrim's Progress*, which personifies virtues and vices.

The Jacobean Age gave us the marvelously witty and cleverly constructed conceits of John Donne's metaphysical sonnets as well as his insightful meditations and his version of sermons or homilies.

"Ask not for whom the bell tolls" and "No man is an island unto himself" are famous epigrams from Donne's *Meditations*. His most famous metaphor compares lovers to a footed compass, traveling seemingly separate but always leaning towards one another and conjoined in "A Valediction: Forbidding Mourning."

Eighteenth Century

Ben Jonson, author of the wickedly droll play, *Volpone*, and the Cavalier *carpe diem* poets Robert Herrick, Sir John Suckling, and Richard Lovelace also wrote during King James I's reign.

The Restoration and Enlightenment reflect the political turmoil surrounding the regicide of Charles I, the Interregnum Puritan government of Oliver Cromwell, and the restoration of the monarchy to England with the coronation of Charles II, who had been given refuge by King Louis XIV of France. Neoclassicism became the preferred writing style, especially for Alexander Pope.

New genres arising in the eighteenth century demonstrate the diversity of expression during this time. They include:

- The diary of Samuel Pepys

- The novels of Daniel Defoe

- The periodical essays and editorials of Joseph Addison and Richard Steele

- Alexander Pope's mock epic *The Rape of the Lock*.

Writers who followed were contemporaries of Dr. Samuel Johnson, the lexicographer of *The Dictionary of the English Language*. Fittingly, this Age of Johnson, which encompasses James Boswell's biography of Dr. Johnson, Robert Burns's Scottish dialect and regionalism in his evocative poetry, and the mystical pre-Romantic poetry of William Blake usher in the Romantic Age and its revolution against Neoclassicism.

Romantic Period

The Romantic Age encompasses two sets of poets: the First Generation Romantics and the Second Generation Romantics.

- William Wordsworth and Samuel Taylor Coleridge collaborated on *Lyrical Ballad*; this defines and exemplifies the tenets of this style of writing.

- The Second Generation Romantics include George Gordon, Lord Byron, Percy Bysshe Shelley, and John Keats. These poets wrote sonnets, odes, epics, and narrative poems—most dealing with homage to nature.

Wordsworth's most famous other works are "Intimations on Immortality" and "The Prelude." Byron's satirical epic *Don Juan* and his autobiographical *Childe Harold's Pilgrimage* are irreverent, witty, self-deprecating, and in part, cuttingly

Read about the Romantic period:

http://www.wwnorton.com/college/english/nael/romantic/welcome.htm

critical of other writers and critics. Shelley's odes and sonnets are remarkable for their sensory imagery. Keats' sonnets, odes, and longer narrative poem *The Eve of St. Agnes* are remarkable for their introspection given the tender age of the poet, who died when he was only twenty-five. In fact, all of the Second Generation Romantics died before their times. Wordsworth, who lived to be eighty, outlived them all, including Coleridge, his friend and collaborator.

Others who wrote during the Romantic Age include the essayist Charles Lamb and the novelist Jane Austen. The Brontë sisters, Charlotte and Emily, wrote one novel each, which are noted as two of the finest ever written: *Jane Eyre* and *Wuthering Heights*. Mary Anne Evans, also known as George Eliot, wrote several important novels: her masterpiece, *Middlemarch;* and *Silas Marner, Adam Bede,* and *Mill on the Floss.*

Nineteenth Century

Read about the Victorian period:

http://www.victorianweb. org/

The Victorian Period is remarkable for the diversity and proliferation of work in poetry, prose, and drama. Poets who are typified as Victorians include Alfred, Lord Tennyson, who wrote *Idylls of the King*, twelve narrative poems about the Arthurian legend; and Robert Browning, who wrote chilling, dramatic monologues such as "My Last Duchess" as well as long, poetic narratives such as *The Pied Piper of Hamlin*. His wife, Elizabeth Barrett Browning, wrote two major works: the epic feminist poem *Aurora Leigh* and her deeply moving and provocative *Sonnets from the Portuguese,* in which she details her deep love for Robert and, to her, his startling reciprocation.

Gerard Manley Hopkins, a Catholic priest, wrote poetry with sprung rhythm. A. E. Housmann, Matthew Arnold, and the Pre-Raphaelites, especially Dante Gabriel Rosetti and his sister, Christina Rosetti, contributed much to round out the Victorian Era poetic scene. The Pre-Raphaelites, a group of nineteenth-century English painters, poets, and critics, reacted against Victorian materialism and the neoclassical conventions of academic art by producing earnest, quasi-religious works. Medieval and early Renaissance painters up to the time of the Italian painter Raphael inspired the group.

Robert Louis Stevenson, the great Scottish novelist, wrote adventure/history lessons for young adults.

Victorian prose ranges from the incomparable, keenly woven plot structures of Charles Dickens to the deeply moving Dorset/Wessex novels of Thomas Hardy, in which women are repressed and life is more struggle than euphoria. Rudyard Kipling wrote about colonialism in India in works like *Kim* and *The Jungle Book* that create exotic locales and convey a specific viewpoint concerning the Raj, the British colonial government during Queen Victoria's reign.

Victorian drama is a product mainly of Oscar Wilde, whose satirical masterpiece *The Importance of Being Earnest* details and lampoons Victorian social mores.

Twentieth Century

The early twentieth century is represented mainly by the towering achievement
of George Bernard Shaw's dramas: *St. Joan, Man and Superman, Major
Barbara,* and *Arms and the Man*, to name a few. Novelists are too numerous to list,
but the following are some of the century's very best:

- Joseph Conrad
- E. M. Forster
- Virginia Woolf
- James Joyce
- Nadine Gordimer
- Graham Greene
- George Orwell
- D. H. Lawrence

Twentieth-century poets of renown and merit include:

- W. H. Auden
- Robert Graves
- T. S. Eliot
- Edith Sitwell
- Stephen Spender
- Dylan Thomas
- Philip Larkin
- Ted Hughes
- Sylvia Plath
- Hugh MacDarmid

World War I, also known as the First World War, the Great War, and The
War to End All Wars, raged from July 1914 until the final Armistice on
November 11, 1918.

More than nine million soldiers died on the various battlefields, and nearly that
many more perished on the participating countries' home fronts as a result of
food shortages and genocide committed under the cover of various civil wars and
internal conflicts. However, more people died of the worldwide influenza out-
break at the end of the war and shortly after than died in the hostilities.

The experiences of the Great War led to a collective national trauma afterwards
for all the participating countries. The optimism of the 1900s was entirely gone,
and those who fought in the war became known as "the Lost Generation" because
they never fully recovered from their experiences. For the next few years, memo-
rials continued to be erected in thousands of European villages and towns. A
sense of disillusionment and cynicism became pronounced, and nihilism became
popular. The world had never before witnessed such devastation, and the depiction in newspapers and on movie screens made the horrors more personal.

War has always spawned creative bursts, and this one was no exception. Poetry, stories, and movies proliferated after World War I. In fact, it's still a fertile subject for art of all kinds, particularly literature and movies. In 2006, young director Paul Gross created, directed, and starred in Passchendaele, based on the stories told him by his grandfather, who was haunted all his life by his killing of a young German soldier in this War to End All Wars.

Literature based on World War I includes:

- "The Soldier," poem by Rupert Brooke
- Goodbye to All That, autobiography by Robert Graves
- "Anthem for Doomed Youth" and "Strange Meeting," poems by Wilfred Owen, published posthumously by Siegfried Sassoon in 1918
- "In Flanders Fields," poem by John McCrae
- *Three Soldiers*, novel by John Dos Passos
- *Journey's End*, play by R. C. Sherriff
- *All Quiet on the Western Front*, novel by Erich Maria Remarque
- *Death of a Hero*, novel by Richard Aldington
- *A Farewell to Arms*, novel by Ernest Hemingway
- *Memoirs of an Infantry Officer*, novel by Siegfried Sassoon

In the Caribbean, Africa, Asia, and the Pacific, postwar decolonization was achieved with almost unseemly haste in the face of increasingly powerful nationalist movements, and Britain rarely fought to retain any territory.

Representative literature includes:

- *Heart of Darkness*, novel by Joseph Conrad
- *Passage to India*, novel by E. M. Forster
- *"Gunga Din,"* poem by Rudyard Kipling

Sample Test Questions and Rationale

(Easy)

1. Charles Dickens, Robert Browning, and Robert Louis Stevenson were:

   A. Victorians

   B. Medievalists

   C. Elizabethans

   D. Absurdists

   The answer is A.

   The Victorian Period is remarkable for the diversity and quality of its literature. Robert Browning wrote chilling monologues, such as "My Last Duchess," and long poetic narratives, such as *The Pied Piper of Hamlin*. Robert Louis Stevenson wrote his works partly for young adults, whose imaginations were quite taken by his *Treasure Island* and *The Case of Dr. Jekyll and Mr. Hyde*. Charles Dickens tells of the misery of the time and the complexities of Victorian society in novels such as *Oliver Twist* or *Great Expectations*.

(Rigorous)

2. The following lines from Robert Browning's poem "My Last Duchess" come from an example of what form of dramatic literature?

   That's my last Duchess painted on the wall,
   Looking as if she were alive. I call
   That piece a wonder, now: Frà Pandolf's hands
   Worked busily a day, and there she stands.
   Will 't please you sit and look at her?

   A. Tragedy

   B. Comic opera

   C. Dramatis personae

   D. Dramatic monologue

   The answer is D.

   A dramatic monologue is a speech given by a character or narrator that reveals characteristics of the character or narrator. This form was first made popular by Robert Browning, a Victorian poet. Tragedy is a form of literature in which the protagonist is overwhelmed by opposing forces. Comic opera is a form of sung music based on a light or happy plot. "Dramatis personae" is the Latin phrase for the cast of a play.

Sample Test Questions and Rationale

(Rigorous)

3. Which author did not write satire?

   A. Joseph Addison

   B. Richard Steele

   C. Alexander Pope

   D. John Bunyan

The answer is D.

John Bunyan was a religious writer, known for his autobiography, *Grace Abounding to the Chief of Sinners*, as well as other books, all religious in their inspiration, such as *The Holy City, or the New Jerusalem* (1665), *A Confession of My Faith*, and *A Reason of My Practice* (1672), or *The Holy War* (1682).

(Rigorous)

4. "Every one must pass through Vanity Fair to get to the Celestial City" is an allusion from a:

   A. Chinese folk tale

   B. Norse saga

   C. British allegory

   D. German fairy tale

The answer is C.

This is a reference to John Bunyan's Pilgrim's Progress from *This World to That Which Is to Come* (Part I, 1678; Part II, 1684), in which the hero, Christian, flees the City of Destruction and must undergo different trials and tests to get to the Celestial City.

SKILL 3.2 Recognizing the relationship of a British or Commonwealth work of prose, poetry, or drama to the historical period or literary movement of which it is a part

Elizabethan Age

The reign of Elizabeth I ushered in a renaissance that led to the end of the medieval age. It was a very fertile literary period.

- The exploration of the new world expanded the vision of all levels of the social order from royalty to peasant

- The rejection of Catholicism by many in favor of Protestantism opened up whole new vistas to thought and daily life

- The manufacture of cloth increased, driving many people from the countryside into the cities

- The population of London exploded, creating a metropolitan business center

- William Caxton brought printing to England in the 1470s

- Literacy increased from 30 percent in the fifteenth century to over 60 percent by 1530

These seem dramatic changes, and they were, but they occurred gradually.

The Italian Renaissance had a great influence on the renaissance in England, and most early sixteenth-century written works were in Latin. It was assumed that a learned person must express his thoughts in that language. However, a determination that vernacular English was valuable in writing began to emerge, and certain scholars began to defend this notion. Elizabeth I's tutor, Roger Ascham, for example, wrote in English.

The publishing of Martin Luther's Ninety-five Theses in 1517 brought on the Reformation—an attempt to return to pure Christianity—and the breakup of western Christendom. This movement eventually led to the secularization of society and the establishment of the king or queen as the head of this new/old church. The Reformation also brought about a new feeling that being religious was also being patriotic; it promoted nationalism.

The ascension of Elizabeth I to the throne also followed a very turbulent period regarding succession, and she ruled for forty-five peaceful years, which allowed arts and literature to flourish.

Although she herself was headstrong and difficult, Elizabeth I happened to have very shrewd political instincts and entrusted power to solid, talented men, most particularly Robert Cecil, her Secretary, and Francis Walsingham, whom she put in charge of foreign policy. She identified with her country as no previous ruler had, and that in itself brought on a period of intense nationalism. Elizabeth I was a symbol of Englishness. The defeat of the Spanish armada in 1588, for example, was the direct result of the strong support she had from her own nation.

Drama was the principal form of literature in this age. Religious plays had been a part of the life of England for a long time, particularly the courtly life. In the Elizabethan age, though, plays became more and more secular and were created primarily for courtly entertainment. By the 1560s, Latin drama, particularly the tragedies of Seneca and the comedies of Plautus and Terence, began to wield an influence in England.

Courtyards of inns became favorite places for the presentation of plays, but in 1576, the Earl of Leicester's Men constructed their own building outside the city and called it The Theatre. Other theatres followed. Each theatre had its own repertory company, and performances were held for the general public as well as for the queen and her court. It is said that Shakespeare wrote *The Merry Wives of Windsor* at the specific command of the queen, who liked Falstaff and wanted to see him in love. It was also for the courtly audience that poetry was introduced into drama.

William Shakespeare and Christopher Marlowe dominated the late 1500s. At the turn of the century, only a few years before Elizabeth I's death, Ben Jonson began writing his series of satirical comedies.

Court favor was notoriously precarious and depended on the whims of the queen and others. Much of the satire of the period reflects the disappointment of writers like Edmund Spenser and John Lyly and the superficiality and treachery of the court atmosphere. "A thousand hopes, but all nothing," wrote Lyly, "a hundred promises, but yet nothing."

Not all literature was dictated by the court, however. The developing middle classes had their own style. Thomas Heywood and Thomas Deloney catered to bourgeois tastes.

The two main universities, Oxford and Cambridge, were also sources for the production of literature. The primary aim of the colleges was to develop ministers, since the break with the Catholic Church had brought about a clergy shortage. However, most university men couldn't make livings as ministers or academics, so they wrote as a way of earning income. Thomas Nashe, Christopher Marlowe, Robert Greene, and George Peele all reveal in their writings how difficult this path was. Remuneration came mostly from patrons.

Greene had sixteen different patrons from seventeen books, whereas Shakespeare had a satisfactory relationship with the Earl of Southampton and didn't need to seek other support. Publishers also would sometimes pay for a manuscript, which they would then own. Unfortunately, if the manuscript did not meet approval with all who could condemn it—the court, the religious leaders, prominent citizens—the author was culpable. Very few writers became as comfortable as Shakespeare did. His success was not only in writing, however, but also from his business acumen.

Writing was seen more as a craft than as an art in this period. There was not great conflict between art and nature, and there was little distinction between literature, sports of the field, or the arts of the kitchen. Balance and control were important in the England of this day, and these concepts are reflected in the era's writing, the poetry in particular. The sestina, a form in which the last words of each line in the first stanza are repeated in a different order in each of the following stanzas, became very popular. Verse forms ranged from the extremely simple four-line ballad stanza to the rather complicated form of the sonnet and the elaborate, beautiful eighteen-line stanza of Spenser's *Epithalamion*.

The term sonnet was used loosely for any short poem. Sonnets were called quatorzains. Quatorzains are fourteen-line poems in iambic pentameter with elaborate rhyme schemes. However, Chaucer's seven-line rhyme royal stanza also survived in the sixteenth century. Shakespeare used this form in *The Rape of Lucrece*. Another innovation was Spenser's nine-line stanza, called the Spenserian stanza, as used in *The Faerie Queene*.

As for themes, some of the darkness that permeated the previous period can still be seen in some Elizabethan literature, such as Shakespeare's *Richard II*. At the same time, however, a spirit of joy, gaiety, innocence, and lightheartedness can be seen in much of the most popular literature of the day, and pastoral themes became popular. The theme of the burning desire for conquest and achievement was also significant in Elizabethan thought.

Important writers of the Elizabethan Age include:

- Sir Thomas More (1478-1535)
- Sir Thomas Wyatt the Elder (1503-1542)
- Edmund Spenser (1552-1599)
- Sir Walter Raleigh (1552-1618)
- Sir Philip Sidney (1554-1586)
- John Lyly (1554-1606)
- George Peele (1556-1596)
- Christopher Marlowe (1564-1593)
- William Shakespeare (1564-1616)

The Industrial Revolution

The Industrial Revolution began in England with the development of the steam engine. However, the steam engine was only one component of the major technological, socioeconomic, and cultural innovations of the early nineteenth century that began in Britain and spread throughout the world. An economy based on manual labor was replaced by one dominated by industry and the manufacture of machinery. Textile industries also underwent rapid growth and change. Canals being built, roads improved, and railways constructed.

Steam power (fueled primarily by coal) and powered machinery (primarily in the manufacture of textiles) drove the remarkable amplification of production capacity. All-metal machine tools were developed by 1820, making it possible to produce more machines.

The exact dates of the Industrial Revolution vary. Some scholars say that the movement began in the 1780s and wasn't fully perceived until the 1830s or 1840s. Others maintain that the beginning was earlier, about 1760, and began

Characteristics of the
Industrial Revolution

- Economy based
  on industry and
  the manufacture of
  machinery
- Steam-powered
  machinery
- Development of a middle
  class
- Exploiting children for
  labor
- Shift from hand-produced
  goods to machine-
  produced goods
- Development of
  organized labor
- Mass migration of rural
  families to urban areas
- Separation of husband
  and wife and changing of
  gender roles
- Rapid increases in
  literacy and political
  participation

to manifest visible changes by 1830. Regardless of the exact dates, the Industrial Revolution's effects spread through Western Europe and North America throughout the nineteenth century, eventually affecting all major countries of the world. The impact on society has been compared to the period when agriculture began to develop and the nomadic lifestyle was abandoned.

The first Industrial Revolution was followed immediately by the second Industrial Revolution around 1850, when the progress in technology and world economy gained momentum with the introduction of steam-powered ships and railways and eventually the internal combustion engine and electrical power generation.

The most noticeable social effect of the Industrial Revolution was the development of a middle class of industrialists and businessmen and a decline in the landed class of nobility and gentry. Although working people had more opportunities for employment in the new mills and factories, working conditions were often less than desirable. Exploiting children for labor wasn't new—it had always existed—but the practice became more apparent and perhaps more egregious as the need for cheap labor increased. In England, laws regarding employment of children began to be developed in 1833.

Another effect of industrialization was the enormous shift from hand-produced goods to machine-produced ones and the loss of jobs among weavers and others, which resulted in violence against the factories and machinery beginning around 1811.

Eventually, the British government took measures to protect industry. Organized labor developed around the same time, too. Because laborers now worked together in factories, mines, and mills, they were better able to organize and gain advantages they felt they deserved. Conditions were bad enough in these workplaces that the energy to bring about change was significant, and trade unions eventually emerged.

Laborers quickly learned to use the weapon of the strike to get what they wanted. The strikes were often violent, and although the managers usually gave in to most of the demands made by strikers, the animosity between management and labor was endemic.

The mass migration of rural families into urban areas also resulted in poor living conditions, long work hours, extensive use of children for labor, and a polluted atmosphere.

Another effect of industrialization was the separation of husband and wife. One person stayed at home and looked after the home and family while the other went off to work—a very different configuration from an agriculture-based economy where the entire family was involved in making a living. Eventually, gender roles began to be defined by the new configuration of labor in this new world order.

The application of industrial processes to printing brought about a great expansion in newspaper and popular book publishing. This development, in turn, was followed by rapid increases in literacy and eventually in demands for mass political participation.

SKILL 3.3 Comparing themes shared in several literary works from the same British or Commonwealth culture or period

There are four major time periods of writings: Neoclassicism, Romanticism, Realism, and Naturalism. Certain authors, among these Chaucer, Shakespeare, and Donne, though writing during a particular literary period, are considered to have a style all their own.

Neoclassicism

NEOCLASSICISM was patterned after the greatest writings of classical Greece and Rome, this type of writing is characterized by a balanced, graceful, well-crafted, refined, elevated style. Major proponents of this style are poet laureates John Dryden and Alexander Pope. The eras in which they wrote are called the Ages of Dryden and Pope, respectively. Neoclassical writing focuses on the group, not the individual.

> **NEOCLASSICISM:** a major time period of writings, patterned after the greatest writings of classical Greece and Rome

Romanticism

ROMANTICISM encompasses writings focused on the individual. Emotions and feelings are validated. Nature acts as an inspiration for creativity; it is a balm of the spirit. Romantics hearken back to medieval, chivalric themes and ambiance. They also emphasize supernatural, Gothic themes and settings, which are characterized by gloom and darkness. Imagination is stressed. New types of writings include detective and horror stories and autobiographical introspection, such as the poems and essays by William Wordsworth.

> **ROMANTICISM:** a major time period of writings, focused on the individual

There are two generations of romantics in British Literature. First Generation Romantics include William Wordsworth and Samuel Taylor Coleridge, whose collaborative, *Lyrical Ballads* defines Romanticism and its components. Wordsworth maintained that the scenes and events of everyday life and the speech of ordinary people were the raw material of which poetry could and should be made. This

Romanticism spread to the United States, where Ralph Waldo Emerson and Henry David Thoreau adopted its tenets in their transcendental romanticism, emphasizing reasoning. Further extensions of this style are found in Edgar Allan Poe's Gothic writings.

Second Generation Romantics include the ill-fated Englishmen Lord Byron, John Keats, and Percy Bysshe Shelley. Byron and Shelley epitomize the romantic poet for some (in their personal lives as well as in their work); they also wrote resoundingly in protest against social and political wrongs and in defense of the struggles for liberty in Italy and Greece. The Second Generation Romantics stressed personal introspection and the love of beauty and nature as requisites of inspiration.

Realism

REALISM: a major time period of writings, focused on the common man and his socioeconomic problems

Unlike classical and neoclassical writing, which often deal with aristocracies and nobility or the gods, writers of **REALISM** discuss the common man and his socioeconomic problems in a nonsentimental way. Muckraking, social injustice, domestic abuse, and inner-city conflicts are examples of writings by writers of Realism. Realistic writers include Thomas Hardy, George Bernard Shaw, and Henrik Ibsen.

Naturalism

NATURALISM: a major time period of writings, focused on the underbelly of society, usually the lower-class struggles

NATURALISM represents Realism pushed to the maximum, writing that exposes the underbelly of society, usually the lower-class struggles. This is the world of penury, injustice, abuse, ghetto survival, hungry children, single parenting, and substance abuse. Émile Zola was inspired by his readings in history and medicine and attempted to apply methods of scientific observation to the depiction of pathological human character, notably in his series of novels devoted to several generations of one French family.

Sample Test Question and Rationale

(Rigorous)

1. **Which choice below best defines naturalism?**

   A. A belief that the writer or artist should apply scientific objectivity in his or her observation and treatment of life without imposing value judgments

   B. The doctrine that teaches that the existing world is the best to be hoped for

   C. The doctrine that teaches that God is not a personality, but that all laws, forces, and manifestations of the universe are God-related

   D. A philosophical doctrine that professes that the truth of all knowledge must always be in question

The answer is A.

Naturalism is a movement that was started by French writers Jules and Edmond de Goncourt with their novel *Germinie Lacerteux* (1865), but its real leader is Emile Zola, who wanted to bring "a slice of life" to his readers. His saga, *Les Rougon Macquart*, consists in twenty-two novels depicting various aspects of social life. English-writing authors representative of this movement include George Moore and George Gissing in England, but the most important naturalist novel in English is Theodore Dreiser's *Sister Carrie*.

SKILL 3.4 Recognizing historical elements, references, and antecedents in British and Commonwealth prose, poetry, and drama

See Skill 3.1

SKILL 3.5 Analyzing the influence of mythic, traditional, or earlier literature on British and Commonwealth prose, poetry, and drama

See Skill 3.1

SKILL 3.6 Demonstrating familiarity with the historical development of British and Commonwealth prose, poetry, and drama

See Skill 3.1

COMPETENCY 4

UNDERSTAND THE PURPOSES, STRUCTURES, ELEMENTS, AND MEANINGS OF WORLD PROSE, POETRY, AND DRAMA OF DIFFERENT MOVEMENTS AND PERIODS

> **SKILL 4.1** Analyzing structures, elements, and themes of world prose, poetry, and drama that are characteristic of particular world cultures, regions, or historical periods

Literary studies expanded beyond the borders of America and Britain to include writing from other cultures.

North American Literature

North American literature is divided between the United States, Canada, and Mexico. Canadian writers of note include feminist Margaret Atwood (*The Hand Maiden's Tale*); Alice Munro, a remarkable short story writer; and W. P. Kinsella, another short story writer whose two major subjects are North American Indians and baseball. Mexican writers include 1990 Nobel Prize– winning poet Octavio Paz (*The Labyrinth of Solitude*) and feminist Rosario Castillanos (*The Nine Guardians*).

Caribbean/Central American Literature

The Caribbean and Central America encompass a vast area and cultures that reflect oppression and colonialism by England, Spain, Portugal, France, and The Netherlands. Caribbean writers include Samuel Selvon from Trinidad and Armando Valladares of Cuba. Central American authors include dramatist Carlos Solorzano from Guatemala, whose plays include Dona Beatriz, The Hapless, The Magician, and The Hands of God.

South American Literature

Chilean Gabriela Mistral was the first Latin American writer to win the Nobel Prize for literature. She is best known for her collection of poetry, *Desolation and Feeling*.

Chile was also home to Pablo Neruda, who also won the Nobel Prize for literature for his poetry. His twenty-nine volumes of poetry have been translated into more than sixty languages, attesting to his universal appeal. His works *Twenty Love Poems* and *Song of Despair* are justly famous. Isabel Allende is carrying on the Chilean literary tradition with her acclaimed novel, *House of Spirits*.

Many literary critics consider Argentine Jorge Luis Borges to be the most important writer of his century from South America. His collections of short stories, *Ficciones*, brought him universal recognition. Also from Argentina, Silvina Ocampo is famed for her poetry and short story collections, which include The Fury and The Days of the Night.

Noncontinental European Literature

Horacio Quiroga represents Uruguay, and Brazil has Joao Guimaraes Rosa, whose novel *The Devil to Pay*, is considered first-rank world literature.

Germany

German poet and playwright Friedrich von Schiller is best known for his history plays *William Tell* and *The Maid of Orleans*. He is a leading literary figure in Germany's Golden Age of Literature. Rainer Maria Rilke, the great lyric poet, is also one of the poets of the unconscious, or stream of consciousness. Germany also has given the world Herman Hesse (*Siddartha*), Gunter Grass (*The Tin Drum*), and the greatest of all German writers, Johann Wolfgang von Goethe.

Scandinavia

Scandinavian literature includes the work of Hans Christian Andersen of Denmark, who advanced the fairy tale genre with such wistful tales as "The Little Mermaid" and "Thumbelina." The social commentary of Henrik Ibsen in Norway startled the world through drama exploring such issues as feminism (*The Doll's House* and *Hedda Gabler*) and the effects of sexually transmitted diseases (*The Wild Duck and Ghosts*). Sweden's Selma Lagerlof is the first woman to win the Nobel Prize for literature. Her novels include *Gosta Berling's Saga* and the world-renowned *The Wonderful Adventures of Nils*, a children's work.

Russia

Russian literature is vast and monumental. Who has not heard of Fyodor Dostoyevski's *Crime and Punishment* and *The Brothers Karamazov* or of Count Leo Tolstoy's *War and Peace*?

Dostoyevski's influence on modern writers cannot be overstressed. Tolstoy's *War and Peace* is the sweeping account of Napoleon's invasion of Russia and taking of Moscow. This novel is called the national novel of Russia. Tolstoy's ability to create realistic and unforgettable female characters, especially Natasha in *War and Peace* and Anna in *Anna Karenina* further advances Tolstoy's greatness.

Aleksandr Pushkin is famous for great short stories; Anton Chekhov for drama (*Uncle Vanya, The Three Sisters, The Cherry Orchard*); and Yvgeny Yvteshenko for poetry (*Babi Yar*). Boris Pasternak won the Nobel Prize (*Dr. Zhivago*). Aleksandr Solzhenitsyn (*The Gulag Archipelago*) returned to Russia after years of expatriation in Vermont. Ilya Varshavsky, who creates fictional dystopias, or the opposite of utopias, represents the genre of science fiction.

France

France has a multifaceted canon of great literature that is broad in scope and almost always champions some social cause, including:

- The poignant short stories of Guy de Maupassant
- The fantastic poetry of Charles Baudelaire (*Fleurs du Mal*)
- The groundbreaking lyrical poetry of Jean Nicolas Arthur Rimbaud and Paul Verlaine
- The existentialism of Jean-Paul Sartre (*No Exit, The Flies, Nausea*), Andre Malraux (*The Fall*), and Albert Camus (*The Stranger and The Plague*), the recipient of the 1957 Nobel Prize for literature

Learn more about Jean Paul Sartre:

http://www.users. muohio.edu/shermalw/ honors_2001_fall/ honors_papers_2001/ detwilerj_Sartre.htm

Drama in France is best represented by Edmond Rostand's *Cyrano de Bergerac* and the neoclassical dramas of Jean Baptiste Racine and Pierre Corneille (*El Cid*). Feminist writers include Simone de Beauvoir and Sidonie-Gabrielle Colette, known for her short stories and novels. The great French novelists include André Gide, Honoré de Balzac (*Cousin Bette*), Stendhal (*The Red and the Black*), and Alexandre Dumas (*The Three Musketeers* and *The Man in the Iron Mask*). Victor Hugo is the Charles Dickens of French literature, having penned the masterpieces *The Hunchback of Notre Dame* and *Les Miserables*. The stream of consciousness of Marcel Proust's *Remembrance of Things Past* and the Absurdist theatre of Samuel Beckett and Eugène Ionesco (*The Rhinoceros*) attest to the groundbreaking genius of the French writers.

Slavic Nations

Austrian writer Franz Kafka (*The Metamorphosis, The Trial,* and *The Castle*)
is considered by many to be the literary voice of the first half of the twentieth
century. Poet Vaclav Havel represents the Czech Republic. Slovakia has dramatist Karel Capek (R.U.R.). Romania is represented by Elie Weisel (*Night*), a
Nobel Prize winner.

Spain

Spain's great writers include Miguel de Cervantes (*Don Quixote*) and Juan
Ramon Jimenez. The anonymous national epic, *El Cid*, has been translated
into many languages.

Italy

Italy's greatest writers include Virgil (*The Aeneid*); Giovanni Boccaccio (The
Decameron); Dante Alighieri (*The Divine Comedy*); and the more contemporary Alberto Moravia.

Ancient Greece

Greece is the cradle not only of democracy, but of literature as well. Greece will
always be prominent in literary stature due to Homer's epics, *The Iliad* and
The Odyssey. Aside from Shakespeare, no secular writer is more often cited. The
works of Plato and Aristotle in philosophy; of Aeschylus, Euripides, and
Sophocles in tragedy; and of Aristophanes in comedy further solidify Greece's
preeminence.

Africa

African literary greats include South Africans Nadine Gordimer (Nobel Prize
for literature) and Peter Abrahams (*Tell Freedom: Memories of Africa*).
Chinua Achebe (*Things Fall Apart*) and the poet Wole Soyinka hail from
Nigeria. Mark Mathabane wrote an autobiography, Kaffir Boy, about growing
up in South Africa. Egyptian writer Naguib Mahfouz and Doris Lessing
from Rhodesia (now Zimbabwe) write about race relations in their respective
countries. Lessing won the 2007 Nobel Prize for literature. Because of her radical
politics, Lessing was once banned from her homeland and the Union of South
Africa; so was Alan Paton, whose seemingly simple story *Cry, the Beloved
Country* brought the plight of African-Americans and the whites' fear of African-
Americans under apartheid to the rest of the world.

*Learn more about
postcolonial literature
in English:*

*http://www.thecore.nus.
edu.sg/post/misc/africov.
html no page*

Far East Literature

Asia has many modern writers who are being translated for the western reading public. India's Krishan Chandar has authored more than 300 stories. Rabindranath Tagore won the Nobel Prize for literature in 1913 (*Song Offerings*). R. K. Narayan, India's most famous writer (*The Guide*), is interested in mythology and legends of India. Santha Rama Rau's work *Gifts of Passage* is her true story of life in a British school where she tries to preserve her Indian culture and traditional home.

Revered as Japan's most famous female author, Fumiko Hayashi (*Drifting Clouds*) had written more than 270 literary works by the time of her death.

The 1968 Nobel Prize for literature was awarded to Yasunari Kawabata (*The Sound of the Mountain, The Snow Country*). His "Palm-of-the-Hand Stories" take the essentials of Haiku poetry and transform them into the short story genre.

Katai Tayama (*The Quilt*) is touted as the father of the Japanese confessional novel. His works, characterized as naturalism, are definitely not for the squeamish. The "slice of life" psychological writings of Ryunosuke Akutagawa gained him acclaim in the western world. His short stories, especially "Rashamon" and "In a Grove," are greatly praised for their style and content.

China, too, has contributed to the literary world. Li Po, the T'ang dynasty poet from China's Golden Age, revealed his interest in folklore by preserving the folk songs and mythology of China. Po further allows his readers to explore the Chinese philosophy of Taoism and to understand feelings against expansionism during the T'ang dynastic rule. The T'ang dynasty, which was one of great diversity in the arts, saw Jiang Fang help create the Chinese version of a short story. His themes often express love between a man and a woman.

Modern feminist and political concerns are written eloquently by Ting Ling, under the pseudonym Chiang Ping-Chih. Her stories reflect her concerns about social injustice and her commitment to the women's movement.

Sample Test Questions and Rationale

(Easy)

1. Considered one of the first feminist plays, this Ibsen drama ends with a door slamming symbolizing the lead character's emancipation from traditional societal norms.

    A. *The Wild Duck*

    B. *Hedda Gabler*

    C. *Ghosts*

    D. *The Doll's House*

The answer is D.

Nora in *The Doll's House* leaves her husband and her children when she realizes her husband is not the man she thought he was. Hedda Gabler, another feminist icon, shoots herself. *The Wild Duck* deals with the conflict between idealism and family secrets. *Ghosts*, considered one of Ibsen's most controversial plays, deals with many social ills, including alcoholism, incest, and religious hypocrisy.

(Average)

2. The writing of Russian naturalists is:

    A. Optimistic

    B. Pessimistic

    C. Satirical

    D. whimsical

The answer is B.

Although the movement, which originated with the critic Vissarion Belinsky, was particularly strong in the 1840s, it can be said that the works of Feodor Dostoevsky, Leo Tolstoy, Anton Chekov, Ivan Turgenev, and Aleksandr Pushkin owe much to it. These authors' works are among the best in international literature, yet they are shrouded in stark pessimism. Tolstoy's *Anna Karenina* or Dostoevsky's *Crime and Punishment* are good examples of this dark outlook.

(Rigorous)

3. Which of the following is the best definition of existentialism?

    A. The philosophical doctrine that matter is the only reality and that everything in the world, including thought, will, and feeling, can be explained only in terms of matter

    B. A philosophy that views things as they should be or as one would wish them to be

    C. A philosophical and literary movement, variously religious and atheistic, stemming from Kierkegaard and represented by Sartre

    D. The belief that all events are determined by fate and are hence inevitable

The answer is C.

Even though there are other very important thinkers in the movement known as existentialism, such as Albert Camus and Maurice Merleau-Ponty, Jean-Paul Sartre remains the main figure in this movement.

SKILL 4.2 **Recognizing the relationship of a work of world prose, poetry, or drama to the historical period or literary movement of which it is a part**

Sumaria

Check out Sumerian art and architecture at:

http://www.crystalinks.com/sumerart.html

Between 7000 BCE and 3000 BCE, the domestication of animals, the development of agriculture, and the establishment of an agricultural surplus led to the invention of writing, thus making possible the emergence of literature and the development of human civilization.

These three developments allowed the small, nomadic groups of hunters and gatherers who had until then existed in pockets all over the world to evolve into larger, stationary communities. The first of these communities developed in an area in the Middle East called Mesopotamia, meaning "Land Between two Rivers," the Tigris and the Euphrates. This ancestor to civilization as we know it was called Sumer, and the Sumerians created the wheel and the first written language.

Perhaps the Sumerians were the first to create so much of what is fundamental to civilization because of their unsurpassed ability to create an agricultural surplus. With their position between two flowing rivers, the Sumerians developed an extensive irrigation system that allowed them to create an abundant surplus. This surplus meant greater economic stability, security, and the ability to support a much larger population within the walls of their cities.

The growing population stimulated the development of governance and specialization. Artisans, governors, builders, regulators, merchants, and priests flourished. Keeping track of all this activity required the development of some kind of record keeping. At first, pictographs (images directly representing concrete objects) were etched into soft clay tablets and allowed to dry.

The scope of record keeping eventually grew from recording how many sacks of barley a farmer brought to the temple to describing in great detail and enthusiasm the exploits of the kings. Thus, with the evolution of the city-state and then the nation, pictographs quickly became insufficient to meet the needs of this new societal structure. Eventually, the Sumerians developed symbols to represent abstract qualities such as courage and love.

Dark Ages

With the destruction of the Roman Empire in the fifth century, the Roman Catholic Church became the dominant and unifying source in Europe. With the ascendancy of the church and the demise of Rome, the social, political, and artistic achievements of the classical age were effectively "lost" for centuries, and Western civilizations entered a time known as the Dark, or Middle, Ages.

Fifteenth and Sixteenth Centuries

By the fifteenth century, however, the lot of the individual had improved dramatically, and the overwhelming influence of the Catholic Church was challenged. This period is known as the Renaissance, which started in Italy in the mid fourteenth century. The Renaissance is associated with the rediscovery and revival of classical Greek and Latin philosophy, literature, and art.

In the fifteenth and early sixteenth centuries, the invention of the printing press (around 1450) and the revolt of Martin Luther, a German Catholic monk, helped to fuel the revival of classical thought and to fuel challenges to the supremacy of the Catholic Church.

The development of paper gave rise to the invention of the printing press. Prior to the development of paper, parchment made from the skin of farm animals was used for writing. Considering that one animal generally produced about four leaves or sheets of parchment, reprinting a book the size of the Bible required the slaughter of at least 300 sheep or calves, making it a very expensive process reserved for the very elite in society.

With the development of paper from rags and the invention of the printing press, printing books and pamphlets became very cheap. In addition, books began to be printed not only in Greek and Latin (the language of scholars and diplomats) but also in the vernacular (the language of the common people). This was very important to the revolutionary success of Martin Luther, who in 1517 nailed his famous *Ninety- Five Theses* to the door of the castle church of Wittenberg.

His Ninety- Five Theses amounted to objections (protestations) regarding the then- pervasive sale of indulgences (pardons for sins) by the Catholic Church throughout Europe, especially in Germany.

Without the printing press, few would have known of or followed Luther's challenge to Roman Catholic authority. The German monk and his supporters turned immediately to the printing press, though, and sent out hundreds of pamphlets explaining his protests against Rome, gaining the support of the German people at all levels of society. As a result, when Luther was excommunicated by the Church in Rome, he and his followers became known as Lutherans, and the first of the Protestant or "protesting" religions was born.

The study of classical texts and advances in science and astronomy aided this break with the Roman Catholic Church by challenging the traditional thinking that had been endorsed and enforced by the Church for generations.

Learn more about Martin Luther at:

http://www.educ.msu. edu/homepages/laurence/ reformation/Luther/Luther. htm

The Renaissance

While the Renaissance revived the classics, the subsequent Age of Reason (also known as The Enlightenment) extolled and emulated the clarity and rational thinking of the great classical writers, thinkers, and artists especially of the Romans. This focus on reason is evident in the writings of John Dryden (1631–1700), in the mathematically exact music of the harpsichord, and in the classical ionic and doric architecture exhibited in palaces and stately homes of this period.

The Romantics

By the late 1700s, however, the Romantics began to challenge this exclusive admiration for the purely intellectual and logical thinking of the neo classicists. Instead of looking to science and rational thought for answers and inspiration, the Romantics celebrated the emotions and the imagination. Romantic poet William Blake (1757–1827) considered science and mathematics to be soulless disciplines that shackled the imagination and inhibited free expression of thought and feelings.

For more information on Percy Bysshe Shelley:

http://www.wam.umd. edu/~djb/shelley/home.htm

The Romantics also preferred nature to the city and distrusted most established institutions, especially the church and the government. In England, people were finding these institutions more and more oppressive. In "The Masque of Anarchy," English poet Percy Bysshe Shelley (1792–1822) encouraged the people of England to stand up against the enslaving establishment:

> *Rise like Lions after slumber*
> *In unvanquishable number —*
> *Shake your chains to earth like dew*
> *Which in sleep had fallen on you —*
> *Ye are many — they are few.*

Sentiments such as Shelley's finally led to reforms in England which, among other changes, eliminated seats in Parliament that had been purchased by wealthy families. Still, it would be fifty years before England passed a reform that allowed men from all economic and social classes to vote, and another fifty years before women were granted the same right.

Nineteenth Century

The nineteenth century is considered by many to be the century of greatest change for Western civilization. Fueled in large part by the Industrial Revolution, this century introduced factories, railroads, and the automobile to civilization.

The Industrial Revolution radically changed the way people lived, allowing them greater and faster mobility and more economic possibilities. Although the growing urbanization created slums and a class of working poor, it also gave rise to a powerful middle class, with surplus wealth and free time in which to spend it.

These developments also created a new deity—"progress"—understood as holding out unlimited hope for the future and for the advancement of human civilization. Religious institutions, which had played such a fundamental role in the public and private lives of peoples in many countries, were forced to take a back seat at this time. The impact of discoveries in astronomy, geology, evolutionary biology, and archeology pushed religion out of the public limelight and into a personal and private sphere.

The Realists

A majority of the literature of this period highlighted contemporary life and manners. By the 1850s, it was known as the literature of reality, or "Realism." The novelist was likened to the scientist, who creates and directs the experiment, but is not part of it. The writer is objective and observational, recording the truth of the reality around him or her.

Writers of the Realism movement include:

- Gustave Flaubert (1821–1880) of France, (*Madame Bovary*)
- Fyodor Dostoevsky (1821–1881) of Russia (*Crime and Punishment*)
- Henry James (1843–1916) of America (*The Aspen Papers, The Turn of the Screw, Daisy Miller,* and *The Bostonians*)

During the first half of the twentieth century, technological advancements and breakthroughs continued. Henry Ford started the world's first automated assembly line in Detroit in 1908, mass producing the famous Model T Ford. The success of this ubiquitous black car was evident, because over 26 million Model T Fords were registered in the United States by 1929.

Radio transmission, telephones, movies, and flying machines all made their debut in the early twentieth century. In the midst of these early advances, the literature produced in these early decades was didactic or instructive in tone. Writers took on issues of the day, such as the function of social classes and professions, female suffrage, the justification of armaments and war, and the morality of empire.

The first half of the twentieth century also witnessed the end of the supremacy of the British Empire, the onset of the Great Depression, and the beginnings of the First World War.

The Modernists

MODERNISM is the term used to describe the literary movement up to the First World War. Considered radical and utopian in nature, this movement was inspired by new ideas in anthropology, psychoanalysis, philosophy, and political science. Rejecting styles and forms of the post-Romantic period, writers of this movement include:

- D. H. Lawrence (1885–1930) of England (*The Rainbow* and *Women in Love*)

- James Joyce (1882–1941) of Ireland (*A Portrait of the Artist as a Young Man* and *Finnegans Wake*)

Lawrence's innovative novels reject traditional narrative styles and use myth and symbols to denounce the horrors of war and the dehumanizing effects of mass industrialization on the individual. Joyce's novels also use symbols, myth, and stream-of-consciousness writing to explore the universality of the human condition and the relationship between the conscious and the unconscious.

The cynicism that followed the horrors of World War I gave rise to a literature that was pessimistic regarding the human potential to survive the horrors and the conveniences of the modern world. In this vein, Aldous Huxley wrote his inventive, anti-utopian novel *Brave New World*.

The onset of World War II in 1939 in Europe halted for a time the great literary movements and inventiveness of the century's first half. The horrors of this second great war, ending with the use of atomic bombs over Japan, so profoundly affected the human spirit that writer William Golding noted, "We have discovered a limit to literature."

The post–World War II era found the United States and Russia as the new world superpowers. Britain was deeply indebted to America and definitely diminished as a world power. Along with this new world order, styles in literature shifted from Modernism to Postmodernism.

Postmodern Literature

POSTMODERN LITERATURE: a movement in literature seen as an extension of the Modernist mode of subjective literature—an inward examination of self

Referred to as a shift, rather than a break, in style, POSTMODERN LITERATURE is seen as an extension of the Modernist mode of subjective literature—of looking inward, of examining and exploring the inner consciousness of the individual and its connection to the whole. During the last half of the twentieth century, the assassinations of political and social leaders, the Cold War, civil rights movements, the feminist movement, the Space Age, the Internet, and all forms of mass media stimulated and heightened the intensity of this inward examination and exploration of self.

In an age of mass information and instant messaging, postmodern literature is still evolving and exploring realities. This literature focuses not only on the reality of the inner self and its relation to the exterior world, but also of multiple realities constructed in time and space at points all over the globe. In spite of the seeming randomness and chaotic nature of such vast and starkly different realties, they remain knowable. Making them so remains the task of the postmodern writer.

SKILL 4.3 Comparing themes shared in several literary works from the same world culture or period

Tales recounting the adventures, exploits, triumphs, and struggles of kings and warriors, as well as stories of creation and the meaning of life, constitute the major themes in ancient world literature.

Although ancient literature began with the Sumerians writing and transcribing their epic tales of heroism and of the all-too-human relationship between themselves and their deities, the body of ancient literature most relevant to the modern world was written between 800 BCE and 400 CE. Ancient Hebrew, Greek, and Latin laid the foundation for most of Western secular and religious thought and for the major themes of Western literature.

The concept of a single, all-powerful God is, perhaps, chief among the foundations of Western thought. A wildly revolutionary idea at the time, monotheism set the Hebrew nation apart from the rest of the ancient world. Concurrent with the theme of a single, omnipotent God, the Hebrew manuscripts also carried the less revolutionary idea of the one who suffers for all. Joseph (who suffered for his family and was then rewarded) and Job (who had everything, lost it all, and because he remained faithful, regained his earthly fortune) exemplify this motif.

The idea of one suffering for all, or of the innocent serving as a scapegoat for the sins of the many, can be found in the most ancient writings and rituals. However, its most profound expression is found in the innocent Hebrew messiah who, "despised and rejected of men," still sought forgiveness for his executioners and chose to make "his grave with the wicked" (Book of Isaiah).

Two masterpieces of ancient Greek literature, the *Iliad* and the *Odyssey*, are attributed to Homer and first existed as part of an oral tradition. War is the graphic subject of the *Iliad*. In this poem, Homer evokes two strong, contradictory, and timeless human emotions: revulsion for war and fascination with violence. In the *Iliad*, Achilles is the ultimate warrior who lives to fight and to die on the battlefield.

The *Odyssey* covers the years after the war described in the *Iliad* and instructs that battles are fought not only on the battlefield but also on the journey home, or on the journey toward a just and honorable life. It is the story of the temptations and obstacles that the soldier Odysseus must overcome before returning to his faithful wife and peaceful home.

The Romans chose first to conquer and then to write. In all matters, the Romans paid highest allegiance not to emotions or to questions of right or wrong, but to what was practical, functional, stable, and lasting. A disciplined and highly organized people, the Romans built a great empire; but for their literary inspirations, they turned to the Greeks.

Although inspired by the Greeks, the Roman poets created distinctly Roman works. In the Latin manuscripts of the Romans, the highest virtues are those that promote adherence to duty and to discipline, as best expressed in the Aeneid by Virgil. In this poem, *Aeneas* is the ideal Roman ruler, devoted to duty above all else. His god-given mission is to found the city that in time will become the seat of the great Roman Empire. To do this, he sacrifices his one and only love and then his life.

Ancient Literary Genres

The major genres employed in ancient literary works include prose, epic poetry, comedic and tragic plays, and satire.

Major genres employed in ancient literary works:
- *Prose*
- *Epic poetry*
- *Comedic plays*
- *Tragic plays*
- *Satire*

Prose

Although ancient novels did exist, the novel as a form of literary expression would not come into its own until the Victorian era. The prose that did exist consisted of historical records (such as Thucydides's account of the Peloponnesian Wars) and the works of philosophers and orators (the speeches of the Greek philosopher Socrates as recorded by his famous student Plato and of the Roman philosopher and orator Cicero).

Epic poetry

The popularity of the epic poem in the ancient world stems from its roots in the oral tradition, in which stories and accounts of wars, kings, warriors, and the gods were shared with the public. Whereas some of the greatest epic poetry is attributed to Homer and Virgil, the Sumerian epic poem Gilgamesh provides the earliest example of this literary genre.

Comedic and tragic plays

Absent in ancient Hebrew and Roman literature, drama had its birth in the fifth century in Athens. Early Greek plays include tragedies by Aeschylus (*Agamemnon*) and Sophocles (*Oedipus Tyrannus*) and comedies by Aristophanes (*Lysistrata*). These Greek dramas grew out of an ancient ritual, a dance to the god Dionysus. The ritual involved a chorus of dancers who sang the familiar songs of their epic heroes in order to honor and please Dionysus and to ensure a bountiful spring.

After the seventh century BCE, a Greek poet, Thespis, decided to add an "actor" into the chorus. The actor Thespian would stand apart from and answer to the chorus. Thus drama, which in Greek means "thing done," was born.

Satire

Whereas the play was unique to the Greeks, satire was unique to Rome. "Satire" was the term the Roman poet Juvenal gave to his poems criticizing the vices and follies of imperial Rome. Chief among these follies was blind ambition, because it caused those afflicted to pray for anything except "a sound mind in a sound body."

> **SKILL 4.4** Recognizing historical elements, references, and antecedents in world prose, poetry, and drama

See Skill 4.1

> **SKILL 4.5** Analyzing the influence of mythic, traditional, or earlier literature in world prose, poetry, and drama

Of the five ancient civilizations (Babylon and Assyria, Egypt, Greece, Rome, and the Israelite culture), the ones identified as having led directly to the development of Western literature are the Greeks, Romans, and Israelites. However, the Egyptians, the Babylonians, and the Assyrians have left their marks indirectly through writings found on papyrus and on clay tablets.

Gilgamesh is recorded on the broken clay tablets of ancient Babylon/Assyria. Written in cuneiform (developed by the Sumerians, who preceded the Babylonians), this epic has survived to echo through the ages. The Babylonians also codified a formal set of laws, the *Code of Hammurabi*, named after a

Babylonian king. Many of these laws were variants on laws inherited from the Sumerians, including the famous "lex talionis," or "an eye for an eye, a tooth for a tooth, a limb for a limb," which the Sumerians learned from the Semites.

Although not considered to be a civilization of great philosophers, Egypt did provide art and writings as evidence of an advanced and complex system of beliefs in a supernatural world, an afterlife, and many gods. The Egyptians also developed high ideals of benevolence and justice. However, these beliefs and standards of behavior were recorded in hieroglyphs on papyrus leaves—neither of which has stood the test of time. Poorly understood by surrounding and subsequent cultures, the direct link between Egyptian literary works and Western thought has been lost.

Myths

The independent development and subsequent contact, interaction, and fusion of attitudes of Greece, Rome, and the Israelites do provide us with a direct link to the origins of Western thought and literature. A significant portion of Western thought is based on these cultures' mythological traditions explaining such matters as creation, the building of civilizations, and the journey one makes from birth to death.

Check out the writings of Joseph Campbell:

http://www.jcf.org/works. php

In *The Power of Myth* by Joseph Campbell and Bill Moyer (1991), Campbell notes that "Greek and Latin and biblical literature used to be part of everyone's education. Now, when these were dropped, a whole tradition of Occidental mythological information was lost. [...] With the loss of that, we've really lost something because we don't have a comparable literature to take its place."

"Mythos" is Greek for "story," but the term refers to not just any story. A myth must involve the relationship between at least one human and a deity. This supernatural relationship has been used to explain the many mysteries of life—the universal truths of love, hate, and fear that have been experienced by humans since the dawn of time. Other characters or archetypes in myths include devils or demons, heroes (almost always male) such as the Greek Hercules, and tricksters (who can be helpful or evil) such as Loki in Norse myths.

The Greeks created their Olympian gods and goddesses, whereas the Romans, who always turned to the Greeks for literary inspiration, borrowed almost all their mythology from the Greeks and gave the Olympian gods distinctive Roman names. Thus, Zeus becomes Jupiter; and Aphrodite, the Greek goddess of love, is transformed into Venus.

Greek and Roman myths present gods or goddesses made in the image of humans. Often the only difference is that the god is immortal, whereas the human is destined to die. Living life comfortably and safely into old age in spite of god-like interference was the goal for most Greeks and Romans. However, in the mythological tradition of the Bible (for Judaism, Christianity, and Islam), there is another, more pressing, element: the fight between good and evil, the need for the individual to transcend the evil in this life in order to attain the spiritual goodness or wholeness that is his or hers by divine right.

Myths common to almost all cultures deal with the creation of the world, the creation of humans, the human fall from grace, and divine anger resulting in the destruction of the world (usually by a flood) except for a chosen male and female whose children will hopefully have learned their lesson.

Folktales

In contrast, whereas the myth has potential for spiritual instruction, folktales are traditional stories told primarily for entertainment, such as the American story of Paul Bunyan. They have been told and retold in the language of the common people: the farmers and peasants, the serfs, and the merchants. Folktales (which can also be instructive) contain heroes, villains, and magical happenings, but they do not involve gods or goddesses.

Taken together, the stories and myths of a people explain and describe their culture with depth, sensitivity, and compassion not possible using mere facts and figures. Myths and folktales describe our common humanity, our origins, and perhaps, if we are careful readers, our destinies.

Sample Test Question and Rationale

(Rigorous)

1. **Hoping to take advantage of the popularity of the Harry Potter series, a teacher develops a unit on mythology comparing the story and characters of Greek and Roman myths with the story and characters of the Harry Potter books. Which of these is a commonality that would link classical literature to popular fiction?**

    A. The characters are gods in human form with human-like characteristics

    B. The settings are realistic places in the world where the characters interact as humans would

    C. The themes center on the universal truths of love and hate and fear

    D. The heroes in the stories are young males and only they can overcome the opposing forces

The answer is C.

Although the gods in Greek and Roman myths take human form, they are immortal as gods must be. The characters in Harry Potter may be wizards, but they are not immortal. Although the settings in these stories have familiar associations, their worlds are vastly different from those inhabited by mortals and Muggles. While male heroes may dominate the action, the females (Hera, Diana, and Hermione) are powerful as well.

SKILL Demonstrating familiarity with the historical development of world
4.6 prose, poetry, and drama

See Skill 4.1

COMPETENCY 5
UNDERSTAND THE PURPOSES, STRUCTURES, ELEMENTS, AND MEANINGS OF INFORMATIONAL AND TECHNICAL TEXTS

SKILL Recognizing various types of informational and technical texts
5.1 *(e.g., newspaper article, editorial, report)*

Twenty-first century Americans read many words every day, both in print and in electronic form. Because of this flood of information, readers should be able to discern the various purposes, structures, elements, and meanings of these expository (informational) texts.

We purchase a new cabinet and read the directions for assembling it. If those directions are not easily understandable, we become frustrated and upset. Installing new software on our computers requires that we read a lot of expository text. The writers of this documentation are not trying to persuade us to read it—they are simply providing information that we might need.

Although many have predicted from time to time that the newspaper will become obsolete (replaced by radio, television, or the Internet), it hasn't happened. The first printed newspaper was published in 1605, and most people still rely on their daily and weekly newspapers to keep in touch with their communities and the world.

Even so, there is some indication that the proliferation of computer access and the high level of accessibility of news from all over the world is, in fact, affecting the newspaper business. Paid circulation is declining in most countries. Advertising revenue, which makes up the bulk of a newspaper's income, is shifting from print to online, resulting in a general decline in newspaper profits. As a result, the predictions that newspapers may vanish are rife again. Only time will tell whether this traditional feature of daily life will end any time soon.

General-interest newspapers are the most common type and are purveyors of current news such as political events, crimes, business, culture, sports, and opinions (editorials, columns, or political cartoons). The first permanent photograph was produced in 1826, and photography eventually became an important part of news stories. Cartoonists also got into the act in 1843 when Punch magazine began to put satirical drawings on its pages. Today, most newspapers include political cartoons.

A newspaper may include the following specific features:

- Weather news and forecasts

- An advice column

- Critical reviews of movies, plays, or restaurants

- Editorial opinions

- A gossip column

- Comic strips and other entertainment, such as crosswords, sudoku, and horoscopes

- A sports column or section

Sample Test Question and Rationale

(Average)

1. **Factors that have caused the decline of newspaper readership include which reason below?**

   A. People are now relying on the Internet for their news, causing a decline in newspaper advertising

   B. Because of environmental concerns and the high cost of paper, people are turning to the radio and television to keep current with the news

   C. Many people think newspapers are too biased in their coverage and seek their information from more credible sources

   D. Newspaper unions have negotiated tough contracts for their workers, and the profits are being negated by high salaries

The answer is A.

Although the death knell for newspapers has sounded before with the advent of radio and television, more analysts are skeptical about the newspaper industry's ability to compete with the Internet. Certainly, the paper supply has an impact on the environment, but this has not caused the decline in newspaper readership. Reading an unbiased newspaper is next to impossible, but responsible readers are critical readers who learn to identify fact from opinion and rely on a variety of sources for their information. Although high wages may affect a newspaper's profit, they do not affect the number of readers.

In reading, comprehending, and interpreting written works, the first important decision to make is to determine the purpose. Why did this writer write this particular document? There are many possibilities. These possibilities often overlap each other, although one may predominate.

- To inform: The writer's purpose here is to present information. The writer may not care whether the reader does anything as a result of reading or listening to this material. The writer only passes on information in case the reader or listener needs or wants the information. College catalogs and news stories in newspapers are examples of expository literature.

- To amuse: The writer's purpose here is to entertain the reader by humorously pointing out the foibles of life. Mark Twain's *Innocents Abroad* relates observations about his travels across Europe and the Holy Land.

- To instruct: The writer's purpose here is to provide directions or guidelines. Examples of instructional writing include a classroom textbook that seeks to provide knowledge, a how-to manual to provide directions, or a sermon to provide moral and ethical guidelines

- To persuade: The writer's purpose here is (1) to change the mind of the reader and lead him or her to accept a particular point of view, or (2) to move the reader to take some action. Politicians and preachers use this form of writing or speaking. The politician may try to persuade the constituency that putting up a fence to protect borders is the appropriate solution to the immigration problem. Persuasive writing and speaking are very much parts of everyday life. Children use persuasion to try to get what they want from their parents.

- To explain: The writer's purpose here is to make something clear and comprehensible. In this attempt to define the nature or meaning of something, the writer establishes its unique characteristics. Jessica Mitford's "Behind the Formaldehyde Curtain" explains the purpose of modern day funeral practices by using examples.

- To describe: The writer may simply wish to share an experience with the reader in such a way that the experience is accessible through one or more of the five senses: seeing, hearing, smelling, tasting, touching. By using descriptive words, the writer seeks to allow the reader to feel that he or she was there at the time. Poets rely heavily on descriptive words to evoke an emotional response, as Alfred, Lord Tennyson does in "Flower in the Crannied Wall":

> *Flower in the crannied wall,*
> *I pluck you out of the crannies*
> *I hold you here, root and all, in my hand,*
> *Little flower—but if I could understand*
> *What you are, root and all, and all in all,*
> *I should know what God and man is.*

- **To tell a story:** A writer uses a narrative style to tell a story (a sequence of events that revolve around some point or theme). For a narrative to be interesting, it should include conflicts of some sort, either between people or between people and some outside force. Narratives also can be about animals or about the recounting of the history of a place. Good narratives generally come to a resolution and convey interesting meaning.

Read the narrative essays of Garrison Keillor at:

http://dir.salon.com/topics/garrison_keillor/

The stories of Garrison Keillor told on his radio show *Prairie Home Companion* and anthologized in various print and electronic media include a wide cast of characters and deal with topics that are current as well as nostalgic.

Sample Test Question and Rationale

(Easy)

1. **What is the main form of discourse in this passage?**

   It would have been hard to find a passer-by more wretched in appearance. He was a man of middle height, stout and hardy, in the strength of maturity; he might have been forty-six or seven. A slouched leather cap hid half his face, bronzed by the sun and wind, and dripping with sweat.

   A. Description

   B. Narration

   C. Exposition

   D. Persuasion

The answer is A.

A description presents a thing or a person in detail and tells the reader about the appearance of whatever it is presenting. Narration relates a sequence of events (the story) told through a process of narration (discourse), in which events are recounted in a certain order (the plot). Exposition is an explanation or an argument within the narration. It can also be the introduction to a play or a story. Persuasion strives to convince either a character in the story or the reader.

SKILL 5.3 Identifying a writer's purpose, main ideas, and supporting details in a given informational or technical text

Sometimes a writer will announce the purpose of a document. The responsibility remains with the reader, however, to determine whether the piece of writing fulfills the announced purpose. If the writer does not state the *point* of the written work, the reader must determine it. It's best to read the entire piece of writing from beginning to end and then to ask the questions: What did the writer accomplish? What did the writer *intend* to accomplish? The point of a piece of writing is called a **THESIS**.

THESIS: the purpose of a piece of writing

Sometimes a piece of writing does not state the thesis anywhere in the text. In these cases, the reader must infer the thesis based on such questions as these:

- Does the writer make a point even though it is not stated?

- What does the paper prove?

- What is the point?

Read more about thesis statements:

http://www.unc.edu/depts/wcweb/handouts/thesis.html

A good thesis statement is very specific. A general thesis statement leads nowhere. Freewriting about a topic often yields several good thesis statements about a particular topic. Once the writer clarifies his or her topic, then the thesis statement needs to be narrowed in scope and intent to fit what the writer wants to accomplish. Composing an effective thesis statement usually requires some whittling and rethinking.

To develop a thesis statement, a writer provides supporting details. These details can include facts, opinions, statistics, examples, or definitions—anything that clarifies the point of the piece of writing.

In the traditional five-paragraph essay taught in schools, the goal is for students to provide depth and breadth to their thesis statements, and they are encouraged to provide three supporting details. However, this standard can often produce limited or artificial support. Writers may choose to focus on one or two supporting details or to provide a much broader range—whatever is needed to develop the thesis clearly and completely.

> **SKILL Applying knowledge of common textual features** (e.g., paragraphs,
> **5.4** topic sentences, tables of contents, step-by-step lists, chapter headings, unit
> summaries) **of informational and technical texts**

Language is hierarchal. The lowest level in the hierarchy consists of sounds (spoken) and letters (written), also known as the **PHONEMIC STAGE** in the hierarchy. The second stage is **MORPHEMES**, or units of meaning that are not words. The third stage in the hierarchy is **WORDS**, which are made out of morphemes.

Words are used to make **SENTENCES** also (which comprise the syntactic level of language). In English, sentences also include *classes* of words (sometimes called parts of speech) that are strictly arranged according to order. English is one of the few languages that depend on word order to convey the intended meaning. For example, Spanish depends on case and inflection in word endings to signal subjects and predicates. Just as the subject of a sentence announces what the topic is, so the verb says something about that subject. The dog (subject) barks (verb).

PARAGRAPHS echo the sentence in that they include a topic sentence that states the subject and include supporting sentences that say something about the topic sentence. The same is true in longer discourses. In an essay, the thesis states the subject of the document. Paragraphs will develop that thesis (say something about the thesis).

As a teacher, keeping in mind that this hierarchical nature of language is innate can be useful; it is embedded in the minds of native speakers, including students. Tapping into this innate characteristic can help students understand the importance of the topic sentence and thesis statement in their own compositions. It's also extremely useful in helping them learn to analyze written text, be it persuasive, expository, descriptive, or narrative. If students understand how language works (including their own) when stating a subject and saying something about it, they can more easily understand how another writer has done that very thing. What is this writer's subject, and what has he or she said about it?

The very notion of a table of contents is based on this hierarchical nature of language. A **TABLE OF CONTENTS** is a map to the arrangement of a document by topic, sub-topics, and sometimes sub-sub topics. If this hierarchy is understood, then creating a table of contents for a written piece comes naturally. For a writer, the table of contents is a natural extension of an outline. It helps the writer stay on target and develop a cohesive and balanced piece of writing. For a reader, the table of contents provides visual clues by establishing the main ideas and supporting details in a hierarchical format.

PHONEMIC STAGE: the lowest level in the language hierarchy—sounds and letters

MORPHEMES: the second level in the language hierarchy—units of meaning that are not words

WORDS: the third level in the language hierarchy—units of meaning, made out of morphemes

SENTENCES: units of meaning, made out of words

PARAGRAPHS: units of meaning made up of a topic sentence and supporting sentences

TABLE OF CONTENTS: a map to the arrangement of a document

To make information easier for readers to comprehend, step-by-step lists help clarify complicated processes or procedures. Just as a cook follows a recipe step by step, so does a mechanic follow an established procedure. These lists can be bulleted or enumerated, depending on the purpose of the list.

When readers have less time to read, they tend to skim. Just as headlines that do not provide accurate clues to the content of a newspaper article can be frustrating, the same is true of inaccurate chapter headings. This is not usually the time to be creative. Effective chapter headings guide readers through material so that they can more easily locate the information they need.

If the student comes to see written and spoken language in the terms delineated above, then summarizing a piece becomes much easier. The summarizer looks for the "bones" of the piece being summarized and bypasses details that flesh out the main points. Students need much practice in this skill because of the tendency to oversimplify. Practice may not make perfect, but it does lead to deeper understanding of how language works.

Sample Test Question and Rationale

(Rigorous)

1. **Which aspect of language is innate?**

   A. Biological capability to articulate sounds understood by other humans

   B. Cognitive ability to create syntactical structures

   C. Capacity for using semantics to convey meaning in a social environment

   D. Ability to vary inflections and accents

The answer is A.

Language ability is innate, and the biological capability to produce sounds lets children learn semantics and syntactical structures through trial and error. Linguists agree that language is first a vocal system of word symbols that enable a human to communicate his or her feelings, thoughts, and desires to other human beings.

SKILL 5.5 **Applying knowledge of common graphic features** *(e.g., graphic organizers, diagrams, captions, illustrations)* **of informational and technical texts**

Writers employ a number of devices, both in text and in pictures, to supplement their informational and technical texts so that readers clearly understand the important ideas.

Tables	Tables depict exact numbers and other data in rows and columns. Repository tables store descriptive information in a form available for general use. They usually contain primary data, which simply summarize raw data. They are not intended to analyze the data, so any analysis is left to the reader or user of the table. A good example of a repository table would be a report of birth statistics by the federal Health and Human Services Department.
Analytical Tables	Analytical tables, on the other hand, are constructed from of the analysis of primary or secondary data, possibly from a repository table or from the raw data itself. An example of an analytical table would be one that compares birth statistics in 1980 to birth statistics in 2005 for the country at large. Such a table might also break the data down into comparisons by state.
Graphs	Graphs depict trends, movements, distributions, and cycles more readily than tables. While graphs can present statistics in a more interesting and comprehensible form than tables, they are less accurate. For this reason, the two are often shown together.
Maps	Although the most obvious use for maps is to locate places geographically, maps can also show specific geographic features such as roads, mountains, and rivers. In addition, maps can show information according to geographic distribution such as population, housing, or manufacturing centers.
Illustrations	A wide range of illustrations, such as pictures, drawings, and diagrams, can be used to illuminate the text in a document. They can also be a part of a graphic layout designed to make the page more attractive.

Some possibilities for the analysis of data, whether presented in tables, charts, graphs, maps, or other illustrations, include:

- Qualitative descriptions: Would drawing conclusions about the quality of a particular treatment or course of action be revealed by the illustration?

- Quantitative descriptions: How much do the results of one particular treatment or course of action differ from another one, and is that variation significant?

- Classification: Is worthwhile information derived from breaking the information down into classifications?

- Estimations: Is it possible to estimate future performance based on the information in the illustration?

- Comparisons: Is it useful to make comparisons based on the data?

- Relationships: Are relationships between components revealed by the scrutiny of the data?

- Cause-and-effect relationships: Are cause-and-effect relationships suggested by the data that were not previously apparent?

- Mapping and modeling: If the data were mapped and a model drawn up, would the point of the document be demonstrated or refuted?

Questions to ask regarding an illustration:

- Why is it in this document?

- What was the writer's purpose in putting it in the document and why at this particular place?

- Does it make a point clearer?

- What implications are inherent in a table that shows birth statistics in all states or even in some selected states?

- What does that have to do with the point and purpose of this piece of writing?

- Is there adequate preparation in the text for the inclusion of the illustration? Does the illustration underscore or clarify any of the points made in the text?

- Is there a clear connection between the illustration and the subject matter of the text?

SKILL 5.6 Applying knowledge of common organizational structures and patterns (e.g., transitions, classification schemes, logical order) of informational and technical texts

Writers use a variety of organizational patterns so that a work has coherence and the relationship of ideas is clear.

The organization of a written work includes two factors: the order in which the writer has chosen to present the different parts of the discussion or argument and the relationships he or she constructs between these parts.

Written ideas need to be presented in a logical order so that a reader can follow the information easily and quickly. There are many different ways in which to order a series of ideas, but they all share one thing in common: to lead the reader along a desired path by giving a clear, strong presentation of the writer's main idea while avoiding backtracking and skipping around. Some of the ways in which a paragraph may be organized are listed in the table below.

Learn more about coherence:

http://www.accd.edu/sac/ english/lirvin/wguides/ Coherence.htm

Sequence of Events	In this type of organization, the details are presented in the order in which they have occurred. Paragraphs that describe a process or procedure, give directions, or outline a given period of time (such as a day or a month) are often arranged chronologically.
Statement Support	In this type of organization, the main idea is stated, and the rest of the paragraph explains or proves it. This organizational structure is also referred to as relative order or order of importance. This type of order can be organized in one of four ways: most to least, least to most, most-least-most, and least-most-least.
Comparison-Contrast	In this type of organization, a paragraph describes the differences between or similarities of two or more ideas, actions, events, or things. Usually, the topic sentence describes the basic relationship between the ideas or items, and the rest of the paragraph explains this relationship.
Classification	In this type of organization, the paragraph presents grouped information about a topic. The topic sentence usually states the general category, and the rest of the sentences show how various elements of the category have a common base and also how they differ from the common base.
Cause and Effect	This pattern describes how two or more events are connected. The main sentence usually states the primary cause(s) and the primary effect(s) and how they are basically connected. The rest of the sentences explain the connection—how one event caused the next.
Spatial/Place	In this type of organization, certain descriptions are organized according to the location of items in relation to each other and to a larger context. The orderly arrangement guides the reader's eye as he or she mentally envisions the scene or place being described.
Example, Clarification, and Definition	These types of organizations show, explain, or elaborate on the main idea. This can be done by showing specific cases, examining meaning multiple times, or extensively describing one term.

Sample Test Question and Rationale

(Rigorous)

1. For their research paper on the use of technology in the classroom, students have gathered data that shows a sharp increase in the number of online summer classes over the past five years. What would be the best way for them to depict this information visually?

   A. A line chart

   B. A table

   C. A pie chart

   D. A flow chart

The answer is A.

A line chart is used to show trends over time and would emphasize the sharp increase. A table is appropriate to show the exact numbers, but it does not have the same impact as a line chart. Not appropriate is a pie chart, which shows the parts of a whole, or a flow chart, which details processes or procedures.

DOMAIN II
READING SKILLS AND STRATEGIES

PERSONALIZED STUDY PLAN

KNOWN MATERIAL/ SKIP IT

PAGE	COMPETENCY AND SKILL	KNOWN MATERIAL/ SKIP IT
99	**6: Understand strategies for the comprehension and interpretation of texts**	☐
	6.1: Applying knowledge of prereading and metacognitive strategies	☐
	6.2: Determining the possible meaning of unfamiliar words and phrases	☐
	6.3: Recognizing how the history of the English language is manifested	☐
	6.4: Identifying accurate summaries, restatements, outlines, and other organizing devices of a text	☐
	6.5: Applying inferential comprehension skills	☐
	6.6: Analyzing how common textual features, graphic features, and organizational structures affect the comprehension and interpretation of texts	☐
	6.7: Applying knowledge of reference resources and skills used to aid comprehension and interpretation	☐
116	**7: Understand strategies for the critical analysis and evaluation of texts**	☐
	7.1: Evaluating the development and use of logic and evidence in an argument	☐
	7.2: Analyzing the effectiveness of a writer's use of language, style, syntax, and rhetorical strategies	☐
	7.3: Distinguishing opinion from fact, conclusion, or inference	☐
	7.4: Discerning the relevance, importance, credibility, and sufficiency of support in a writer's argument	☐
	7.5: Determining how a writer uses tone and style	☐
	7.6: Demonstrating knowledge of the effect of the cultural, political, and social environment on a writer's use of language	☐
132	**8: Understand skills for effective reading across the curriculum**	☐
	8.1: Recognizing the relationships of messages, themes, and ideas from one subject area to those from another	☐
	8.2: Applying knowledge of a writer's purpose, the academic context, and prior learning	☐
	8.3: Applying knowledge of organizational structures and patterns, graphic features, and textual features	☐
	8.4: Recognizing how certain words and concepts are related to multiple subjects and how similes, metaphors, and analogies are used to compare ideas	☐

COMPETENCY 6
UNDERSTAND STRATEGIES FOR THE COMPREHENSION AND INTERPRETATION OF TEXTS

SKILL 6.1 Applying knowledge of prereading and metacognitive strategies used to enhance the comprehension of challenging texts

Jumping into a reading assignment may be tempting. Most students just want to get the assignment done and are unwilling to add any steps. Persuading them that they will save time in the end if they take the time to do some preliminary preparation for reading a piece will be worth the classroom time.

What can be done ahead of time?

- Looking at the date of publication is useful. Knowing that a story, was published in 1930 or in 2005 can reveal a lot about the setting and characters. Knowing what was going on in the world at the time of publication would help a reader, and an encyclopedia can provide a quick overview. Also, knowing something about the author is useful. Most well-known authors have at least a short biography in an appropriate encyclopedia.

- A quick overview of the story before beginning to read might help. Are there chapters with headings? If not, a quick survey of the sections, either chapters or paragraphs, will yield clues that will guide reading and improve comprehension. If the reading assignment is an essay, a quick skimming for paragraph topic sentences and a look at the conclusion will provide useful information before beginning the actual reading. Students should be warned not to make premature judgments based on any of these pre-reading activities, however, and should be advised to let the story or essay speak for itself.

Assuming that the students in your classroom do not have reading disabilities, reading comprehension skills can be taught. This works particularly well if reading comprehension instruction goes hand-in-hand with teaching writing skills. Students need to practice looking for the point of a written discourse just as they need to learn to focus their writing. What was the writer's aim or purpose? Can the writing be said to be persuasive in nature, for instance, or is it simply conveying useful (or not useful) information? Is the piece purely expressive, with the intention of opening up an experience for the reader?

> *Check out different reading strategies:*
>
> *http://www.greece. k12.ny.us/instruction/ ela/6-12/OKOKReading/ Reading%20Strategies/ reading%20strategies%20 index.htm*

These skills will be taught in the writing classroom and can be reinforced in the reading classroom. If students understand what the possible structures are in a piece of writing, they will be more skilled at comprehending what is being said.

Another tool for comprehension is learning to react to the written information. What does this piece have to do with me? Do I agree or disagree with this writer? Once a reader gets to that point, the ability to comprehend has matured to a useful level.

Sample Test Questions and Rationale

(Average)

1. Written on the sixth grade reading level, most of S. E. Hinton's novels (for instance, *The Outsiders*) have the greatest reader appeal with:

   A. sixth graders

   B. ninth graders

   C. twelfth graders

   D. adults

   The answer is B.

   Adolescents are concerned with their changing bodies, their relationships with each other and adults, and their place in society. Reading *The Outsiders* makes them confront different problems that they are only now beginning to experience as teenagers, such as gangs and social identity. The book is universal in its appeal to adolescents.

(Average)

2. Which teaching method would best engage underachievers in the required senior English class?

   A. Assign use of glossary work and extensively footnoted excerpts of great works

   B. Have students take turns reading aloud the anthology selection

   C. Let students choose which readings they'll study and write about

   D. Use a chronologically arranged, traditional text, but also assign group work, panel presentations, and portfolio management

   The answer is C.

   Allowing students to choose the readings they'll study encourages them to react honestly to literature. Students should take notes on what they're reading so they will be able to discuss the material. They should not only react to literature, but also experience it. Small-group work is a good way to encourage them. The other answers are not fit for junior high or high school students. They should be encouraged, however, to read critics of works in order to understand critical work.

Sample Test Questions and Rationale (cont.)

(Average)

3. Which of the following would be the most significant factor in teaching Homer's *Iliad* and *Odyssey* to any particular group of students?

    A. Identifying a translation on the appropriate reading level

    B. Determining the students' interest level

    C. Selecting an appropriate evaluative technique

    D. Determining the scope and delivery methods of background study

The answer is A.

Students will learn the importance of these two works if the translation reflects both the vocabulary that they know and their reading level. Greece will always be foremost in literary assessments due to Homer's works. Homer is the most often cited author, after Shakespeare. Greece is the cradle of both democracy and literature. This is why it is so crucial that Homer be included in the works assigned.

(Average)

4. The students in Mrs. Cline's seventh grade language arts class have been invited to attend a performance of *Romeo and Juliet* presented by the drama class at the high school. To best prepare, they should:

    A. Read the play as a homework exercise

    B. Read a synopsis of the plot and a biographical sketch of the author

    C. Examine a few main selections from the play to become familiar with the language and style of the author

    D. Read a condensed version of the story and practice attentive listening skills

The answer is D.

By reading a condensed version of the story, students will know the plot and therefore be able to follow the play on stage. It is also important for them to practice listening techniques such as one-to-one tutoring and peer-assisted reading.

(Rigorous)

5. After watching a movie of a train derailment, a child exclaims, "Wow, look how many cars fell off the tracks. There's junk everywhere. The engineer must have really been asleep." Using the facts that the child is impressed by the wreckage and assigns blame to the engineer, a follower of Piaget's theories would estimate the child to be about:

    A. Ten years old

    B. Twelve years old

    C. Fourteen years old

    D. Sixteen years old

The answer is A.

According to Piaget's theory, children seven to eleven years old begin to apply logic to concrete things and experiences. They can combine performance and reasoning to solve problems. They have internalized moral values and are willing to confront rules and adult authority.

SKILL 6.2 Determining the possible meaning of unfamiliar words and phrases using context clues and/or structural analysis and applying knowledge of roots, etymology, and word structure to interpret words with multiple meanings, strong connotations, misleading cognates, and similar characteristics

For students to understand difficult or complex passages, they must use skills to define unfamiliar words and infer meaning by surrounding text. By understanding how words are formed, students will be better able to analyze challenging vocabulary and phrases.

Learn more about monitoring comprehension:

http://www.indiana. edu/~l517/monitoring.html

Context Clues

Context clues help readers determine the meaning of words with which they are not familiar. The context of a word consists of the sentence or sentences that surround that word. Read the following sentences and attempt to determine the meanings of the words in bold print.

> The **luminosity** of the room was so incredible that there was no need for lights.

If there was no need for lights, then one must assume that the word luminosity has something to do with giving off light. The definition of "luminosity," therefore, is the emission of light.

> Jamie could not understand Joe's feelings. His mood swings made understanding him an **enigma**.

The fact that he could not be understood made him somewhat of a puzzle. The definition of "enigma" is a mystery or puzzle.

Another way to determine meaning is to identify common morphemes, prefixes, and suffixes. Familiarity with word roots (the basic elements of words) and with prefixes can also help one determine the meanings of unknown words.

Root words

ROOT WORD: a word from which another word is developed

A ROOT WORD is a word from which another word is developed. The second word can be said to have its "root" in the first. This structural component nicely lends itself to the illustration of a tree with roots, so that students can use a concrete image for an abstract concept. Students may also want to construct root words literally by using cardboard trees and/or actual roots from plants to create word family models. This way, students have the opportunity to own their root words.

An example of a root word is "bene," which means "good" or "well." English words from this Latin root include "benefit," "beneficial," "beneficent," and "beneficiary."

Base words

A **BASE WORD** is a stand-alone linguistic unit that cannot be deconstructed or broken down into smaller words. For example, in the word "retell," the base word is "tell."

Contractions

CONTRACTIONS are shortened forms of two words in which one or more letters have been deleted. These deleted letters have been replaced by an apostrophe. For example, "hasn't" is the contraction for "has not."

Prefixes

PREFIXES are beginning units of meaning that can be added (or "affixed") to a base word or root word. They cannot stand alone. Prefixes are also sometimes known as "bound morphemes," meaning that they cannot stand alone as a base word. Some examples of prefixes are "pre," "ex," "trans," and "sub."

Suffixes

A **SUFFIX** is an ending unit of meaning that can be affixed to a root or base word. Suffixes transform the original meanings of base and root words. Like prefixes, they are also known as bound morphemes, because they cannot stand alone as words. Some examples of suffixes are "ing," "ful," "ness," and "er."

Inflectional endings

INFLECTIONAL ENDINGS are types of suffixes that impart a new meaning to the base or root word. These endings in particular change the gender, number, tense, or form of the base or root words. Just like other suffixes, these are also termed "bound morphemes." Some examples are "ette," "es," and "ed."

Compound words

COMPOUND WORDS occur when two or more base words are connected to form a new word. The meaning of the new word is in some way connected with that of the base words. "Bookkeeper," besides being the only English word with three double letters in a row, is an example of a compound word.

BASE WORD: a stand-alone linguistic unit that cannot be deconstructed or broken down into smaller words

CONTRACTIONS: shortened forms of two words in which one or more letters have been deleted

Learn more about word analysis:

http://www.orangeusd.k12.ca.us/yorba/word_analysis.htm

PREFIXES: beginning units of meaning that can be added to a base word or rootword hich another word is developed

SUFFIX: an ending unit of meaning that can be affixed to a root or base word suffix

INFLECTIONAL ENDINGS: types of suffixes that impart a new meaning to the base word or root word

COMPOUND WORDS: words that occur when two or more base words are connected to form a new word

Following is a partial list of roots and prefixes. Reviewing these might be useful to you.

Root	Meaning	Example
aqua	water	aqualung
astro	stars	astrology
bio	life	biology
carn	meat	carnivorous
circum	around	circumnavigate
geo	earth	geology
herb	plant	herbivorous
mal	bad	malicious
neo	new	neonatal
tele	distant	telescope

Prefix	Meaning	Example
un-	not	unnamed
re-	again	reenter
il-	not	illegible
pre-	before	preset
mis-	incorrectly	misstate
in-	not	informal
anti-	against	antiwar
de-	opposite	derail
post-	after	postwar
ir-	not	irresponsible

Word forms

Sometimes a very familiar word can appear as a different part of speech. You may have heard that *fraud* involves a criminal misrepresentation, so when it appears as the adjective form *fraudulent* ("He was suspected of fraudulent activities"), you can make an educated guess. You probably know that something out of date is *obsolete*; therefore, when you read about "built-in *obsolescence*," you can detect the meaning of the unfamiliar word.

Practice Exercise

Read the following sentences and attempt to determine the meanings of the underlined words.

1. **Farmer John got a two-horse plow and went to work. Straight furrows stretched out behind him.**

   The word <u>furrows</u> means:

   A. Long cuts made by plow

   B. Vast, open fields

   C. Rows of corn

   D. Pairs of hitched horses

2. **The survivors struggled ahead, shambling through the terrible cold, doing their best not to fall.**

   The word <u>shambling</u> means:

   A. Frozen in place

   B. Running

   C. Shivering uncontrollably

   D. Walking awkwardly

Answer Key

1. **A**

   "Long cuts made by plow" is the correct answer. The words "straight" and the expression "stretched out behind him" are your clues

2. **D**

   "Walking awkwardly" is the correct answer. The words "ahead" and "through" are your clues.

   The context for a word is the written passage that surrounds it. Sometimes the writer offers synonyms—words that have nearly the same meaning. Context clues also can appear within the sentence itself, within the preceding and/or following sentence(s), or in the passage as a whole.

Sentence clues

Often, a writer will actually define a difficult or particularly important word for the reader the first time it appears in a passage. Phrases like *that is, such as, which is,* or *is called* might announce the writer's intention to give the definition. Occasionally, a writer will simply use a synonym or near-synonym joined by the word *or*. Look at the following examples:

> The **credibility**, that is to say, the believability, of the witness was called into question by evidence of previous perjury.
>
> Nothing would **assuage** or lessen the child's grief.

Punctuation

At the sentence level, punctuation is often a clue to the meaning of a word. Commas, parentheses, quotation marks, and dashes tell the reader that a definition is being offered by the writer.

> A tendency toward **hyperbole**, extravagant exaggeration, is a common flaw among persuasive writers.
>
> Political **apathy**—lack of interest—can lead to the death of the state.

A writer might simply give an explanation in other words that you can understand in the same sentence.

> The **xenophobic** townspeople were suspicious of every foreigner.

Writers also explain a word in terms of its opposite at the sentence level.

> His **incarceration** was ended, and he was elated to be out of jail.

Adjacent sentence clues

The context for a word goes beyond the sentence in which it appears. At times, the writer uses adjacent sentences to present an explanation or definition.

> The $200 for the car repair would have to come out of the **contingency** fund. Fortunately, Angela's father had taught her to keep some money set aside for just such emergencies.

The second sentence offers a clue to the definition of *contingency* as used in this sentence: emergencies. Therefore, a fund for contingencies would be money tucked away for unforeseen and/or urgent events.

Entire passage clues

On occasion, one must look at an entire paragraph or passage to figure out the definition of a word or term. In the following paragraph, notice how the word *nostalgia* undergoes a form of extended definition throughout the selection rather than in just one sentence.

> The word **nostalgia** links Greek words for away from home and pain. If you're feeling **nostalgic**, then you are probably in some physical distress or discomfort, suffering from a feeling of alienation and separation from loved ones or loved places. **Nostalgia** is that awful feeling you remember from the first time you went away to camp or spent the weekend with a friend's family—homesickness, or some condition even more painful than that. But in common use, **nostalgia** has come to have more sentimental associations. A few years back, for example, a **nostalgia** craze had to do with the 1950s. We resurrected poodle skirts and saddle shoes, built new restaurants to look like old ones, and tried to make chicken a la king just as mother probably never made it. In TV situation comedies, we recreated a pleasant world that probably never existed and relished our **nostalgia**, longing for a homey, comfortable lost time.

Sample Test Questions and Rationale

(Easy)

1. To understand the origins of a word, one must study its:

   A. Synonyms

   B. Inflections

   C. Phonetics

   D. Etymology

   The answer is D.

   Etymology is the study of word origins. A synonym is an equivalent of another word and can substitute for it in certain contexts. Inflection is a modification of words according to their grammatical functions, usually by employing variant word endings to indicate such qualities as tense, gender, case, and number. Phonetics is the science devoted to the physical analysis of the sounds of human speech, including their production, transmission, and perception.

(Average)

2. The synonyms "gyro," "hero," and "submarine" reflect which influence on language usage?

   A. Social

   B. Geographical

   C. Historical

   D. Personal

   The answer is B.

   These words are interchangeable, but their use depends on the region of the United States, not on the social class of the speaker. Nor is there any historical context around any of them. The usage can be personal, but it will most often vary with the region.

Sample Test Questions and Rationale (cont.)

(Rigorous)

3. **Which word in the following sentence is a bound morpheme: "The quick brown fox jumped over the lazy dog"?**

   A. The

   B. Fox

   C. Lazy

   D. Jumped

The answer is D.

The suffix "–ed" is an affix that cannot stand alone as a unit of meaning. Thus it is bound to the free morpheme "jump." "The" is always an unbound morpheme since no suffix or prefix can alter its meaning. As written, "fox" and "lazy" are unbound, but their meaning is changed with affixes, such as "foxes" or "laziness."

SKILL 6.3 Recognizing how the history of the English language is manifested in modern vocabulary, word structures, spelling, and pronunciation

Perhaps the most basic principle about language is a simple one: Language inevitably changes over time. If a community speaking a homogeneous language and dialect is for some reason separated with no contact between the two resulting communities, the people will be speaking different dialects within a few generations and eventually will have difficulty understanding each other.

Language changes in all its manifestations. At the phonetic level, the sounds of a language change along with its orthography (spelling). The vocabulary level will probably manifest the greatest changes. Changes in syntax are slower and less likely to occur.

English has changed in response to the influences of many other languages and cultures as well as internal cultural changes; however, its syntax still relies on word order. It has not shifted to an inflected system even though many of the cultures that have affected it do have an inflected language.

The most significant influence on a language is the blending of cultures. The Norman conquest that brought the English speakers in the British Isles under the

Causes of change in English:

- Influences of other languages
- Influences of other cultures
- Internal cultural changes
- Blending of cultures
- Colonization of other countries
- Introduction of television
- Computerization of the world

rule of French speakers changed the language, but English speakers did not adopt the language of the ruling class. They did not become speakers of French. Even so, many vocabulary words entered the language in that period. The Great Vowel Shift that occurred between the fourteenth and sixteenth centuries is generally attributed to the migration to southeast England following the bubonic plague. The Great Vowel Shift largely accounts for the discrepancy between orthography and speech—the difficult spelling system in modern English.

Colonization of other countries has also brought new vocabulary into the English language. Indian English has its own easily recognizable attributes, as do Australian and North American English; these cultural interactions have added to meanings of individual words and in the language at large. The fact that English is the most widely spoken and understood language all over the world in the twenty-first century implies that it is constantly being changed by the globalized world.

Other influences, of course, affect language. The introduction of television and its domination by the United States have had a great influence on the English that is spoken and understood all over the world. The same is true of the computerizing of the world (Tom Friedman called it "flattening" in his *The World is Flat: A Brief History of the Twenty-first Century*). New terms have been added ("blog"), old terms have changed meaning ("mouse"), and nouns have become verbs ("prioritize").

SKILL 6.4 Identifying accurate summaries, restatements, outlines, and other organizing devices of a text and recognizing how these devices aid in comprehension of the content, organization, and reasoning of a written text

One way to determine students' level of understanding is to have them summarize a passage. To do so, they must be able to determine the main ideas and supporting details and then identify the underlying structure. This skill can be developed through practice and repetition. Here's an example.

Sample Passage

Chili peppers may turn out to be the wonder drug of the decade. The fiery fruit comes in many sizes, shapes, and colors, all of which grow on plants that are genetic descendants of the tepin plant, originally native to the Americas. Connoisseurs of the regional cuisines of the Southwest and Louisiana are already well aware that food flavored with chilies can cause a good sweat, but medical researchers are learning more every day about the medical power of capsaicin, the ingredient in the peppers that produces the heat.

Capsaicin as a pain medication has been a part of folk medicine for centuries. It is, in fact, the active ingredient in several currently available, over-the-counter liniments for sore muscles. Recent research has been examining the value of the compound for the treatment of other painful conditions. Capsaicin shows some promise in the treatment of phantom-limb syndrome, shingles, and some types of headaches. Additional research focuses upon the use of capsaicin to relieve pain in postsurgical patients. Scientists speculate that application of the compound to the skin causes the body to release endorphins—natural pain relievers manufactured by the body itself. An alternative theory holds that capsaicin somehow interferes with the transmission of signals along the nerve fibers, thus reducing the sensation of pain.

In addition to its well-documented history as a painkiller, capsaicin has recently received attention as a phytochemical, one of the naturally occurring compounds from foods that show cancer-fighting qualities. Like the phytochemical sulfoaphane found in broccoli, capsaicin might turn out to be an agent capable of short-circuiting the actions of carcinogens at the cell level before they can cause cancer.

Learn more about writing a summary or précis:

http://www. webenglishteacher.com/ summary.html

Summary

Chili peppers contain a chemical called capsaicin, which has proved useful for treating a variety of ailments. Recent research reveals that capsaicin is a phytochemical, a natural compound that may help fight cancer.

Outline

- Chili peppers could be the wonder drug of the decade
- Chili peppers contains capsaicin
- Capsaicin can be used as a pain medication
- Capsaicin is a phytochemical
- Phytochemicals show cancer-fighting qualities
- Capsaicin might be able to short-circuit the effects of carcinogens

SKILL 6.5 Applying inferential comprehension skills to draw conclusions from a given passage and interpret implied information

An **INFERENCE** is sometimes called an "educated guess" because it requires that you go beyond the obvious to create additional meaning by taking the text one logical step further. Inferences and conclusions are based on the content of the passage—that is, on what the passage says or how the writer says it—and are derived by reasoning.

> **INFERENCE:** an "educated guess"

Inference is an essential and automatic component of most reading activities. For example, making educated guesses about the meaning of unknown words, about the author's main idea, or about whether the author is writing with a bias all involve the use of inference. Such is the essence of inference: You use your own ability to reason in order to figure out what the writer implies. As a reader, then, you must often logically extend meaning that is only implied.

Consider the following example. Assume you are an employer and are reading over the letters of reference submitted by a prospective employee for the position of clerk/typist in your real estate office. The position requires the applicant to be neat, careful, trustworthy, and punctual. You come across this letter of reference submitted by an applicant:

> *Todd Finley has asked me to write a letter of reference for him. I am well qualified to do so because he worked for me for three months last year. His duties included answering the phone, greeting the public, and producing some simple memos and notices on the computer. Although Todd initially had few computer skills and little knowledge of telephone etiquette, he did acquire some during his stay with us. Todd's manner of speaking, both on the telephone and with the clients who came to my establishment, could be described as casual. He was particularly effective when communicating with peers. Please contact me by telephone if you wish to have further information about my experience.*

Here the writer implies, rather than openly states, the main idea. This letter calls attention to itself because there's a problem with its tone. A truly positive letter would say something like "I have the distinct honor of recommending Todd Finley." Here, however, the letter simply verifies that Todd worked in the office. Second, the praise is obviously lukewarm. For example, the writer says that Todd "was particularly effective when communicating with peers." An educated guess translates that statement into a nice way of saying Todd was not serious about his communication with clients.

In order to draw inferences and make conclusions, a reader must use prior knowledge and apply it to the current situation. A conclusion or inference is never stated. You must rely on your common sense.

Practice Exercise

Read the following passages and select an answer.

1. Tim Sullivan had just turned fifteen. As a birthday present, his parents had given him a guitar and a certificate for ten guitar lessons. He had always shown a love of music and a desire to learn an instrument. Tim began his lessons and, before long, he was making up his own songs. At the music studio, Tim met Josh, who played the piano, and Roger, whose instrument was the saxophone. They all shared the same dream, to start a band, and each was praised by his teacher as having real talent.

   From this passage, one can infer that:

   A. Tim, Roger, and Josh are going to start their own band

   B. Tim is going to give up his guitar lessons

   C. Tim, Josh, and Roger will no longer be friends

   D. Josh and Roger are going to start their own band

2. The Smith family waited patiently around carousel number 7 for their luggage to arrive. They were exhausted after their five-hour trip and were anxious to get to their hotel. After about an hour, they realized that they no longer recognized any of the other passengers' faces. Mrs. Smith asked the person who appeared to be in charge if they were at the right carousel. The man replied, "Yes, this is it, but we finished unloading that baggage almost half an hour ago."

   From the man's response, we can infer that:

   A. The Smiths were ready to go to their hotel

   B. The Smiths' luggage was lost

   C. The man had their luggage

   D. They were at the wrong carousel

Answer Key

1. **A**

   Given the facts that Tim wanted to be a musician and start his own band, after meeting others who shared the same dreams, we can infer that they joined together in an attempt to make their dreams become a reality.

2. **B**

   Since the Smiths were still waiting for their luggage, we know that they were not yet ready to go to their hotel. From the man's response, we know that they were not at the wrong carousel and that he did not have their luggage. Therefore, though not directly stated, the reader can infer that the luggage was lost.

Sample Test Questions and Rationale

(Rigorous)

1. Based on the excerpt below from Kate Chopin's short story "The Story of an Hour," what can students infer about the main character?

She did not stop to ask if it were or were not a monstrous joy that held her. A clear and exalted perception enabled her to dismiss the suggestion as trivial. She knew that she would weep again when she saw the kind, tender hands folded in death; the face that had never looked save with love upon her, fixed and gray and dead. But she saw beyond that bitter moment a long procession of years to come that would belong to her absolutely. And she opened and spread her arms out to them in welcome.

A. She dreaded her life as a widow

B. Although she loved her husband, she was glad that he was dead for he had never loved her

C. She worried that she was too indifferent to her husband's death

D. Although they had both loved each other, she was beginning to appreciate that opportunities had opened because of his death

The answer is D.

Dismissing her feeling of "monstrous joy" as insignificant, the young woman realizes that she will mourn her husband who had been good to her and had loved her. But that "long procession of years" does not frighten her; instead, she recognizes that this new life belongs to her alone, and she welcomes it with open arms.

(Rigorous)

2. Recognizing empathy in literature is mostly a/an:

A. Emotional response

B. Interpretive response

C. Critical response

D. Evaluative response

The answer is C.

In critical responses, students make value judgments about the quality and atmosphere of a text. Through class discussion and written assignments, students react to and assimilate a writer's style and language.

SKILL 6.6 Analyzing how common textual features, graphic features, and organizational structures *(e.g., paragraphs, topic sentences, tables of contents, step-by-step lists, chapter headings, unit summaries)* affect the comprehension and interpretation of texts

We've all had the experience of reading an article, an essay, or a report and scratching our heads while wondering what the piece said. Sometimes, the reading might even have been enjoyable because of language use, humor, and anecdotes. Even so, if the meaning, purpose, intent, and message have not been communicated clearly, the reader is left feeling that his or her time has been wasted and will not be willing to read anything else by that writer.

A successful piece of writing or speech makes a point, has a purpose, and leaves the reader with some feelings about it, even if the reader rejects the point that has been made. Teaching students the value and validity of writing paragraphs with clearly stated topic sentences and essays with clear thesis statements is one of the most important things a teacher of English—writing, composition, and speech— can accomplish, and much of the classroom time must be devoted to this.

How does one write effective topic sentences? First of all, although many effective paragraphs have topic sentences at the end or in the middle, developing writers are better served by putting their topic sentences at the beginning of their paragraphs. Teachers are encouraged to make this placement a requirement when working on this stage of the composition process.

Prose that lacks unity usually fails for one of the following reasons: it lacks a clear statement of a main idea; the opening statement misdirects the reader because it makes a commitment that the writing does not—perhaps cannot—meet; or subdivisions are not selected or phrased so that they clarify their relation to the main idea. A good topic statement works for the writer because it appropriately directs the writer's commitment. A topic sentence is only effective if the details that follow develop it.

- The details may cite particulars, instances, examples, and illustrations. Probably the easiest way to clarify a topic sentence is to provide instances.

- An incident or extended illustration can also be used effectively. The writer may establish the topic sentence by telling a story or describing a single illustration in some detail. This extended illustration might be an analogy.

- Yet another way to develop a topic sentence is by using cause-and-effect speculations.

- Comparison and contrast are often used very effectively in establishing a point.

- Not used as often, but still a viable alternative, is a restatement and amplification of the topic sentence itself.

See Skill 5.4 for an explanation of the table of contents, chapter headings, and summaries.

SKILL Applying knowledge of reference resources and skills used to aid
6.7 comprehension and interpretation

Titles listed in the resource list at the end of this guide are current reference materials with which all language arts teachers should be familiar.

Though the list of literature text publishers is extensive, the following is a tried-and-true list that meets the needs of students in grades 6–12. Teachers should familiarize themselves with the texts adopted by their own districts and select those resources that best reflect the district's scope and sequence.

- Heritage Edition Series by Harcourt Brace Jovanovich
- Norton Anthologies
- Bedford Introduction to Literature
- *Sound and Sense—Introduction to Poetry*, by Laurence Perrine and R. Arp
- *Sound and Sense—Literature Structure*
- *Literary Cavalcade, Read,* and *Scholastic Magazine*

To be life-long learners, students should learn to conduct their own research. Thus, they need to know what resources are available to them and how to use them.

Dictionaries are useful for spelling, writing, and reading. Looking up a word in the dictionary should be expected behavior for students, not a punishment or busy work that has no reference to their current reading assignment.

Model the correct way to use the dictionary, since some students have never been taught proper dictionary skills. As the teacher, you need to demonstrate that as an adult reader and writer, you routinely and happily use the dictionary.

Encyclopedias in print or online are the beginning point for many research projects. Although these entries may sometimes lack timeliness, they do provide students with general background information.

Databases hold billions of records, so students should be taught effective search techniques like using key words and Boolean operators. Learning that "and" and "or" will increase the number of hits while "not" or "and not" will decrease the number of hits can save researchers time and effort.

The Internet is a multifaceted gold mine of information, but students must be careful to discriminate between reliable and unreliable sources. Use sites that are associated with an academic institution, such as a university or a scholarly organization. Typical domain names will end in "edu" or "org."

Students (and everyone) should evaluate any piece of information gleaned from the Internet. The information should be validated by at least three sources. Wikipedia is very useful, but it can be changed by anyone who chooses; so any information on it should be supported by other sources.

Sample Test Question and Rationale

(Average)

1. **If a student has a poor vocabulary, the teacher should recommend first that:**

   A. The student read newspapers, magazines, and books on a regular basis

   B. The student enroll in a Latin class

   C. The student write the words repetitively after looking them up in the dictionary

   D. The student use a thesaurus to locate synonyms and incorporate them into his or her vocabulary

The answer is A.

It is up to the teacher to help the student choose reading material, but the student must be able to choose where to search for the reading pleasure indispensable for enriching vocabulary.

COMPETENCY 7
UNDERSTAND STRATEGIES FOR THE CRITICAL ANALYSIS AND EVALUATION OF TEXTS

SKILL 7.1 Evaluating the development and use of logic and evidence in an argument

Effective argumentative discourse is based on the strength of the writer's supporting information. Using reliable and relevant facts, an argument can convince or motivate.

An **ARGUMENT** is a generalization that is proven or supported with facts. If the facts are not accurate, the generalization remains unproven. Using inaccurate "facts" to support an argument is called a **FALLACY** in reasoning.

Accuracy

Some factors to consider in judging whether the facts used to support an argument are accurate include the following:

- Are the facts current, or are they out of date? For example, if the argument includes the proposition that "birth defects in babies born to drug-using mothers are increasing," then the supporting data must include the most recent available statistics.

- Where was the data obtained, and is that source reliable?

- The calculations on which certain facts are based may be unreliable. Before using a piece of derived information, can you repeat the results by making your own calculations?

Relevance

Even facts that are true and have a sharp impact on the argument may not be relevant to the case at hand. Some examples of irrelevant supporting information are:

- Health statistics from an entire state may have no relevance, or little relevance, to a particular county or zip code. Statistics from an entire country cannot be used to prove very much about a particular state or county.

- An analogy can be useful in making a point, but the comparison must match up in all characteristics. Analogy should be used very carefully. It is just as likely to destroy an argument as it is to strengthen it.

Importance

The importance or significance of a fact may not strengthen an argument. For example, of the millions of immigrants in the United States, using a single family to support a solution to the immigration problem will not make much difference overall, even though such single-example arguments are often used to support one approach or another. They may achieve a positive reaction, but they will not prove that one solution is better than another. If enough cases were cited from a variety of geographical locations, however, the information might be significant.

ARGUMENT: a generalization that is proven or supported with

FALLACY: an argument that is supported using inaccurate "facts"

Learn more about post hoc fallacy:

http://www.sjsu.edu/ depts/itl/graphics/adhom/ posthoc.html

Sufficiency

How much supporting evidence is enough? Generally speaking, three strong supporting facts are sufficient to establish the thesis of an argument. For example:

> *Conclusion: All green apples are sour.*
> - *When I was a child, I bit into a green apple from my grandfather's orchard, and it was sour.*
> - *I once bought green apples from a roadside vendor, and when I bit into one, it was sour.*
> - *My grocery store had a sale on green Granny Smith apples last week. I bought several, only to find that they were sour when I bit into one.*

The fallacy in the above argument is that the sample was insufficient. A more exhaustive search will probably turn up some green apples that are not sour.

Sometimes more than three supporting facts are too many. However, it's not unusual to hear public speakers, particularly politicians, who cite a long litany of facts to support their positions.

A writer makes choices about which facts to use and which to discard when developing an argument. Those choices may exclude anything that does not support the point of view the writer is taking. It's always a good idea for the reader to do some research to spot the omissions and to ask whether they have an impact on the acceptance of the point of view presented in the argument.

A good example of the omission of facts in an argument is the résumé of an applicant for a job. The applicant is arguing that he or she should be awarded a particular job. The application form will ask for information about past employment, and unfavorable dismissals from jobs in the past may be omitted by the applicant. If the argument seems too neat or too compelling, there are probably facts that might be relevant that have not been included.

Sample Test Question and Rationale

(Rigorous)

1. **Which of the following is not a fallacy in logic?**

   A. All students in Ms. Suarez's fourth period class are bilingual.
   Beth is in Ms. Suarez's fourth period.
   Beth is bilingual.

   B. All bilingual students are in Ms. Suarez's class.
   Beth is in Ms. Suarez's fourth period.
   Beth is bilingual.

   C. Beth is bilingual.
   Beth is in Ms. Suarez's fourth period.
   All students in Ms. Suarez's fourth period are bilingual.

   D. If Beth is bilingual, then she speaks Spanish.
   Beth speaks French.
   Beth is not bilingual.

The correct answer is A.

The second statement, or premise, is tested against the first premise. Both premises are valid and the conclusion is logical. In Answer B, the conclusion is invalid because the first premise does not exclude other students. In Answer C, the conclusion cannot be logically drawn from the preceding premises—that is, you cannot conclude that all students are bilingual based on one example. In Answer D, the conclusion is invalid because the first premise is faulty.

SKILL 7.2 Analyzing the effectiveness of a writer's use of language, style, syntax, and rhetorical strategies for specific purposes and audiences

Tailoring language for a particular audience is an important skill. Writing to be read by a business associate surely sounds different from writing to be read by a younger sibling. Not only are the vocabularies different, but the formality or informality of the discourse needs to be adjusted.

Two characteristics that determine language style are degree of formality and word choice. The most formal language does not use contractions or slang, while the most informal language probably features a casual use of common sayings and anecdotes. Formal language uses longer sentences and does not sound like a conversation. Informal language uses shorter sentences (not necessarily simple sentences, but shorter constructions) and may sound like a conversation.

TONE: the writer's attitude toward the material and/or readers

CONNOTATIONS: affective meanings attached to words

In both formal and informal writing, there exists a **TONE**, the writer's attitude toward the material and/or readers. Tone may be playful, formal, intimate, angry, serious, ironic, outraged, baffled, tender, serene, depressed, and so on. The overall tone of a piece of writing is dictated by both the subject matter and the audience. Tone is also related to the actual word choices that make up the document, as we attach affective meanings to words, called their **CONNOTATIONS**. Gaining this conscious control over language makes it possible to use language appropriately in various situations and to evaluate its uses in literature and other forms of communication. By evoking the proper responses from readers or listeners, we can prompt them to take action.

Using the following questions is an excellent way to assess the audience and tone of a given piece of writing:

- Who is your audience (friend, teacher, businessperson, someone else)?

- How much does this person know about you and/or your topic?

- What is your purpose (to prove an argument, to persuade, to amuse, to register a complaint, to ask for a raise, and so on)?

- What emotions do you have about the topic (nervous, happy, confident, angry, sad, no feelings at all)?

- What emotions do you want to register with your audience (anger, nervousness, happiness, boredom, interest)?

- What persona do you need to create in order to achieve your purpose?

- What choice of language is best suited to achieving your purpose with this particular subject (slang, friendly but respectful, formal)?

- What emotional quality do you want to transmit to achieve your purpose (matter of fact, informative, authoritative, inquisitive, sympathetic, angry), and to what degree do you want to express this tone?

Sample Test Questions and Rationale

(Average)

1. **Which of the following responses to literature typically gives middle school students the most problems?**

   A. Interpretive

   B. Evaluative

   C. Critical

   D. Emotional

   The answer is B.

   Middle school readers will exhibit both emotional and interpretive responses. In middle/junior high school, organized study models enable students to identify main ideas and supporting details, to recognize sequential order, to distinguish fact from opinion, and to determine cause/effect relationships. Also, a child's ability to say why a particular book was boring or why a particular poem made him/her sad evidences critical reactions on a fundamental level. It is a bit early for evaluative responses, however. These depend on the reader's consideration of how the piece represents its genre, how well it reflects the social/ethical mores of a given society, and how well the author has approached the subject for freshness and slant. Evaluative responses are made only by a few advanced high school students.

(Average)

2. **Which of the following is not one of the four forms of discourse?**

   A. Exposition

   B. Description

   C. Rhetoric

   D. Persuasion

   The answer is C.

   Rhetoric is an umbrella term for techniques of expressive and effective speech. Rhetorical figures are ornaments of speech such as anaphora, antithesis, metaphor, and so on. The other three choices are specific forms of discourse.

(Rigorous)

3. **The arrangement and relationship of words in sentences or sentence structures best describes**

   A. Style

   B. Discourse

   C. Thesis

   D. Syntax

   The answer is D.

   Syntax is the grammatical structure of sentences. Style refers to the way something is written. Discourse, broadly, means communication. A thesis is the main idea that holds an essay together.

SKILL
7.3 **Distinguishing opinion from fact, conclusion, or inference in a passage**

Your students will enjoy sharing their opinions. Some of them may be voicing what they have heard from others, while some are discovering their own voices. All of them, though, are trying to make sense of their worlds. Helping students distinguish between fact and opinion, realize conclusions, and make inferences develops critical reasoning.

Facts and Opinions

FACT: a statement that is verifiable

OPINION: a statement that must be supported in order to be accepted

JUDGMENT: a type of opinion; a decision or declaration based on observation or reasoning that expresses approval or disapproval

FACTS are statements that are verifiable. OPINIONS are statements that must be supported in order to be accepted. Facts are used to support opinions. For example, "Jane is a bad girl" is an *opinion*. However, "Jane hit her sister with a baseball bat" is a *fact* upon which the opinion is based. JUDGMENTS are opinions—decisions or declarations based on observation or reasoning that express approval or disapproval. Facts report what has happened or exists, and they come from observation, measurement, or calculation. Facts can be tested and verified, whereas opinions and judgments cannot. They can only be supported with facts. Most statements cannot be so clearly distinguished. "I believe that Jane is a bad girl" is a fact. The speaker knows what he or she believes. However, the statement obviously includes a judgment that could be disputed by another person who might believe otherwise. Judgments are not usually so firm. They are, rather, plausible opinions that provoke thought or lead to factual development.

Use the chart below to identify both facts and opinions in a text and be sure to explain how you know the details you write down are either facts or opinions.

FACT VS. OPINION		
	Text Details and Direct Quotes From the Text	**Explain How You Know Whether the Details Are Facts or Opinions**
Facts		
Opinions		

http://www.greece.k12.ny.us/instruction/ela/6-12/Tools/factvsopinion

Conclusions

CONCLUSIONS are drawn as a result of a line of reasoning. Whether inductive or deductive, a conclusion is an analysis of what the data means. Given all the facts, all the opinions, and all the details, the reader can draw a conclusion.

> CONCLUSION: an analysis drawn as a result of a line of reasoning

> *Joe DiMaggio, a Yankees center fielder, was replaced by Mickey Mantle in 1952.*

This is a fact. If necessary, evidence can be produced to support this.

> *First-year players are more ambitious than seasoned players.*

This is an opinion. There is no proof to support that every first-year player feels this way.

Practice Exercise

1. The Inca were a group of Indians who ruled an empire in South America.

   A. Fact

   B. Opinion

2. The Inca were clever.

   A. Fact

   B. Opinion

3. The Inca built very complex systems of bridges.

   A. Fact

   B. Opinion

Answer Key

1. **A**

   Research can prove this statement true.

2. **B**

   It is doubtful that all people who have studied the Inca agree with this statement. Therefore, no proof is available.

3. **A**

   As with question number one, research can prove this statement true.

Sample Test Question and Rationale

(Rigorous)

1. Students have been asked to write a research paper on automobiles and have brainstormed a number of questions they will answer based on their research findings. Which of the following is not an interpretive question to guide research?

   A. Who were the first ten automotive manufacturers in the United States?

   B. What types of vehicles will be used fifty years from now?

   C. How do automobiles manufactured in the United States compare and contrast with each other?

   D. What do you think is the best solution for the fuel shortage?

The answer is A.

The question asks for objective facts. Answer B is a prediction that asks how something will look or be in the future, based on the way it is now. Answer C asks for similarities and differences, which is a higher-level research activity that requires analysis. Answer D is a judgment question that requires informed opinion.

SKILL 7.4 Discerning the relevance, importance, credibility, and sufficiency of support in a writer's argument

See Skill 7.1

SKILL 7.5 Determining how a writer uses tone and style to present a particular point of view or to hold the interest of readers

Tone

TONE: the author's attitude toward the subject matter

The **TONE** of a written passage is the author's attitude toward the subject matter. The tone is revealed through the qualities of the writing itself and is a direct product of such stylistic elements as language and sentence structure.

Often, writers have an emotional stake in their subjects; their purpose, either explicitly or implicitly, is to convey those feelings to the reader. In such cases, the writing is generally subjective; that is, it stems from opinions, judgments, values, ideas, and feelings. Both sentence structure (syntax) and word choice (diction) are instrumental tools in creating tone.

Tone may be thought of generally as positive, negative, or neutral. Below is a statement about snakes that demonstrates tone:

> *Many species of snakes live in Florida. Some of those species, both poisonous and nonpoisonous, have habitats that coincide with those of human residents of the state.*

The tone of the writer in this statement is neutral. The sentences are declarative (not exclamations or fragments or questions). The adjectives are few and nondescript: many, some, poisonous (balanced with nonpoisonous). Nothing much in this brief paragraph would alert the reader to the writer's feelings about snakes. The paragraph has a neutral, objective, detached, impartial tone.

Then again, if the writer's attitude toward snakes involves admiration, or even affection, the tone would generally be positive:

> *Florida's snakes are a tenacious bunch. When they find their habitats invaded by humans, they cling to their home territories as long as they can, as if vainly attempting to fight off the onslaught of the human hordes.*

An additional message emerges in this paragraph: the writer quite clearly favors snakes over people. The writer uses adjectives like tenacious to describe his or her feelings about snakes. The writer also humanizes the reptiles, making them brave, beleaguered creatures.

If the writer's attitude toward snakes involves active dislike and fear, then the tone would also reflect that attitude by being negative:

> *Countless species of snakes, some more dangerous than others, still lurk on the urban fringes of Florida's towns and cities. They will often invade domestic spaces, terrorizing people and their pets.*

Here, obviously, the snakes are the villains. They lurk, they invade, and they terrorize. The tone of this paragraph might be said to be distressed regarding snakes.

In the same manner, a writer can use language to portray characters as good or bad. A writer uses positive and negative adjectives, as seen above, to convey the manner of a character.

Style

STYLE: a distinctive manner of expression, applying to all levels of language

In literature, STYLE means a distinctive manner of expression and applies to all levels of language. At the phonemic level, style is evident in word choices, alliteration, assonance, and others. Style at the syntactic level is characterized by length of sentences, choice of structure and phraseology, and patterns—even extending beyond the sentence to paragraphs and chapters. Critical readers determine what is distinctive about the writer's use of these elements.

Sample Test Questions and Rationale

(Easy)

1. **Which definition is the best for defining diction?**

   A. The specific word choices of an author to create a particular mood or feeling in the reader

   B. Writing that explains something thoroughly

   C. The background, or exposition, for a short story or drama

   D. Word choices that help teach a truth or moral

   The answer is A.

   Diction refers to an author's choice of words, expressions, and style to convey his or her meaning.

(Average)

2. **Overcrowded classes prevent the individual attention needed to facilitate language development. This drawback can be best overcome by:**

   A. Dividing the class into independent study groups

   B. Assigning more study time at home

   C. Using more drill practice in class

   D. Team teaching

   The answer is A.

   Dividing a class into small groups fosters peer enthusiasm and evaluation, and sets an atmosphere of warmth and enthusiasm. It is much preferable to divide the class into smaller study groups than to lecture, which bores students and therefore fails to facilitate curricular goals. Also, it is preferable to do this than to engage the whole class in a general teacher-led discussion because such discussion favors the loquacious and inhibits the shy.

Sample Test Questions and Rationale (cont.)

(Average)

3. **Which event triggered the beginning of Modern English?**

   A. Conquest of England by the Normans in 1066

   B. Introduction of the printing press to the British Isles

   C. Publication of Samuel Johnson's lexicon

   D. American Revolution

   The answer is B.

With the arrival of the written word, reading matter became mass produced, so the public tended to adopt the speech and writing habits printed in books and the language became more stable.

(Average)

4. **Which of the following is not true about the English language?**

   A. English is the easiest language to learn

   B. English is the least inflected language

   C. English has the most extensive vocabulary of any language

   D. English originated as a Germanic tongue

   The answer is A.

Just like any other language, English has inherent difficulties that make it difficult to learn, even though English has no declensions such as those found in Latin, Greek, or contemporary Russian, or a tonal system such as in Chinese.

(Rigorous)

5. **What was responsible for the standardizing of dialects across America in the twentieth century?**

   A. With the immigrant influx, America became a melting pot of languages and cultures

   B. Trains enabled people to meet other people of different languages and cultures

   C. Radio, and later, television, used actors and announcers who spoke without pronounced dialects

   D. Newspapers and libraries developed programs to teach people to speak English with an agreed-upon common dialect

   The answer is C.

The growth of immigration in the early part of the twentieth century created pockets of language throughout the country. Coupled with regional differences already in place, the number of dialects grew. Transportation enabled people to move to different regions, where languages and dialects continued to merge. With the growth of radio and television, however, people were introduced to a standardized dialect through actors and announcers who spoke so that anyone across America could understand them. Newspapers and libraries never developed programs to standardize spoken English.

Sample Test Questions and Rationale (cont.)

(Rigorous)

6. The most significant drawback to applying learning theory research to classroom practice is that:

A. Today's students do not acquire reading skills with the same alacrity as when greater emphasis was placed on reading classical literature

B. Development rates are complicated by geographical and cultural factors

C. Homogeneous grouping has contributed to faster development of some age groups

D. Social and environmental conditions have contributed to an escalated maturity level than research done twenty or more years ago would seem to indicate

The answer is D.

Because of rapid social changes, topics that did not use to interest younger readers are now topics of books for even younger readers. There are many books dealing with difficult topics, and it is difficult for the teacher to steer students toward books that they are ready for and to try to keep them away from books whose content, although well written, is not yet appropriate for their level of cognitive and social development. There is a fine line between this and censorship.

SKILL 7.6 Demonstrating knowledge of the effect of the cultural, political, and social environment on a writer's use of language

Learn more about the history of the English language:

http://ebbs.english.vt.edu/hel/hel.html

English is an Indo-European language that has evolved through several periods. The origin of English dates to the settlement of the British Isles in the fifth and sixth centuries by Germanic tribes called the Angles, Saxons, and Jutes. The original Britons spoke a Celtic tongue, whereas the Angles spoke a Germanic dialect.

Modern English derives from the speech of the Anglo-Saxons, who imposed not only their language but also their social customs and laws on their new land. From the fifth to the tenth century, Britain's language was the tongue we now refer to as Old English. During the next four centuries, the many French attempts at English conquest introduced many French words to English. However, the grammar and syntax of the language remained Germanic.

Middle English, most evident in the writings of Geoffrey Chaucer, dates loosely from 1066 to 1509. Old English words required numerous inflections to indicate noun cases, plurals, and verb conjugations. Middle English continued the use of many inflections and pronunciations that treated these inflections as separately pronounced syllables. English in 1300 would have been written "Olde Anglishe" with the e's at the ends of the words pronounced as our short a vowel. Even adjectives had plural inflections: "long dai" became "longe daies," pronounced "long-a day-as." Spelling was phonetic; thus every vowel had multiple pronunciations, a fact that continues to affect the language.

Modern English dates from the introduction of The Great Vowel Shift, which created guidelines for spelling and pronunciation. Before the printing press, books were copied laboriously by hand; the language was subject to the individual interpretation of the scribes. Printers and subsequently lexicographers like Samuel Johnson and America's Noah Webster influenced the guidelines. As reading matter was mass produced, the reading public was forced to adopt the speech and writing habits developed by those who wrote and printed books.

Despite many students' insistence to the contrary, Shakespeare's writings are in Modern English. Teachers should stress to students that language, like customs, morals, and other social factors, is constantly subject to change. Immigration, inventions, and cataclysmic events change language as much as any other facet of life is affected by these changes.

The domination of one race or nation over others can change a language significantly. Beginning with the colonization of the New World by England and Spain, English and Spanish became dominant languages in the Western hemisphere.

American English today is somewhat different in pronunciation and vocabulary from British English. The British call a truck a "lorry," a baby carriage a "pram" (short for "perambulator"), and an elevator a "lift." The two languages have very few syntactical differences, though, and even the tonal qualities that were once so clearly different are converging.

Although Modern English is less complex than Middle English, it is still considered difficult to learn because of its many exceptions to the rules. English has become, however, the world's dominant language by reason of the great political, military, and social power of England from the fifteenth to the nineteenth centuries and of America in the twentieth and twenty-first centuries.

Modern inventions—the telephone, phonograph, radio, television, and motion pictures—have especially affected English pronunciation. Regional dialects, once a hindrance to clear understanding, have fewer distinct characteristics. The speakers from different parts of the United States of America can be identified by their accents, but as educators and media personalities stress uniform pronunciations and proper grammar, the differences are diminishing.

The English language has a more extensive vocabulary than any other language. Ours is a language of synonyms, words borrowed from other

> *Check out the learning resources of the OED:*
>
> *hhttp://www.oed.com/learning/*

languages, and coined words, many of them introduced by the rapid expansion of technology.

Students should understand that language is in constant flux. They can demonstrate this when they use language for specific purposes and audiences. Negative criticism of a student's errors in word choice or sentence structures will inhibit creativity. Positive criticism that suggests ways to enhance communication skills will encourage exploration.

Geographical Influences

Dialect differences occur mainly in pronunciation. Bostonians say "pahty" for "party," and Southerners blend words like "you all" into "y'all." Besides the dialect differences already mentioned, the biggest geographical factors in American English stem from minor word choice variances. Depending on the region, when you order a carbonated, syrupy beverage most generically called a soft drink, you might ask for a "soda" in the South, or a "pop" in the Midwest. If you order a soda in New York, then you will get a scoop of ice cream in your soft drink, while in other areas you would have to ask for a "float."

Social Influences

Social influences on language are mostly those imposed by family, peer groups, and mass media. The economic and educational levels of families determine language use. Exposure to adults who encourage and assist children to speak well enhances readiness for other areas of learning and contributes to their ability to communicate their needs.

Historically, children learned language, speech patterns, and grammar from members of the extended family just as they learned the rules of conduct within their family unit and community. In modern times, the mother in a nuclear family became the dominant force in influencing children's development. With increasing social changes, many children are not receiving the proper guidance in all areas of development, especially language.

Those who are fortunate to be in educational day-care programs like Head Start or in certified preschools develop better language skills than those whose care is entrusted to untrained care providers. Once children enter elementary school, they are also greatly influenced by peer language. This peer influence becomes significant in adolescence as the use of teen jargon gives teenagers a sense of identity within their chosen group(s) and independence from the influence of adults. In some lower socioeconomic groups, children use Standard English in school and street language outside the school. Some children of immigrant families become bilingual by necessity if no English is spoken in the home.

Research has shown a strong correlation between socioeconomic characteristics and all areas of intellectual development. Traditional measurement instruments rely on verbal ability to establish intelligence. Research findings and test scores reflect that children reared in nuclear families providing cultural experiences and individual attention become more language proficient than those who are denied that security and stimulation.

Personal Influences

The rate of physical development and identifiable language disabilities also influence language development. Nutritional deficiencies, poor eyesight, and conditions such as stuttering or dyslexia can inhibit children's ability to master language. Unless diagnosed early, these conditions can hamper communication into adulthood. They can also stymie the development of self-confidence and, therefore, the willingness to learn or to overcome the handicap. Children should receive proper diagnosis and positive corrective instruction for these issues.

In adolescence, children's choice of role models and decisions about their future determine the growth of identity. Rapid physical and emotional changes and the stress of coping with the pressure of sexual awareness make concentration on any educational pursuits difficult. The easier the transition from childhood to adulthood, the better the competence will be in all learning areas.

Middle school and junior high school teachers are confronted by a student body ranging from fifth graders, who are still childish, to eighth or ninth graders, who if not in fact, at least in their minds, are young adults. Teachers must approach language instruction as a social development tool with more emphasis on vocabulary acquisition, reading improvement, and speaking/writing skills.

High school teachers can deal with the more formalized instruction of grammar, usage, and literature meant for older adolescents whose social development allows them to pay more attention to studies that will improve their chances for a better adult life.

As a tool, language must have relevance to students' real environment. Many high schools have developed practical English classes for business/vocational students, whose specific needs are determined by their desire to enter the workforce upon graduation. More emphasis is placed upon accuracy of mechanics and understanding verbal and written directions, because these are skills desired by employers. Writing résumés, completing forms, reading policy and operations manuals, and generating reports are some of the desired skills. Emphasis is placed on higher-level thinking skills, including inferential thinking and literary interpretation, in literature classes for college-bound students.

Sample Test Question and Rationale

(Easy)

1. **The Elizabethans wrote in:**

    A. Celtic

    B. Old English

    C. Middle English

    D. Modern English

The answer is D.

There is no document written in Celtic in England, and a work such as *Beowulf* is representative of Old English in the eighth century. It is also the earliest Teutonic written document. Before the fourteenth century, little literature is known to have appeared in Middle English, which had absorbed many words from the Norman French spoken by the ruling class, but at the and of the fourteenth century there appeared the works of Geoffrey Chaucer, John Gower, and the novel *Sir Gawain and The Green King*. The Elizabethans wrote in modern English, and their legacy is very important: They imported the Petrarchan, or Italian, sonnet, which Sir Thomas Wyatt and Sir Philip Sydney illustrated in their works. Sir Edmund Spencer invented his own version of the Italian sonnet and wrote *The Faerie Queene*. The literature of the time includes the hugely important works of William Shakespeare and Christopher Marlowe.

Check out this link on teaching literature— story response/writing:

http://www. teachingliterature.org/

COMPETENCY 8
UNDERSTAND SKILLS FOR EFFECTIVE READING ACROSS THE CURRICULUM

SKILL **Recognizing the relationships of messages, themes, and ideas**
8.1 **from one subject area to those from another subject area and to life experiences**

Human nature compels us to compare objects, ideas, and even people to look for commonalities. This naturally occurring phenomenon can be very useful in literary analysis. For example, in *The Five People You Meet in Heaven*, Mitch Albom's theme of giving one's life to save another alludes to the biblical teaching that the greatest love is to give up one's life for a friend. The same theme can be found in newspapers as well. For example, a man in New York City risked his life to rescue a homeless man from the wheels of a train. Stories of animals that show extraordinary bravery to save their masters or mistresses are very popular, too.

War is a very popular theme for literature of all kinds. Ernest Hemingway's novels, written based on his experience in the Spanish Civil War, make familiar and poignant statements about the effects of war. Much poetry has been written about this theme: "Johnny, I Hardly Know Ye," an anonymous eighteenth-century Irish ballad; Wilfred Owen's World War I poem "Dulce et Decorum Est"; and Richard Lovelace's seventeenth century "To Lucasta," to name a few examples. Comparing the treatment of such a common theme by different writers adds depth and interest to an interpretation of a literary work. One's own experience is useful in interpreting war literature, too. Few of us have had the privilege of living our lives without experiencing our country at war and of seeing its destructive effects on human beings.

In analyzing literature and in looking for ways to bring a work to life for an audience, the use of comparable themes and ideas from other pieces of literature and from one's own life experiences, including from reading the daily newspaper, is very important and useful.

Sample Test Question and Rationale

(Average)

1. **To explore the relationship of literature to modern life, which of these activities would not enable students to explore comparable themes?**

    A. After studying various world events, such as the Palestinian-Israeli conflict, students write an updated version of *Romeo and Juliet* using modern characters and settings

    B. Before studying *Romeo and Juliet*, students watch *West Side Story*

    C. Students research the major themes of *Romeo and Juliet* by studying news stories and finding modern counterparts for the story

    D. Students explore and compare the romantic themes of *Romeo and Juliet* and *The Taming of the Shrew*

The answer is D.

By comparing the two plays by Shakespeare, students focus on the culture of the period in which the plays were written. In Answer A, students should be able to recognize modern parallels with current culture clashes. In Answer B, by comparing *Romeo and Juliet* to the 1950s update of *West Side Story*, students can study how the themes are similar in two completely different historical periods. In Answer C, students can study local, national, and international news for comparable stories and themes.

SKILL 8.2 Applying knowledge of a writer's purpose, the academic context, and prior learning to the comprehension of ideas in the subject areas

Thinking about and drawing conclusions about a writer's purpose in creating a work of fiction is important when attempting to understand and appreciate the piece. Why did this writer write this particular work at this particular time?

We know that John Steinbeck wrote *The Grapes of Wrath* out of his own concern that his fellow Americans were suffering and that their suffering could be traced to greed and indifference on the parts of those who brought on and perpetuated the state of affairs that had led to the Great Depression. Prior learning about the history and political situation in the 1930s is very useful in interpreting writing from that period of time, including Steinbeck's masterpiece. What led him to these conclusions? Was it his brief education at Stanford? Was it because of reading that he had done? These are important questions for an interpreter to ask about a writer and the literature he or she produces.

SKILL 8.3 Applying knowledge of organizational structures and patterns, graphic features, and textual features to the comprehension of ideas in the subject areas

When reading a piece of writing for comprehension, you should first determine, exactly what its purpose is. Was the piece written to persuade the reader to a point of view or to get a reader to take some action? Was it written simply to communicate information, such as a news feature on a local institution? A college catalog may include some parts that encourage students to enroll and attend; however, for the most part, college catalogs are written to inform. A piece of writing might be intended to communicate an experience the writer has had in such a way that the reader might also experience it, such as the destructive force of a flood. This is called descriptive writing. Another possibility is that the piece of writing is intended simply to tell a story—a chronological approach.

PERSUASIVE WRITING: writing that has a thesis, either sated or implied

PERSUASIVE WRITING has a thesis, either stated or implied, so look first for that. What does this writer want you to believe or do? Once the thesis has been determined, the supporting reasons should be isolated and examined. Are they adequate to persuade? Can this reasoning be accepted, or is it flawed or fallacious? Can this writer be trusted to write objectively about this topic, or is there bias? Is this writer knowledgeable enough to write reliably about this topic? These questions can be answered only after carefully picking out the reasons the writer gives for you to accept his or her point of view or advice.

In understanding an **INFORMATIVE** piece of writing—one whose purpose is not to persuade but simply to give information—you should determine the organizational structure of the piece of writing. Is the information presented spatially, chronologically, or visually? What are the steps in the information-giving process? Are they in logical order? Are they understandable enough that you could explain the information to another person?

> **INFORMATIVE WRITING:** writing whose purpose is to give informattion

In reading **DESCRIPTIVE** writing, the main question to ask is whether you can experience what the writer is attempting to share with you. Can you see what the writer is describing? Can you hear it, smell it, and so on? Are the descriptions complete enough for comprehension and reaction? A good example of effective and powerful descriptive writing is Wilfred Owen's poem "Dulce et Decorum Est." Read some of the lines:

> **DESCRIPTIVE WRITING:** writing whose purpose is to communicate an experience

Bent double, like old beggars under sacks,
Knock-kneed, coughing like hags, we cursed through sludge,
Till on the haunting flares we turned our backs
And towards our distant rest began to trudge.
Men marched asleep. Many had lost their boots
But limped on, blood-shod. All went lame; all blind;
Drunk with fatigue; deaf even to the hoots
Of tired, outstripped Five-Nines (gas shells) that dropped behind.

Someone has said that "war is hell," but this poem lets us see and feel how bad it truly is from those who have experienced it first hand, fulfilling the purpose of descriptive language.

In reading a **NARRATIVE**, the main question to ask is whether the incidents lead to a resolution. What is the purpose of the story? What is the meaning? Why did the writer write it?

> **NARRATIVE WRITING:** writing whose purpose is to tell a story

Sample Test Question and Rationale

(Average)

1. **Which of the following is a formal reading-level assessment?**

    A. A standardized reading test

    B. A teacher-made reading test

    C. An interview

    D. A reading diary

The answer is A.

If assessment is standardized, it has to be objective. Answers B, C, and D are all subjective assessments.

SKILL 8.4 Recognizing how certain words and concepts are related to multiple subjects and how similes, metaphors, and analogies are used to compare ideas across subject areas

Teachers and students easily fall into the attitude that the study of literature and writing is confined to the English classroom and curriculum, but nothing could be further from the truth. When teachers in English classes work with history, sociology, psychology, and science teachers, student skills can make leaps.

Check out this detailed lesson plan on The Grapes of Wrath:

http://www.neabigread.org/ books/grapesofwrath

Using Steinbeck's *The Grapes of Wrath* again for an example, if English teachers and social studies teachers cooperate in helping students see that literature is real and emerges out of human experience, then students will begin to write papers of a different quality. American people and politicians used many of the same themes that Steinbeck used in his book during the run-up to the election in 1932 to defeat President Hoover and elect President Roosevelt. Understanding the history and geography of the Dust Bowl states and of migration west dating from the time of the Louisiana Purchase is very useful for reading this piece of literature with greater depth and understanding.

Check out this assortment of literary analysis lesson plans:

http://www.teach-nology. com/teachers/lesson_ plans/language_arts/ literary/

Identifying similes, metaphors, and analogies in a piece of writing is made easier by relating these figures of speech to other subject areas such as history and geography. The title of Steinbeck's story, *The Grapes of Wrath*, is an allusion to a popular and well-known hymn, "The Battle Hymn of the Republic." The allusion introduces Steinbeck's theme of injustice. The hymn suggests that God will rid the world of that kind of injustice:

> *Mine eyes have seen the glory of the coming of the Lord:*
> *He is trampling out the vintage where the grapes of wrath are stored;*
> *He hath loosed the fateful lightning of His terrible swift sword:*
> *His truth is marching on.*

Teaching literary analysis, particularly taking students to the point where they can see such things as metaphors and allusions, is a slow and difficult process. Using across-the-curriculum tools increases student growth in this area.

Sample Test Question and Rationale

(Rigorous)

1. How will literature help students in a science class be able to understand the following passage?

   Just as was the case more than three decades ago, we are still sailing between the Scylla of deferring surgery for too long and risking irreversible left ventricular damage and sudden death, and the Charibdas of operating too early and subjecting the patient to the early risks of operation and the later risks resulting from prosthetic valves.

   —E. Braunwald, *European Heart Journal,*
   July 2000

   A. They will recognize the allusion to Scylla and Charibdas from Greek mythology and understand that the medical community has to select one of two unfavorable choices

   B. They will recognize the allusion to sailing and understand its analogy to doctors as sailors navigating unknown waters

   C. They will recognize that the allusion to Scylla and Charibdas refers to the two islands in Norse mythology where sailors would find themselves shipwrecked and understand how the doctors feel isolated by their choices

   D. They will recognize the metaphor of the heart and relate it to Eros, the character in Greek mythology who represents love. Eros was the love child of Scylla and Charibdas

The answer is A.

Scylla and Charibdas were two sea monsters guarding a narrow channel of water. Sailors trying to elude one side would face danger by sailing too close to the other side. The allusion indicates two equally undesirable choices.

DOMAIN III

WRITING CONVENTIONS AND THE WRITING PROCESS

PERSONALIZED STUDY PLAN

KNOWN MATERIAL/ SKIP IT

PAGE	COMPETENCY AND SKILL	
141	**9: Understand the conventions of Standard American English**	☐
	9.1: Applying an extensive knowledge of Standard American English	☐
	9.2: Recognizing and evaluating the appropriateness of grammar	☐
	9.3: Recognizing appropriate and inappropriate use of words, phrases, and clauses in written texts	☐
	9.4: Demonstrating knowledge of standard sentence construction	☐
	9.5: Demonstrating knowledge of Standard American English mechanics	☐
189	**10: Understand writing as a process**	☐
	10.1: Recognizing techniques for generating and organizing ideas	☐
	10.2: Demonstrating knowledge of techniques for selecting and presenting detailed evidence as support for ideas	☐
	10.3: Recognizing methods for developing ideas into a well-organized composition	☐
	10.4: Demonstrating knowledge of revision, editing, and proofreading methods and standards	☐
204	**11: Understand the use of research and technology in writing**	☐
	11.1: Recognizing the differences between primary and secondary sources	☐
	11.2: Identifying various sources of information and using technology in research	☐
	11.3: Recognizing methods for verifying accuracy	☐
	11.4: Assessing the credibility, objectivity, and reliability of a source of information	☐
	11.5: Synthesizing information from multiple sources and perspectives	☐
	11.6: Applying knowledge of ethical principles and appropriate formats for quotations, citations, and bibliographies	☐
	11.7: Recognizing how the medium of presentation can affect a reader's construction of meaning from a text	☐

COMPETENCY 9
UNDERSTAND THE CONVENTIONS OF STANDARD AMERICAN ENGLISH

**SKILL Applying an extensive knowledge of Standard American English
9.1 grammar, semantics, syntax, morphology, and phonology**

Understanding the history and development of their language is one part of students' study of the English language. They should also understand the features and characteristics of their language's structure.

Phonological Awareness

PHONOLOGICAL AWARENESS refers to the ability of the reader to recognize the sound of spoken language. This recognition includes how these sounds can be blended together, segmented (divided up), and manipulated (switched around). This awareness then leads to **PHONICS**, a method for teaching students to read. Phonics helps students "sound out words."

Instructional methods to teach phonological awareness may include auditory games and drills during which students recognize and manipulate the sounds of words, separate or segment the sounds of words, take out sounds, blend sounds, add in new sounds, or take apart sounds to recombine them in new formations. These drills and games are good ways to foster phonological awareness.

**SKILL Recognizing and evaluating the appropriateness of grammar that
9.2 does not conform to Standard American English in written texts**

The dynamism of Standard American English is one of its distinguishing characteristics. Standard American English reflects the culture of the time, and as the culture changes, so does the language. No longer in vogue, "neato" will date someone as fast as bell bottoms and paisley shirts. Just because most of us understand "ain't" doesn't make it an appropriate word for every situation.

SLANG is defined as "very informal usage in vocabulary and idiom that is characteristically more metaphorical, playful, elliptical, vivid, and ephemeral than

---

Check out a continuum of complexity of phonological awareness activities:

http://www.ldonline.org/article/6254

PHONOLOGICAL AWARENESS: the ability of a reader to recognize the sound of spoken language

PHONICS: a method for teaching reading that helps students "sound out words"

Check out this link—Do you speak American?

http://www.pbs.org/speak/seatosea/standardamerican/hamlet/

SLANG: very informal usage in vocabulary and idiom

ordinary language, as [in the phrase] *Hit the road.*" Slang is fine in conversation between friends, but it is extremely inappropriate in formal writing. Because of its colloquial nature, slang can be easily misunderstood. Moreover, using slang can affect how seriously a reader regards your writing. The only time that slang may be appropriate in formal writing is when it is used in a quote or dialogue.

JARGON: the language peculiar to a particular trade, profession, or group

JARGON is defined as "the language, [especially] the vocabulary, peculiar to a particular trade, profession, or group: *medical jargon.*" Jargon pertains to the vocabulary used by a limited or specialized group of people. As a result, using jargon can affect clear and effective communication to a general reading public. Jargon, like slang, has its own time and place.

If you are writing for a specialized audience, jargon will communicate meaning effectively and show the audience that you are familiar with the terms associated with that specialized field. If, however, you are writing for a more general audience, jargon will be unintelligible gibberish and, perhaps, even offensive. If readers feel that an author is being pretentious or boastful, they may find the passage distasteful.

CLICHÉ: a trite, stereotyped expression

A **CLICHÉ** is defined as "a trite, stereotyped expression; a sentence or phrase, usually expressing a popular or common thought or idea, that has lost originality, ingenuity, and impact by long overuse, as [in] *sadder but wiser*, or *strong as an ox.*" Due to lack of creativity, thoughtfulness, and personal perspective, the use of clichés weakens writing.

Clichés are boring and sometimes even offensive. Writers should avoid using clichés when writing an original work. Rather than using tired expressions to convey an idea, rethink the idea that is being conveyed, and reword it with correct vocabulary and specific details.

Sample Test Questions and Rationale

For Question 1, circle the choice that best corrects the underlined error without changing the meaning of the original sentence.

(Easy)

1. There were <u>fewer pieces</u> of evidence presented during the second trial.

   A. fewer peaces

   B. less peaces

   C. less pieces

   D. fewer pieces

The answer is D.

Use "fewer" for countable items; use "less" for amounts and quantities, such as fewer minutes but less time. "Peace" is the opposite of war, not a "piece" of evidence.

(Easy)

2. "Clean as a whistle" or "easy as falling off a log" are examples of:

   A. Semantics

   B. Parody

   C. Irony

   D. Clichés

The answer is D.

A cliché is a phrase or expression that has become dull due to overuse. Semantics relates to the meanings of words. A parody is a work that imitates another, usually satirically. Irony is the relationship between what is said and what is meant.

SKILL 9.3 **Recognizing appropriate and inappropriate use of words, phrases, and clauses in written texts**

An **IDIOMATIC EXPRESSION** is a group of words whose meaning, when considered as a whole, is something entirely different from the meaning of each individual word. This feature of idioms is called noncompositionality. For example, the expression "hit the hay" has nothing to do with literally hitting hay; it means to go to bed. In addition, idioms display nonsubstitutability, which means that one cannot replace a word in an idiom and maintain the idiom's meaning. For example, one cannot say "hit the straw" instead of "hit the hay," even though straw and hay could be considered synonyms. Lastly, idioms are nonmodifiable; if an idiom is modified with syntactic transformations, it loses its idiomatic meaning. "Katie hit the bale of hay with her car" changes the meaning.

> **IDIOMATIC EXPRESSION:** a group of words whose meaning, when considered as a whole, is something entirely different from the meaning of each individual word

Idioms are not hard and fast grammatical rules; rather, idioms are verbal habits that have become ingrained in standard English language usage. Learning correct usage of idiomatic expressions is about learning to trust your ear. Idioms come in the form of expressions such as "rain check" or "a penny for your thoughts" as well as phrases such as "in contrast to" and "not only … but."

SOME IDIOMS	
abide by	discriminate against
agreed to	in charge of
as…as	in contrast to
among	insist upon
between	neither… nor
concerned with	not only…. but also
different from	rely upon

Error: *I am having trouble deciding between the chocolate, vanilla, and strawberry milkshakes.*

Problem: Here, more than two items are being distinguished. In this case, you must use *among*, as *between* should only be used when comparing two items.

Correction: *I am having trouble deciding among the chocolate, vanilla, and strawberry milkshakes.*

Error: *Eugena has less game tokens than Charlie.*

Problem: *Less* is used to answer the question *"How much?"*, whereas *fewer* is used to answer the question *"How many?"*

Correction: *Eugena has fewer game tokens than Charlie.*

Error: *Sheryl is considered as the top executive in her field.*

Problem: This sentence sounds awkward. The proper expression would be *considered the* instead of *considered as the*.

Correction: *Sheryl is considered the top executive in her field.*

Error: *The geography final exam featured such topics like state capitals, the seven seas, and world climate.*

Problem: The correct expression should be *such…as* instead of *such… like.* *Like* should be used only with a direct comparison: Cara looks a lot like her sister.

Correction: *The geography final exam featured such topics as state capitals, the seven seas, and world climate.*
—OR—
The geography final exam featured topics such as state capitals, the seven seas, and world climate.

Practice Exercise

Choose the option that explains the meaning of the underlined portion.

1. My parents took everyone out for my birthday and agreed to <u>foot the bill</u>.

   A. Kick the receipt

   B. Leave without paying

   C. Pay

2. On the first day of school, the teacher had planned several "getting-to-know-you" activities to help break the ice.

   A. Break up a block of ice

   B. Put everyone at ease

   C. Learn names

3. My boss gave me <u>the green light</u> to begin the project I'd proposed last week.

   A. Permission to start

   B. A large sum of money

   C. A hug

Answer Key

1. C

2. B

3. A

Practice Exercise: Word Choice I

Choose the most effective word or phrase within the context suggested by the sentences.

1. The defendant was accused of _____ money from his employer.

   A. stealing

   B. borrowing

   C. robbing

2. O.J. Simpson's angry disposition _____ his ex-wife Nicole.

   A. mortified

   B. intimidated

   C. frightened

3. Many tourists are attracted to the Paradise Island because of its _____ climate.

   A. friendly

   B. peaceful

   C. balmy

4. The woman was angry because the tomato juice left an _____ stain on her brand new carpet.

   A. unsightly

   B. ugly

   C. unpleasant

5. After disobeying orders, the army private was _____ by his superior officer.

   A. degraded

   B. attacked

   C. reprimanded

6. Sharon's critical evaluation of the student's book report left the student feeling _____, which caused him to want to quit school.

   A. surprised

   B. depressed

   C. discouraged

7. The life-saving medication created by the scientist had a _____ impact on further developments in the treatment of cancer.

   A. beneficial

   B. fortunate

   C. miraculous

8. *The Phantom of the Opera* is one of Andrew Lloyd Webber's most successful musicals, largely because of its _____ themes.

   A. romantic

   B. melodramatic

   C. imaginary

9. The massive Fourth of July fireworks display _____ the partygoers with lots of colored lights and sound.

   A. disgusted

   B. captivated

   C. captured

10. Many of the residents of Grand Forks, North Dakota, were forced to _____ their homes because of the flood.

    A. escape

    B. evacuate

    C. exit

Answer Key

1.	A	5.	C	8.	A
2.	C	6.	C	9.	B
3.	C	7.	A	10.	B
4.	A				

Practice Exercise: Word Choice II

Choose the sentence that expresses the thought most clearly and most effectively and that is structurally correct in grammar and syntax.

1. A. The movie was three hours in length, featuring interesting characters,and moved at a fast pace.

    B. The movie was three hours long, featured interesting characters, and moved at a fast pace.

    C. Moving at a fast pace, the movie was three hours long and featured interesting characters.

2. A. We were so offended by the waiter's demeanor that we left the restaurant without paying the check.

    B. The waiter's demeanor offended us so much that without paying the check, we left the restaurant.

    C. We left the restaurant without paying the check because we were offended by the waiter's demeanor.

3. A. In today's society, information about our lives is provided to us by computers.

    B. We rely on computers in today's society to provide us information about our lives.

    C. In today's society, we rely on computers to provide us with information about our lives.

4. A. Folding the sides of the tent carefully, Jack made sure to be quiet so none of the other campers would be woken up.

    B. So none of the other campers would be woken up, Jack made sure to be quiet by folding the sides of the tent carefully.

    C. Folding the sides of the tent carefully, so none of the other campers would wake up, Jack made sure to be quiet.

Answer Key

1.	B	3.	C
2.	A	4.	A

Practice Exercise: Word Choice III

Choose the most effective word or phrase within the context suggested by the sentence(s).

1. The six hundred employees of General Electric were _____ by the company due to budgetary cutbacks.

   A. released

   B. terminated

   C. downsized

2. The force of the tornado _____ the many residents of the town of Russell, Kansas.

   A. intimidated

   B. repulsed

   C. frightened

3. Even though his new car was easy to drive, Fred _____ to walk to work every day because he liked the exercise.

   A. needed

   B. preferred

   C. considered

4. June's parents were very upset over the school board's decision to suspend her from Adams High for a week. Before they filed a lawsuit against the board, they _____ with a lawyer to help them make a decision.

   A. consulted

   B. debated

   C. conversed

5. The race car driver's _____ in handling the automobile was a key factor in his victory.

   A. patience

   B. precision

   C. determination

6. After impressing the judges with her talent and charm, the beauty contestant _____ more popularity by singing an aria from *La Bohème*.

   A. captured

   B. scored

   C. gained

7. The stained-glass window was _____ when a large brick flew through it during the riot.

   A. damaged

   B. cracked

   C. shattered

8. The class didn't know what happened to the professor until the principal _____ why the professor dropped out of school.

   A. informed

   B. discovered

   C. explained

9. The giant penthouse at the top of the building enables the billionaire industrialist _____ the citizens on the street.

   A. to view from above

   B. the chance to see

   C. to glance at

10. Sally's parents _____ her to attend the dance after she promised to return by midnight.

    A. prohibited

    B. permitted

    C. asked

Answer Key

1.	C	5.	B	9.	C
2.	C	6.	C	10.	B
3.	B	7.	C		
4.	A	8.	C		

Practice Exercise: Word Choice IV

The following passages contain irrelevant, repetitive, and/or wordy expressions. Select the underlined word or word group that is unnecessary to the context of the passage.

1. Some children decide to participate <u>actively</u> in <u>extracurricular</u> activities, such as after-school sports and <u>various</u> clubs. Many teachers and administrators <u>willingly</u> volunteer to supervise the activities during their <u>spare</u> time.

   A. actively

   B. extracurricular

   C. various

   D. willingly

   E. spare

2. Our high school reunion was held at the <u>swanky</u> Boca Hilton, which is known for its elegance and <u>glamour</u>. We arrived in a <u>rented</u> stretch limo and prepared to dance and have a good time, <u>reminiscing</u> with our <u>dear</u> friends.

   A. swanky

   B. glamour

   C. rented

   D. reminiscing

   E. dear

3. Once we reached <u>the top of</u> the mountain, a <u>powerful</u> storm came from <u>out of</u> nowhere, bringing rain and <u>large</u> hailstones from the dark <u>black</u> skies above.

   A. the top of

   B. powerful

   C. out of

   D. large

   E. black

4. Police officers often undergo a rigorous, <u>harsh</u> training period to prepare them <u>adequately</u> for the <u>intense</u> dangers and stresses of the job. <u>Only</u> the most physically fit candidates are capable of handling the challenges of dealing with the <u>criminal</u> elements of our society.

   A. harsh

   B. adequately

   C. intense

   D. Only

   E. criminal

Practice Exercise: Word Choice IV (cont.)

The following passages contain irrelevant, repetitive, and/or wordy expressions. Select the underlined word or word group that is unnecessary to the context of the passage.

5. The <u>early morning</u> hurricane struck at dawn, knocking out power lines and <u>ripping the roofs from</u> buildings <u>all</u> throughout Broward County. <u>Massive</u> winds and rain wreaked havoc, and terrified residents ran <u>madly</u> for shelter and safety.

    A. early morning

    B. ripping the roofs from

    C. all

    D. Massive

    E. madly

6. Alan's alcoholism affected the entire family <u>deeply</u>. When his father asked <u>him to</u> stop drinking, he <u>refused and</u> drove off in his sister's car, which he crashed into a utility pole. <u>Fortunately</u>, Alan miraculously survived and now is undergoing intensive treatment in a top-notch facility <u>that is well-regarded</u>.

    A. deeply

    B. him to

    C. refused and

    D. Fortunately

    E. that is well-regarded

7. Soap operas are popular among <u>many</u> television viewers because of their ability to <u>blend</u> real issues such as drug abuse, infidelity, and AIDS <u>with melodramatic plots</u> concerning lust, greed, vanity, and revenge. <u>These shows</u> often have very devoted followings among viewers who watch them <u>faithfully</u> every day.

    A. many

    B. blend

    C. with melodramatic plots

    D. These shows

    E. faithfully

8. Walt Disney World <u>is one of</u> the most visited tourist attractions in the United States. Its success <u>and prosperity</u> can be attributed to the <u>blend of</u> childhood fantasy and adult imagination. The park features rides and <u>attractions</u> that hold considerable appeal for <u>both</u> children and adults.

    A. is one of

    B. and prosperity

    C. blend of

    D. attractions

    E. both

Practice Exercise: Word Choice IV (cont.)

The following passages contain irrelevant, repetitive, and/or wordy expressions. Select the underlined word or word group that is unnecessary to the context of the passage.

9. Jason was the best <u>baseball</u> player on the Delray Beach High School baseball team; in fact, he was known as the star <u>of the team</u>. He could play several positions on the field <u>with enthusiasm and skill</u>, but his strength was hitting balls <u>out of the park</u>. When Jason was at the plate, the coach expected him to score a home run <u>every time</u>.

   A. baseball

   B. of the team

   C. with enthusiasm and skill

   D. out of the park

   E. every time

10. Many of the major cities in the United States are grappling with <u>a variety of</u> problems, such as crime, crumbling roadways, a shortage of <u>funding for</u> schools and healthcare, and a lack of jobs. There are <u>no easy</u> solutions to these problems, but mayors who have <u>strong</u> leadership abilities <u>work to</u> create good ideas to deal with them.

    A. a variety of

    B. funding for

    C. no easy

    D. strong

    E. work to

Answer Key

1. D	5. A	9. A
2. A	6. E	10. E
3. E	7. E	
4. A	8. B	

Recognize Commonly Confused or Misused Words or Phrases

Students frequently encounter problems with homonyms. Strictly speaking, a HOMONYM is a word that is spelled and pronounced just like another word but that has a different meaning. An example is the word *mean*, which can be a verb—"to intend"; an adjective—"unkind"; or a noun or adjective—"average."

HOMONYM: a word that is spelled and pronounced just like another word but that has a different meaning

HOMOGRAPHS: words that share the same spelling, regardless of how they are pronounced, and have different meanings

HOMOPHONES: words that are pronounced the same but may or may not have different spellings

HETERONYMS: (sometimes called heterophones) share the same spelling but have different pronunciations and meanings

CAPITONYMS: words that are spelled the same but have different meanings when capitalized

HOMOGRAPHS are words that share the same spelling, regardless of how they are pronounced, and have different meanings. Words that are pronounced the same but may or may not have different spellings are called **HOMOPHONES**. **HETERONYMS** (sometimes called heterophones) share the same spelling but have different pronunciations and meanings. For example, the homographs *desert* (abandon) and *desert* (arid region) are heteronyms (pronounced differently), but the homographs *mean* (intend) and *mean* (average) are homophones because they are pronounced the same (they are also homonyms).

CAPITONYMS are words that are spelled the same but have different meanings when capitalized. A capitonym may or may not have different pronunciations; for example, *polish* (to make shiny) and *Polish* (from Poland).

Some of the most troubling homophones are those that are spelled differently but that sound the same. Some examples include its (third person singular neuter pronoun) and *it's* ("it is"); *there* (a location), *their* (third person plural pronoun), and *they're* ("they are"). Another common example is *to, too,* and *two*.

Some homonyms/homographs are particularly intriguing. *Fluke*, for instance, refers to a fish, a flatworm, the end parts of an anchor, the fins on a whale's tail, and a stroke of luck.

COMMONLY MISUSED WORDS		
Accept is a verb meaning "to receive or to tolerate."	**Except** is usually a preposition meaning "excluding."	**Except** is also a verb meaning "to exclude."
Advice is a noun meaning "recommendation."	**Advise** is a verb meaning "to recommend."	
Affect is usually a verb meaning "to influence."	**Effect** is usually a noun meaning "result." Effect can also be a verb meaning "to bring about."	
An **allusion** is "an indirect reference."	An **illusion** is "a misconception or false impression."	
Add is a verb meaning "to put together."	**Ad** is a noun that is the abbreviation for the word "advertisement."	
Ain't is a common, nonstandard contraction for the contraction "aren't."		

Table continued on next page

Allot is a verb meaning "to distribute."	**A lot** can act as an adverb that means "often," "to a great degree," or "a large quantity." (Example: She shops a lot.)	
Allowed is used as an adjective that means "permitted."	**Aloud** is an adverb that means "audible."	
Bare is an adjective that means "naked" or "exposed." It can also indicate a minimum.	As a noun, **bear** is a large mammal.	As a verb, **bear** means "to carry a heavy burden."
Capital refers to a city; capitol to "a building where lawmakers meet."	**Capital** also refers to "wealth" or "resources."	
A **chord** is a noun that refers to "a group of musical notes."	**Cord** is a noun meaning "rope" or "a long electrical line."	
Compliment is a noun meaning "a praising or flattering remark."	**Complement** is a noun that means "something that completes or makes perfect."	
Climactic is derived from climax, "the point of greatest intensity in a series or progression of events."	**Climatic** is derived from climate; it refers to meteorological conditions.	
Discreet is an adjective that means "tactful" or "diplomatic".	**Discrete** is an adjective that means "separate" or "distinct."	
Dye is a noun or verb used to indicate artificial coloring.	**Die** is a verb that means "to pass away."	**Die** is also a noun that means "a cube-shaped game piece."
Effect is a noun that means "outcome."	**Affect** is a verb that means "to influence."	
Elicit is a verb meaning "to bring out" or "to evoke."	**Illicit** is an adjective meaning "unlawful."	
Emigrate means "to leave one country or region to settle in another."	**Immigrate** means "to enter another country and reside there."	
Gorilla is a noun meaning "a large great ape."	**Guerrilla** is "a member of a band of irregular soldiers."	

Table continued on next page

Hoard is a verb that means "to accumulate" or "store up."	A **horde** is "a large group."	
Lead is a verb that means "to guide" or "to serve as the head of." It is also a noun that is a type of metal.		
Medal is a noun that means "an award that is strung round the neck."	**Meddle** is a verb that means "to involve oneself in a matter without right or invitation."	**Metal** is "an element such as silver or gold." **Mettle** is a noun meaning "toughness" or "courage."
Morning is a noun indicating "the time between midnight and midday."	**Mourning** is a verb or noun pertaining to "the period of grieving after a death."	
Past is a noun meaning "a time before now" (past, present, and future).	**Passed** is the past tense of the verb "to pass."	
Piece is a noun meaning "portion."	**Peace** is a noun meaning "the opposite of war or serenity."	
Peak is a noun meaning "the tip" or "height to reach the highest point."	**Peek** is a verb that means "to take a brief look."	**Pique** is a verb meaning "to incite or raise interest."
Principal is a noun most commonly meaning "the chief or head," and it also means "a capital sum of money."	**Principle** is a noun meaning "a basic truth or law."	
Rite is a noun meaning "a special ceremony."	**Right** is an adjective meaning "correct" or "the opposite direction of left."	**Write** is a verb meaning "to compose in writing."
Than is a conjunction used in comparisons; **then** is an adverb denoting time. Examples: That pizza is more <u>than</u> I can eat. Tom laughed, and <u>then</u> we recognized him.	To remember the correct use of these words, you can use the following: **Than** is used to *compare*; both words have the letter a in them. **Then** tells *when*; both words are spelled the same, except for the first letter.	
There is an adverb specifying place; it is also an expletive. Adverb: Sylvia is lying there unconscious. Expletive: <u>There</u> are two plums left.	**Their** is a possessive pronoun.	**They're** is a contraction of "they are." Fred and Jane finally washed <u>their</u> car. <u>They're</u> later than usual today.
To is a preposition.	**Too** is an adverb.	**Two** is a number.
Your is a possessive pronoun;	**You're** is a contraction of "you are."	

PROBLEM PHRASES	
CORRECT	**INCORRECT**
Supposed to	Suppose to
Used to	Use to
Toward	Towards
Anyway	Anyways
Couldn't care less	Could care less
For all intents and purposes	For all intensive purposes
Come to see me	Come and see me
En route	In route
Regardless	Irregardless
Second, Third	Secondly, Thirdly

Other confusing words

Lie is an intransitive verb meaning to recline or rest on a surface. Its principal parts are *lie, lay,* and *lain.* **Lay** is a transitive verb meaning "to put or place." Its principal parts are *lay, laid,* and *laid.*

> *Birds lay eggs.*
> *I lie down for bed around 10 p.m.*

Set is a transitive verb meaning "to put or to place." Its principal parts are *set, set,* and *set.* **Sit** is an intransitive verb meaning "to be seated." Its principal parts are *sit, sat,* and *sat.*

> *I set my backpack down near the front door.*
> *They sat in the park until the sun went down.*

Among is a preposition to be used with three or more items. **Between** is to be used with two items.

> *Between you and me, I cannot tell the difference among those three Johnson sisters.*

As is a subordinating conjunction used to introduce a subordinating clause. **Like** is a preposition and is followed by a noun or a noun phrase.

> *As I walked to the lab, I realized that the recent experiment findings were much like those we found last year.*

Can is a verb that means "to be able." **May** is a verb that means "to have permission." "Can" and "may" are only interchangeable in cases of possibility.

> *I can lift 250 pounds.*
> *May I go to Alex's house?*

Sample Test Questions and Rationale

DIRECTIONS: Choose the most effective word within the context of the sentence.

(Average)

1. Many of the clubs in Boca Raton are noted for their _____ elegance.

   A. vulgar

   B. tasteful

   C. ordinary

   Answer: B. tasteful

   Tasteful means beautiful or charming, which would correspond to an elegant club. The words *vulgar* and *ordinary* have negative connotations.

(Average)

2. When a student is expelled from school, the parents are usually _____ in advance.

   A. rewarded

   B. congratulated

   C. notified

   Answer: C. notified

   Notified means informed or told, which fits into the logic of the sentence. The words *rewarded* and *congratulated* are positive actions, which do not make sense regarding someone being expelled from school.

(Average)

3. Before appearing in court, the witness was _____ the papers requiring her to show up.

   A. condemned

   B. served

   C. criticized

   Answer: B. served

   Served means given, which makes sense in the context of the sentence. *Condemned* and *criticized* do not make sense within the context of the sentence.

Sample Test Questions and Rationale (cont.)

DIRECTIONS: Choose the underlined word or phrase that is unnecessary within the context of the passage.

(Easy)

4. The <u>expanding</u> number of television channels has prompted cable operators to raise their prices, <u>even though</u> many consumers do not want to pay a higher <u>increased</u> amount for their service.

   A. expanding

   B. prompted

   C. even though

   D. increased

   Answer: D. increased

   The word *increased* is redundant with *higher* and should be removed. All the other words are necessary within the context of the sentence.

(Average)

5. <u>Considered by many to be</u> one of the worst <u>terrorist</u> incidents <u>on American soil</u> was the bombing of the Oklahoma City Federal Building, which will be remembered <u>for years to come</u>.

   A. Considered by many to be

   B. terrorist

   C. on American soil

   D. for years to come

   Answer: A. Considered by many to be

   Considered by many to be is a wordy phrase and unnecessary in the context of the sentence. All other words are necessary within the context of the sentence.

(Average)

6. The <u>flu</u> epidemic struck <u>most of</u> the <u>respected</u> faculty and students of the Woolbright School, forcing the Boynton Beach School Superintendent to close it down <u>for two weeks</u>.

   A. flu

   B. most of

   C. respected

   D. for two weeks

   Answer: C. respected

   The fact that the faculty might have been *respected* is not necessary to mention in the sentence. The other words and phrases are all necessary to complete the meaning of the sentence.

Sample Test Questions and Rationale (cont.)

DIRECTIONS: Choose the most effective word or phrase within the context suggested by the sentence.

(Average)

7. Because George's _____ bothering him, he apologized for crashing his father's car.

   A. feelings were

   B. conscience was

   C. guiltiness was

   Answer: B. conscience was

   Option B shows the correct word choice because a *conscience* would motivate someone to confess. Option A is incorrect because *feelings* is not as accurate as *conscience*. Option C is incorrect because *guiltiness* is less descriptive of George's motive for confession than conscience.

(Rigorous)

8. The charity art auction _____ every year at Mizner Park has a wide selection of artists showcasing their work.

   A. attended

   B. presented

   C. displayed

   Answer: B. presented

   The word *presented* makes more sense in the context of the sentence than *attended* or *displayed*.

SKILL 9.4 **Demonstrating knowledge of standard sentence construction** *(e.g., subordination, parallel structure, use and placement of modifiers)*

Writers who understand the complexities of syntax clearly appreciate the impact of sentence structure on their writing and subsequent perception of its meaning. While students may not yet share this appreciation, they can still benefit from the knowledge and use of varied sentence structure.

Sentence Structure

Students should recognize simple, compound, complex, and compound-complex sentences. They need to use dependent (subordinate) and independent clauses correctly to create these sentence structures.

A **SIMPLE SENTENCE** consists of one independent clause.

> *Joyce wrote a letter.*

A **COMPOUND SENTENCE** consists of two or more independent clauses usually connected by a coordinating conjunction preceded by a comma (and, but, or, nor, for, so, yet). Compound sentences are sometimes connected by semicolons, with or without a coordinating conjunction.

> *Joyce wrote a letter, and Dot drew a picture.*

A **COMPLEX SENTENCE** consists of an independent clause and one or more dependent clauses. The dependent clauses may precede the independent clause or follow it.

> *While Joyce wrote a letter, Dot drew a picture.*
> *Dot drew picture while Joyce wrote a letter.*

A **COMPOUND-COMPLEX SENTENCE** consists of one or more dependent clauses plus two or more independent clauses.

> *When Mother asked the girls to demonstrate their new-found skills, Joyce wrote a letter, and Dot drew a picture.*

Note: Do not confuse compound sentence elements with compound sentences.

Simple sentence with compound subject:

> *<u>Joyce</u> and <u>Dot</u> wrote letters.*
> *The <u>girl</u> in row three and the <u>boy</u> next to her were passing notes across the aisle. asked the girls to demonstrate their new-found skills, Joyce wrote a letter, and Dot drew a picture.*

Simple sentence with compound predicate:

> *Joyce wrote letters and drew pictures.*
> *The captain of the high school debate team graduated with honors and studied broadcast journalism in college.*

Simple sentence with compound object of preposition:

> *Coleen graded the students' essays for <u>style</u> and <u>mechanical accuracy</u>.*

SIMPLE SENTENCE: a sentence consisting of one independent clause

COMPOUND SENTENCE: a sentence consisting of two or more independent clauses

COMPLEX SENTENCE: a sentence consisting of an independent clause and one or more dependent clauses

COMPOUND-COMPLEX SENTENCE: a sentence consisting of one or more dependent clauses plus two or more independent clauses

Types of Clauses

CLAUSES are connected word groups that are composed of at least one subject and one verb. (A subject is the doer of an action or the element that is being joined. A verb conveys either the action or the link.)

CLAUSES: connected word groups composed of at least one subject and one verb

> *Students are waiting for the start of the assembly.*
> *Subject   Verb*
>
> *At the end of the play, students wait for the curtain to come down.*
>   *Subject   Verb*

Clauses can be independent or dependent. **INDEPENDENT CLAUSES** can stand alone or can be joined to other clauses.

INDEPENDENT CLAUSES: clauses that can stand alone or can be joined to other clauses

Comma and coordinating conjunction

Independent clause	, for	Independent clause
	, and	Independent clause
	, nor	Independent clause
	, but	Independent clause
	, or	Independent clause
	, yet	Independent clause
	, so	Independent clause

Semicolon

Independent clause	;	Independent clause

Subordinating conjunction, dependent clause, and comma

Dependent clause	,	Independent clause

Independent clause followed by a subordinating conjunction that introduces a dependent clause

Independent clause	Dependent clause

DEPENDENT CLAUSES, by definition, contain at least one subject and one verb. However, they cannot stand alone as a complete sentence. They are structurally dependent on the main clause.

DEPENDENT CLAUSES: clauses that cannot stand alone as a complete sentence

There are two types of dependent clauses: (1) those with a subordinating conjunction, and (2) those with a relative pronoun.

Sample subordinating conjunctions

Although   When   If   Unless   Because

<u>*Unless*</u> *a cure is discovered,* <u>*many more people will die of the disease*</u>

Dependent clause   +   Independent clause

Sample relative pronouns

Who Whom Which That

<u>*The White House has an official website,*</u> <u>*which*</u> *contains press releases, news updates, and biographies of the President and Vice-President.*

<u>*(Independent clause*</u> *+* <u>*relative pronoun*</u> *+* <u>*relative dependent clause)*</u>

Fragments

Fragments occur (1) if word groups standing alone are missing either a subject or a verb, and (2) if word groups containing a subject and verb and standing alone are actually made dependent because of the use of subordinating conjunctions or relative pronouns.

Error: *The teacher waiting for the class to complete the assignment.*

Problem: This sentence is not complete because the "ing" word alone does not function as a verb. When a helping verb is added (for example, was waiting), the fragment will become a sentence.

Correction: *The teacher was waiting for the class to complete the assignment.*

Error: *Until the last toy was removed from the floor.*

Problem: Words such as "*until,*" "*because,*" "*although,*" "*when,*" and "*if*" make a clause dependent and thus incapable of standing alone. An independent clause must be added to make the sentence complete.

Correction: *Until the last toy was removed from the floor, the kids could not go outside to play.*

Error: *The city will close the public library. Because of a shortage of funds.*

Problem: *The problem is the same as above. The dependent clause must be joined to the independent clause.*

Correction: *The city will close the public library because of a shortage of funds.*

Fragments are tested in sentences tied to a passage. Items will be in one of two formats.

Format A

Forensics experts conclude that the residents died from chemical radiation. Or from a mixture of toxic substances and asphyxiation.

A. *radiation; or*

B. *radiation or*

C. *radiation or,*

D. *No change is necessary*

Format B

Forensics experts conclude that the residents died from chemical radiation. Or from a mixture of toxic substances and asphyxiation.

A. *Forensic's*

B. *radiation or*

C. *asphyxiation*

D. *No change is necessary*

In each case, you must consider the punctuation between radiation and or. The punctuation decision is difficult if you do not understand that the second group of words, the one that begins with Or, is not a sentence. Although these questions may appear to be only about punctuation, they are also about fragments.

The answer in both formats is B. The word group *Or perhaps from a mixture of toxic substances and asphyxiation* lacks a subject and a complete verb. It must be joined to the preceding sentence. A comma is not necessary since the word residents is the subject of the verb phrase *died from chemical radiation and of asphyxiation.*

Practice Exercise

Choose the option that corrects the underlined portion(s) of the sentence. If no error exists, choose "No change is necessary."

1. Despite the lack of funds in the **budget it** was necessary to rebuild the roads that were damaged from the recent floods.

   A. budget: it

   B. budget, it

   C. budget; it

   D. No change is necessary

2. After determining that the fire was caused by faulty **wiring, the** building inspector said the construction company should be fined.

   A. wiring. The

   B. wiring the

   C. wiring; the

   D. No change is necessary

3. Many years after buying a grand **piano Henry** decided he'd rather play the violin instead.

   A. piano: Henry

   B. piano, Henry

   C. piano; Henry

   D. No change is necessary

4. Computers are being used more and more **frequently. because** of their capacity to store information.

   A. frequently because

   B. frequently, because

   C. frequently; because

   D. No change is necessary

5. Doug washed the floors **every day. to** keep them clean for the guests.

   A. every day to

   B. every day,

   C. every day;

   D. No change is necessary.

Answer Key

1. B

The clause that begins with *despite* is independent and must be separated with the clause that follows by a comma. Option A is incorrect because a colon is used to set off a list or to emphasize what follows. In Option B, a comma incorrectly suggests that the two clauses are dependent.

2. D

In the test item, a comma correctly separates the dependent clause *After...wiring* at the beginning of the sentence from the independent clause that follows. Option A incorrectly breaks the two clauses into separate sentences, whereas Option B omits the comma, and Option C incorrectly suggests that the phrase is an independent clause.

3. B

The phrase *Many years... piano* must be joined to the independent clause. Option A incorrectly puts a colon before Henry decided, and Option C incorrectly separates the phrase as if it were an independent clause.

4. A

The second clause *because... information* is dependent and must be joined to the first independent clause. Option B is incorrect because a comma is not necessary since the dependent clause comes at the end of the sentence rather than at the beginning. In Option C, a semicolon incorrectly suggests that the two clauses are independent.

5. A

The second clause *to keep... guests* is dependent and must be joined to the first independent clause. Option B is incorrect because a comma is not necessary since the dependent clause comes at the end of the sentence rather than at the beginning. In Option C, a semicolon incorrectly suggests that the two clauses are independent.

Run-on Sentences and Comma Splices

Comma splices appear when two sentences are joined by only a comma. Fused or run-on sentences appear when two sentences are run together with no punctuation at all.

Error   *Dr. Sanders is a brilliant scientist, his research on genetic disorders won him a Nobel Prize.*

Problem: A comma alone cannot join two independent clauses. The two clauses can be joined by a semicolon, or they can be separated by a period.

Correction: *Dr. Sanders is a brilliant scientist; his research on genetic disorders won him a Nobel Prize.*
OR
Dr. Sanders is a brilliant scientist. His research on genetic disorders won him a Nobel Prize.

Error: *Florida is noted for its beaches they are long, sandy, and beautiful.*

Problem: The first sentence ends with the word beaches, and the second sentence cannot be joined with the first. The fused sentence error can be corrected in several ways: (1) one clause may be made dependent on another with a subordinating conjunction or a relative pronoun; (2) a semicolon may be used to combine two equally important ideas; (3) the two independent clauses may be separated by a period.

Correction: *Florida is noted for its beaches, which are long, sandy, and beautiful*
OR
Florida is noted for its beaches; they are long, sandy, and beautiful.
OR
Florida is noted for its beaches. They are long, sandy, and beautiful.

Error: *The number of hotels has increased, however, the number of visitors has grown also.*

Problem: The first sentence ends with the word increased, and a comma is not strong enough to connect it to the second sentence. The adverbial transition however does not function the same way as a coordinating conjunction and cannot be used with commas to link two sentences. Several different corrections are available.

Correction: *The number of hotels has increased; however, the number of visitors has grown also.*
[Two separate but closely related sentences are created with the use of the semicolon.]
OR
The number of hotels has increased. However, the number of visitors has grown also.
[Two separate sentences are created.]
OR

Although the number of hotels have increased, the number of visitors has grown also.
[One idea is made subordinate to the other and separated with a comma.]
OR
The number of hotels have increased, but the number of visitors has grown, also.
[The comma before the coordinating conjunction but is appropriate. The adverbial transition however does not function the same way as the coordinating conjunction but does.]

Practice Exercise

Choose the option that corrects an error in the underlined portion(s). If no error exists, choose "No change is necessary."

1. Scientists are excited at the ability to clone a sheep; however, it is not yet known if the same can be done to humans.

   A. sheep, however,

   B. sheep. However,

   C. sheep, however;

   D. No change is necessary

2. Because of the rising cost of college tuition the federal government now offers special financial assistance, such as loans, to students.

   A. tuition, the

   B. tuition; the

   C. such as loans

   D. No change is necessary

3. As the number of homeless people continues to rise, the major cities like New York and Chicago, are now investing millions of dollars in low-income housing.

   A. rise. The major cities

   B. rise; the major cities

   C. New York and Chicago

   D. No change is necessary

4. Unlike in the 1950s, most households find the husband and wife in many different career fields working full-time to make ends meet.

   A. the 1950s; most

   B. the 1950s most

   C. ends meet, in many

   D. No change is necessary

Answer Key

1. **B**

   Option B correctly separates two independent clauses. The comma in Option A after the word *sheep* creates a run-on sentence. The semicolon in Option C does not separate the two clauses but occurs at an inappropriate point.

2. **A**

   The comma in Option A correctly separates the independent clause and the dependent clause. The semicolon in Option B is incorrect because one of the clauses is independent. Option C requires a comma to prevent a run-on sentence.

3. **C**

   Option C is correct because a comma creates a fragment. Option A is incorrect because the first clause is dependent. The semi-colon in Option B incorrectly divides the dependent clause from the independent clause.

4. **D**

   Option D correctly punctuates the sentence. Option A incorrectly uses a semicolon. The lack of a comma in Option B violates the rule that an introductory phrase requires a comma after it. Option C puts a comma in an inappropriate place.

Faulty Parallelism

Two or more elements stated in a single clause should be expressed with the same (or parallel) structure (e.g., all adjectives, all verb forms or all nouns).

Error: *She needed to be beautiful, successful, and have fame.*

Problem: The phrase to be is followed by two different structures: beautiful and successful are adjectives, and have fame is a verb phrase.

Correction: *She needed to be <u>beautiful</u>, <u>successful</u>, and <u>famous</u>.*
                  (adjective) (adjective)   (adjective)
      OR
      She needed <u>beauty</u>, <u>success</u>, and <u>fame</u>.
              (noun) (noun)   (noun)

Error: *I plan either to sell my car during the spring or during the summer.*

Problem: Paired conjunctions (also called correlative conjunctions—such as either-or, both-and , neither-nor, not only-but also) need to be followed with similar structures. In the sentence above, *either* is followed by to *sell my car during the spring*, while or is followed only by the phrase *during the summer*.

Correction: *I plan to sell my car during either the spring or the summer.*

Error: *The president pledged to lower taxes and that he would cut spending to lower the national debt.*

Problem: An infinitive phrase *to lower taxes* follows the verb *pledged*, and then a relative clause, *that he would cut spending*, stands in the same relation to *pledged*.

Correction: *The president pledged to lower taxes and to cut spending to lower the national debt.*
OR
The president pledged that he would lower taxes and cut spending to lower the national debt.

Practice Exercise

Choose the sentence that expresses the thought most clearly and effectively and that has no error in structure.

1. **A.** Andy found the family tree, researches the Irish descendents, and he was compiling a book for everyone to read.

   B. Andy found the family tree, researched the Irish descendents, and compiled a book for everyone to read.

   C. Andy finds the family tree, researched the Irish descendents, and compiled a book for everyone to read.

2. **A.** In the last ten years, computer technology has advanced so quickly that workers have had difficulty keeping up with the new equipment and the increased amount of functions.

   B. Computer technology has advanced so quickly in the last ten years that workers have had difficulty to keep up with the new equipment and by increasing amount of functions.

   C. In the last ten years, computer technology has advanced so quickly that workers have had difficulty keeping up with the new equipment and the amount of functions are increasing.

3. **A.** The Florida State History Museum contains exhibits honoring famous residents, a video presentation about the state's history, an art gallery featuring paintings and sculptures, and they even display a replica of the Florida Statehouse.

   B. The Florida State History Museum contains exhibits honoring famous residents, a video presentation about the state's history, an art gallery featuring paintings and sculptures, and even a replica of the Florida Statehouse.

   C. The Florida State History Museum contains exhibits honoring famous residents, a video presentation about the state's history, an art gallery featuring paintings and sculptures, and there is even a replica of the Florida Statehouse.

Practice Exercise (cont.)

Choose the sentence that expresses the thought most clearly and effectively and that has no error in structure.

4. A. Either the criminal justice students had too much practical experience and limited academic preparation or too much academic preparation and little practical experience

    B. The criminal justice students either had too much practical experience and limited academic preparation or too much academic preparation and little practical experience.

    C. The criminal justice students either had too much practical experience and limited academic preparation or had too much academic preparation and little practical experience.

5. A. Filmmaking is an arduous process in which the producer hires the cast and crew, chooses locations for filming, supervisers the actual production, and guides the editing

    B. Because it is an arduous process, filmmaking requires the producer to hire a cast and crew and choose locations, supervise the actual production, and guides the editing.

    C. Filmmaking is an arduous process in which the producer hires the cast and crew, chooses locations for filming, supervises the actual production, and guided the editing.

Answer Key

1. **B**

    Option B uses parallelism by presenting a series of past tense verbs *found, researched,* and *compiled.* Option A interrupts the parallel structure of past tense verbs: found, researches, and *he was compiling.* Option C uses present tense verbs and then shifts to past tense: *finds, researched,* and *compiled.*

2. **A**

    Option A uses parallel structure at the end of the sentence: *the new equipment and the increased amount of functions.* Option B creates a faulty structure with *to keep up with the new equipment and by increasing amount of functions.* Option C creates faulty parallelism with *the amount of functions are increasing.*

3. **B**

    Option B uses parallelism by presenting a series of noun phrases acting as objects of the verb contains. Option A interrupts that parallelism by inserting *they even display,* and Option C interrupts the parallelism with the addition of *there is.*

Answer Key (cont.)

4. **C**

In the either-or parallel construction, look for a balance on both sides. Option C creates that balanced parallel structure: *either had...or had.* Options A and B do not create the balance. In Option A, the structure is *Either the students . . . or too much.* In Option B, the structure is *either had . . . or too much.*

5. **A**

Option A uses parallelism by presenting a series of verbs with objects: *hires the cast and crew, chooses locations for filming, supervises the actual production, and guides the editing.* The structure of Option B incorrectly suggests that filmmaking chooses locations, supervises the actual production, and guides the editing. Option C interrupts the series of present tense verbs by inserting the participle *guided,* instead of the present tense *guides.*

Misplaced and Dangling Modifiers

Phrases that are not placed near the one word they modify often result in misplaced modifiers. Phrases that do not relate to the subject being modified result in dangling modifiers.

Error: *Weighing the options carefully, a decision was made regarding the punishment of the convicted murderer.*

Problem: Who is weighing the options? No one capable of weighing is named in the sentence; thus, the participle phrase weighing the options carefully dangles. This problem can be corrected by adding a subject to the sentence who is capable of doing the action.

Correction: *Weighing the options carefully, the judge made a decision regarding the punishment of the convicted murderer.*

Error: *Returning to my favorite watering hole brought back many fond memories.*

Problem: The person who returned is never indicated, and the participle phrase dangles. This problem can be corrected by creating a dependent clause from the modifying phrase.

Correction: *When I returned to my favorite watering hole, many fond memories came back to me.*

Error: *One damaged house stood only to remind townspeople of the hurricane.*

Problem: The placement of the modifier *only* suggests that the sole reason the house remained was to serve as a reminder. The misplaced modifier creates ambiguity. This problem can be corrected by moving the modifier.

Correction: *Only one damaged house stood, reminding townspeople of the hurricane.*

Error: *Recovered from the five-mile hike, the obstacle course was a piece of cake for the Boy Scout troop.*

Problem: The obstacle course is not recovered from the five-mile hike, so the modifying phrase must be placed closer to the word, that it modifies, troop.

Correction: *The obstacle course was a piece of cake for the Boy Scout troop, which had just recovered from a five-mile hike.*

Practice Exercise

Choose the sentence that expresses the thought most clearly and effectively and that has no error in structure.

1. A. Attempting to remove the dog from the well, the paramedic tripped and fell in also.

    B. As the paramedic attempted to remove the dog from the well, he tripped and fell in also.

    C. The paramedic tripped and fell in also attempting to remove the dog from the well.

2. A. To save the wounded child, a powerful explosion ripped through the operating room as the doctors worked.

    B. In the operating room, as the wounded child was being saved, a powerful explosion ripped through.

    C. To save the wounded child, the doctors worked as an explosion ripped through the operating room.

3. A. One hot July morning, a herd of giraffes screamed wildly in the jungle next to the wildlife habitat.

    B. One hot July morning, a herd of giraffes screamed in the jungle wildly next to the wildlife habitat.

    C. One hot July morning, a herd of giraffes screamed in the jungle next to the wildlife habitat, wildly.

4. A. Looking through the file cabinets in the office, the photographs of the crime scene revealed a new suspect in the investigation.

    B. Looking through the file cabinets in the office, the detective discovered photographs of the crime scene that revealed a new suspect in the investigation.

    C. A new suspect in the investigation was revealed in photographs of the crime scene that were discovered while looking through the file cabinets in the office.

Answer Key

1. **B**

    Option B corrects the dangling participle *attempting to remove the dog from the well* by creating a dependent clause introducing the main clause. In Option A, the introductory participle phrase *Attempting . . . well* does not refer to a paramedic, the subject of the main clause. The word *also* in Option C incorrectly implies that the paramedic was doing something besides trying to remove the dog.

2. **C**

    Option C corrects the dangling modifier *to save the wounded child by* adding the concrete clause *doctors worked*. Option A infers that an explosion was working to save the wounded child. Option B never tells who was trying to save the wounded child.

3. **A**

    Option A places the adverb *wildly* closest to the verb *screamed*, which it modifies. Both Options B and C incorrectly place the modifier away from the verb.

4. **B**

    Option B corrects the modifier *looking* through the file cabinets in the *office* by placing it next to the detective who is doing the looking. Option A sounds as though the photographs were looking; Option C has no one doing the looking.

Sample Test Questions and Rationale

For questions 1 through 6, circle the choice that best corrects the underlined error without changing the meaning of the original sentence.

(Average)

1. <u>Mixing the batter for cookies</u>, the cat licked the Crisco from the cookie sheet.

   A. While mixing the batter for cookies

   B. While the batter for cookies was mixing

   C. While I mixed the batter for cookies

   D. While I mixed the cookies

   The answer is C.

   Answer A gives the impression that the cat was mixing the batter (it is a "dangling modifier"). Answer B implies that the batter was mixing itself. Answer D lacks precision: It is the batter that was being mixed, not the cookies themselves.

(Average)

2. Mr. Smith <u>respectfully submitted his resignation and had</u> a new job.)

   A. respectfully submitted his resignation and has

   B. respectfully submitted his resignation before accepting

   C. respectfully submitted his resignation because of

   D. respectfully submitted his resignation and had

   The answer is C.

   Answer A eliminates any relationship of causality between submitting the resignation and having the new job. Answer B just changes the sentence and does not indicate the fact that Mr. Smith had a new job before submitting his resignation. Answer D means that Mr. Smith first submitted his resignation and then got a new job.

(Average)

3. The teacher <u>implied</u> from our angry words that there was conflict <u>between you and me</u>.

   A. implied… between you and I

   B. inferred… between you and I

   C. inferred… between you and me

   D. implied… between you and me

   The answer is C.

   The difference between the verb "to imply" and the verb "to infer" is that implying is directing an interpretation toward other people; to infer is to deduce an interpretation from someone else's discourse. Moreover, "between you and I" is grammatically incorrect: After the preposition "between," the object (or 'disjunctive' with this particular preposition) pronoun form, "me," is needed.

Sample Test Questions and Rationale (cont.)

(Rigorous)

4. The Taj Mahal <u>has been designated</u> one of the Seven Wonders of the World, and people <u>know it</u> for its unique architecture.

   A. The Taj Mahal has been designated one of the Seven Wonders of the World, and it is known for its unique architecture.

   B. People know the Taj Mahal for its unique architecture, and it has been designated one of the Seven Wonders of the World

   C. People have known the Taj Mahal for its unique architecture, and it has been designated of the Seven Wonders of the World

   D. The Taj Mahal has designated itself one of the Seven Wonders of the World

The answer is A.

In the original sentence, the first clause is passive voice and the second clause is active voice, causing a voice shift. Answer B merely switches the clauses but does not correct the voice shift. In Answer C, only the verb tense in the first clause has been changed but is still active voice. Sentence D changes the meaning. In Answer A, both clauses are passive voice.

(Rigorous)

5. A teacher <u>must know not only her subject matter but also</u> the strategies of content teaching.

   A. must not only know her subject matter but also the strategies of content teaching

   B. not only must know her subject matter but also the strategies of content teaching

   C. must not know only her subject matter but also the strategies of content teaching

   D. must know not only her subject matter but also the strategies of content teaching

The answer is D.

"Not only" must come directly after "know" because the intent is to create the clearest meaning link with the "but also" predicate section later in the sentence.

(Rigorous)

6. Walt Whitman was famous for <u>his composition, *Leaves of Grass*, serving as a nurse during the Civil War, and a devoted son.</u>

   A. *Leaves of Grass*, his service as a nurse during the Civil War, and a devoted son

   B. composing *Leaves of Grass*, serving as a nurse during the Civil War, and being a devoted son

   C. his composition, *Leaves of Grass*, his nursing during the Civil War, and his devotion as a son

   D. his composition, *Leaves of Grass*, serving as a nurse during the Civil War, and a devoted son

The answer is B.

In order to be parallel, the sentence needs three gerunds. The other sentences use both gerunds and nouns, which results in a lack of parallelism.

Sample Test Questions and Rationale (cont.)

(Average)

7. **Which of the following sentences contains a subject-verb agreement error?**

   A. Both mother and her two sisters were married in a triple ceremony.

   B. Neither the hen nor the rooster is likely to be served for dinner.

   C. My boss, as well as the company's two personnel directors, have been to Spain.

   D. Amanda and the twins are late again

The answer is C.

The reason for this is that the true subject of the verb is "My boss," not "two personnel directors."

SKILL 9.5 **Demonstrating knowledge of Standard American English mechanics** *(e.g., spelling, capitalization, punctuation)*

Spelling correctly is not always easy, because English not only uses an often inconsistent spelling system but also uses many words derived from other languages. Good spelling is important because incorrect spelling damages the physical appearance of writing and may puzzle your reader.

The following list of words are frequently misspelled:

• commitment	• patience	• height	• guarantee
• succeed	• obstinate	• leisurely	• tropical
• necessary	• achievement	• shield	• misfortune
• connected	• responsibility	• foreign	• particular
• opportunity	• prejudice	• innovative	• yield
• embarrassed	• familiar	• similar	• possession
• occasionally	• hindrance	• proceed	• accumulate
• receive	• controversial	• contemporary	• hospitality
• their	• publicity	• beneficial	• judgment
• accelerate	• prescription	• attachment	• conscious

Spelling Plurals and Possessives

If the multiplicity and complexity of spelling rules based on phonics, letter doubling, and exceptions to rules are not mastered by adulthood, writers should use a good dictionary to achieve correctness. As spelling mastery is usually difficult for adolescents, our recommendation for them is the same. Learning the use of a dictionary and thesaurus will be a more rewarding use of time than laboring to master each obscure rule and exception.

Most nouns that end in hard consonants or hard consonant sounds followed by a silent *e* are made plural by adding *s*. Some words ending in vowels only add *s*.

> *fingers, numerals, banks, bugs, riots, homes, gates, radios, bananas*

Nouns that end in soft consonant sounds such as *s, j, x, z, ch*, and *sh*, are made plural by adding *es*. Some nouns ending in *o* add *es*.

> *dresses, waxes, churches, brushes, tomatoes, potatoes*

Nouns ending in *y* preceded by a vowel are made plural by adding *s*.

> *boys, alleys*

Nouns ending in y preceded by a consonant are made plural by changing the *y* to *i* and adding *es*.

> *babies, corollaries, frugalities, poppies*

Some nouns plurals are formed irregularly or remain the same.

> *sheep, deer, children, leaves, oxen*

Some nouns derived from foreign words, especially Latin, may make their plurals in two different ways—one of them Anglicized. Sometimes, the meanings are the same; other times, the two plurals are used in slightly different contexts. It is always wise to consult the dictionary.

> *appendices, appendixes*   *criterion, criteria*
> *indexes, indices*   *crisis, crises*

Make the plurals of closed (solid) compound words in the usual way, except for words ending in *ful*, which make their plurals from the root word.

> *timelines, hairpins*

Make the plurals of open or hyphenated compound words by adding the change in inflection to the word that changes in number.

> *fathers-in-law, courts-martial, masters of art, doctors of medicine*

Make the plurals of letters, numbers, and abbreviations by adding s.

> *fives and tens, IBMs, 1990s, ps and qs (Note that letters are italicized.)*

When in doubt, consult a dictionary.

I before E

i before *e*	grieve, fiend, niece, friend
except after *c*	receive, conceive, receipt
or when sounded like "a"	as in reindeer and weight, and reign
Exceptions:	weird, foreign, seize, leisure

Practice Exercise: ei/ie Words

Circle the correct spelling of the word in each parenthesis.

1. The (sheild, shield) protected the gladiator from serious injury.

2. Tony (received, recieved) an award for his science project.

3. Our (neighbors, nieghbors), the Thomsons, are in the Witness Protection Program.

4. Janet's (friend, freind), Olivia, broke her leg while running the marathon.

5. She was unable to (conceive, concieve) a child after her miscarriage.

6. Rudolph the Red-Nosed (Riendeer, Reindeer) is my favorite Christmas song.

7. The farmer spent all day plowing his (feild, field).

8. Kat's (wieght, weight) loss plan failed, and she gained twenty pounds!

9. They couldn't (beleive, believe) how many people showed up for the concert.

10. Ruby's (niece, neice) was disappointed when the movie was sold out.

Answer Key

1. shield
2. received
3. neighbors
4. friend
5. conceive

6. reindeer
7. field
8. weight
9. believe
10. niece

Practice Exercise: Spelling Rules

Add suffixes to the following words and write the correct spelling form in the blanks.

1. swing + ing = _____
2. use + able = _____
3. choke + ing = _____
4. furnish + ed = _____
5. punish + ment = _____
6. duty + ful = _____
7. bereave + ment = _____
8. shovel + ing = _____
9. argue + ment = _____

10. connect + ed = _____
11. remember + ed = _____
12. treat + able = _____
13. marry + s = _____
14. recycle + able = _____
15. waste + ful = _____
16. pray + ing = _____
17. reconstruct + ing = _____
18. outrage + ous = _____

Answer Key

1. swinging
2. useable
3. choking
4. furnished
5. punishment
6. dutiful
7. bereavement
8. shoveling
9. argument

10. connected
11. remembered
12. treatable
13. marries
14. recyclable
15. wasteful
16. praying
17. reconstructing
18. outrageous

Commas

COMMAS indicate a brief pause. They are used to set off dependent clauses and long introductory word groups, to separate words in a series, to set off incidental information that interrupts the flow of the sentence, and to separate independent clauses joined by conjunctions.

> **COMMAS:** punctuation marks that indicate a brief pause

Error: *After I finish my master's thesis I plan to work in Chicago.*

Problem: A comma is needed after an introductory dependent clause containing a subject and verb.

Correction: *After I finish my master's thesis, I plan to work in Chicago.*

Error: *I washed waxed and vacuumed my car today.*

Problem: Nouns, phrases, or clauses in a list, as well as two or more coordinate adjectives that modify one word, should be separated by commas. Although a comma after the word *and* is sometimes considered optional, it is often necessary to clarify the meaning.

Correction: *I washed, waxed, and vacuumed my car today.*

Error: *She was a talented dancer but she is mostly remembered for her singing ability.*

Problem: A comma is needed before a conjunction that joins two independent clauses (complete sentences).

Correction: *She was a talented dancer, but she is mostly remembered for her singing ability.*

Error: *This incident is I think typical of what can happen when the community remains so divided.*

Problem: Commas are needed between nonessential words or words that interrupt the main clause.

Correction: *This incident is, I think, typical of what can happen when the community remains so divided.*

Semicolons and Colons

SEMICOLONS:
punctuation marks that
separate two or more
closely related independent
clauses

COLONS: punctuation
marks that introduce
lists and emphasize what
follows

SEMICOLONS are needed to separate two or more closely related independent clauses when the second clause is introduced by a transitional adverb. (These clauses may also be written as separate sentences, preferably by placing the adverb within the second sentence). **COLONS** are used to introduce lists and to emphasize what follows.

Error: *I climbed to the top of the mountain, it took me three hours.*

Problem: A comma alone cannot separate two independent clauses. Instead, a semicolon is needed to separate two related sentences.

Correction: *I climbed to the top of the mountain; it took me three hours.*

Error: *In the movie, asteroids destroyed Dallas, Texas, Kansas City, Missouri, and Boston, Massachusetts.*

Problem: Semicolons are needed to separate items in a series that already contains internal punctuation.

Correction: *In the movie, asteroids destroyed Dallas, Texas; Kansas City, Missouri; and Boston, Massachusetts.*

Error: *Essays will receive the following grades, A for excellent, B for good, C for average, and D for unsatisfactory.*

Problem: A colon is needed to emphasize the information or list that follows.

Correction: *Essays will receive the following grades: A for excellent, B for good, C for average, and D for unsatisfactory.*

Error: *The school carnival included: amusement rides, clowns, food booths, and a variety of games.*

Problem: The material preceding the colon and the list that follows is not a complete sentence. Do not separate a verb (or preposition) from the object.

Correction: *The school carnival included amusement rides, clowns, food booths, and a variety of games.*

Apostrophes

APOSTROPHES are used to show either contractions or possession.

Error: *She shouldnt be permitted to smoke cigarettes in the building.*

Problem: An apostrophe is needed in a contraction in place of the missing letter.

Correction: *She shouldn't be permitted to smoke cigarettes in the building.*

Error: *My cousins motorcycle was stolen from his driveway.*

Problem: An apostrophe is needed to show possession.

Correction: *My cousin's motorcycle was stolen from his driveway. (Note: The use of the apostrophe before the letter s means that there is just one cousin. The plural form would read the following way: My cousins' motorcycle was stolen from their driveway.)*

Error: *The childrens new kindergarten teacher was also a singer.*

Problem: An apostrophe is needed to show possession.

Correction: *The children's new kindergarten teacher was also a singer. (Note: children is plural, so the apostrophe comes between the n and the s.)*

Error: *Children screams could be heard for miles.*

Problem: An apostrophe and the letter s are needed in the sentence to show whose screams they are.

Correction: *Children's screams could he heard for miles. (Note: children is plural, so the apostrophe comes between the n and the s.)*

Quotation Marks

The more troublesome punctuation marks involve the use of quotations.

Using terminal punctuation in relation to quotation marks

In a quoted statement that is either declarative or imperative, place the period inside the closing quotation marks.

Check out this guide to grammar and writing:

http://grammar.ccc. commnet.edu/grammar/

"The airplane crashed on the runway during takeoff."

If the quotation is followed by other words in the sentence, place a comma inside the closing quotations marks and a period at the end of the sentence.

"The airplane crashed on the runway during takeoff," said the announcer.

In most instances in which a quoted title or expression occurs at the end of a sentence, the period is placed before either the single or double quotation marks

"The middle school readers were unprepared to understand Bryant's poem 'Thanatopsis.'"

Early book-length adventure stories like Don Quixote and The Three Musketeers were known as "picaresque novels."

There is an instance in which the final quotation mark would precede the period if the content of the sentence were about a speech or quote so that the understanding of the meaning would be confused by the placement of the period.

The first thing out of his mouth was "Hi, I'm home."

but

The first line of his speech began "I arrived home to an empty house".

In sentences that are interrogatory or exclamatory, the question mark or exclamation point should be positioned outside the closing quotation marks if the quote itself is a statement, command, or cited title.

Who decided to lead us in the recitation of the "Pledge of Allegiance"?

Why was Tillie shaking as she began her recitation, "Once upon a midnight dreary. . ."?

I was embarrassed when Mrs. White said, "Your slip is showing"!

In sentences that are declarative but the quotation is a question or an exclamation, place the question mark or exclamation point inside the quotation marks.

The hall monitor yelled, "Fire! Fire!"

"Fire! Fire!" yelled the hall monitor.

Cory shrieked, "Is there a mouse in the room?" (In this instance, the question supersedes the exclamation.)

Using double quotation marks with other punctuation

Quotations—whether words, phrases, or clauses—should be punctuated according to the rules of the grammatical function they serve in the sentence.

> *The works of Shakespeare, "the bard of Avon," have been contested as originating with other authors.*
>
> *"You'll get my money," the old man warned, "when 'Hell freezes over'."*
>
> *Sheila cited the passage that began "Four score and seven years ago . . ." (Note the ellipsis followed by an enclosed period.)*
>
> *Old Ironsides inspired the preservation of the U.S.S. Constitution.*

Use quotation marks to enclose the titles of shorter works: songs, short poems, short stories, essays, and chapters of books. (See "Using Italics" for punctuating longer titles.)

> "The Tell-Tale Heart" (short story)
>
> "Casey at the Bat" (poem)
>
> "America the Beautiful" (song)

Dashes

Use dashes to denote sudden breaks in thought.

> *Some periods in literature—the Romantic Age, for example—spanned different time periods in different countries.*

Use dashes instead of commas if commas are already used elsewhere in the sentence for amplification or explanation.

> *The Fireside Poets included three Brahmans—James Russell Lowell, Henry David Wadsworth, Oliver Wendell Holmes—and John Greenleaf Whittier.*

Use italics to punctuate the titles of long works of literature, names of periodical publications, musical scores, works of art and motion picture television, and radio programs. (When unable to write in italics, you can instruct students to underline in their own writing where italics would be appropriate.)

> *The Idylls of the King*   *Hiawatha*   *The Sound and the Fury*
>
> *Mary Poppins*   *Newsweek*   *The Nutcracker Suite*

Capitalization

Capitalize all proper names (including persons, specific organizations, and agencies of government); places (countries, states, cities, parks, and specific geographical areas); things (political parties, structures, historical and cultural terms, and calendar and time designations); and religious terms (any deity, revered person or group, and sacred writings).

> *Percy Bysshe Shelley, Argentina, Mount Rainier National Park, Grand Canyon, League of Nations, the Sears Tower, Birmingham, Lyric Theater, Americans, Midwesterners, Democrats, Renaissance, Boy Scouts of America, Easter, God, Bible, Dead Sea Scrolls, Koran*

Capitalize proper adjectives and titles used with proper names.

> *California gold rush, President John Adams, French fries, Homeric epic, Romanesque architecture, Senator John Glenn*

Note: Some words that represent titles and offices are not capitalized unless used with a proper name.

Capitalized	Not Capitalized
Congressman McKay	*the congressman from Florida*
Commander Alger	*commander of the Pacific Fleet*
Queen Elizabeth	*the queen of England*

Capitalize all main words in titles of works of literature, art, and music.

Error: *Emma went to Dr. Peters for treatment since her own Doctor was on vacation.*

Problem: The use of capital letters with Emma and Dr .Peters is correct since they are specific (proper) names; the title Dr. is also capitalized. However, the word doctor is not a specific name and should not be capitalized.

Correction: *Emma went to Dr. Peters for treatment since her own doctor was on vacation.*

Error: *Our Winter Break does not start until next wednesday.*

Problem: Days of the week are capitalized, but seasons are not capitalized.

Correction: *Our winter break does not start until next Wednesday.*

Error: *The exchange student from israel who came to study biochemistry spoke spanish very well.*

Problem: Languages and the names of countries are always capitalized. Courses are also capitalized when they refer to a specific course; they are not capitalized when they refer to courses in general.

Correction: *The exchange student from Israel who came to study Biochemistry spoke Spanish very well.*

Practice Exercise

Choose the option that corrects an error in the underlined portion(s). If no error exists, choose "No change is necessary."

1. <u>Greenpeace</u> is an <u>Organization</u> that works to preserve the <u>world's</u> environment.

   A. greenpeace

   B. organization

   C. worlds

   D. No change is necessary

2. When our class travels to <u>France</u> next <u>year</u>, we will see the <u>country's</u> many famous landmarks.

   A. france

   B. year; we

   C. countries

   D. No change is necessary

3. <u>New York City</u>, the heaviest populated city <u>in America</u> has more than eight million people living there <u>every day</u>.

   A. new york city

   B. in America, has

   C. Everyday

   D. No change is necessary

4. The <u>television</u> show The X-Files has gained a huge <u>following because</u> it focuses on paranormal phenomena, extraterrestrial life, and the oddities of <u>human existence</u>.

   A. Television

   B. following, because

   C. Human existence

   D. No change is necessary

5. Being a <u>Policeman</u> requires having many <u>qualities</u>: physical <u>agility</u>, good reflexes, and the ability to make quick decisions.

   A. policeman

   B. qualities;

   C. agility:

   D. No change is necessary

Answer Key

1. **B**

   In the sentence, the word organization does not need to be capitalized due to the fact that it is a general noun. In Option A, the name of the organization should be capitalized. In Option C, the apostrophe is used to show that one world is being protected, not more than one.

2. **D**

   In Option A, France is capitalized because it is the name of a country. In Option B, the comma, not the semicolon, should separate a dependent clause from the main clause. In Option C, the use of an apostrophe and an s indicates only one country is being visited.

3. **B**

   In Option A, New York City is capitalized because it is the name of a place. In Option B, a comma is needed to separate the noun America from the verb has. In Option C, the phrase every day needs no capitalization.

4. **D**

   In Option A, television does not need to be capitalized because it is a noun. In Option B, a comma is necessary to separate an independent clause from the main clause. In Option C, human existence is a general term that does not need capitalization.

5. **A**

   In Option A, policeman does not need capitalization because it is a general noun. In Option B, a colon, not a semicolon, is needed because the rest of the sentence is related to the main clause. In Option C, a comma, not a colon, is needed to separate the adjectives.

Sample Test Questions and Rationale

For questions 1 and 2, circle the choice that best corrects the underlined error without changing the meaning of the original sentence.

(Easy)

1. Joe <u>didn't hardly know</u> his cousin Fred who'd had a rhinoplasty.

    A. hardly did know his cousin Fred

    B. didn't know his cousin Fred hardly

    C. hardly knew his cousin Fred

    D. didn't know his cousin Fred

    E. didn't hardly know his cousin Fred

The answer is C.

Using the adverb "hardly" to modify the verb creates a negative, and adding "not" creates the dreaded double negative.

(Average)

2. Wally <u>groaned, "Why</u> do I have to do an oral interpretation <u>of "The Raven</u>."

    A. groaned, "Why… of 'The Raven'?"

    B. groaned "Why… of "The Raven"?

    C. groaned ", Why… of "The Raven?"

    D. groaned, "Why… of "The Raven."

The answer is A.

The question mark in a quotation that is an interrogation should be within the quotation marks. Also, when quoting a work of literature within another quotation, one should use single quotation marks ('…') for the title of this work, and the single quotation marks should close before the final quotation mark.

(Rigorous)

3. <u>The coach offered her assistance but the athletes wanted</u> to practice on their own.

    A. The coach offered her assistance, however, the athletes wanted to practice on their own

    B. The coach offered her assistance: furthermore, the athletes wanted to practice on their own

    C. Having offered her assistance, the athletes wanted to practice on their own.

    D. The coach offered her assistance; however, the athletes wanted to practice on their own

The answer is D.

A semicolon precedes a transitional adverb that introduces an independent clause. Answer A is a comma splice. In Answer B, the colon is used incorrectly, since the second clause does not explain the first. In Answer C, the opening clause confuses the meaning of the sentence. In answer D, the semicolon is used correctly before however.

Sample Test Questions and Rationale (cont.)

(Easy)

4. A punctuation mark indicating omission, interrupted thought, or an incomplete statement is a/an:

   A. Ellipsis

   B. Anachronism

   C. Colloquy

   D. Idiom

The answer is A.

With the use of an ellipsis, a word or words that would clarify the sentence's message are missing, yet it is still possible to understand them from the context.

(Easy)

5. Which of the following sentences is properly punctuated?

   A. The more you eat; the more you want.

   B. The authors—John Steinbeck, Ernest Hemingway, and William Faulkner—are staples of modern writing in American literature textbooks.

   C. Handling a wild horse, takes a great deal of skill and patience.

   D. The man, who replaced our teacher, is a comedian.

The answer is B.

Dashes should be used instead of commas when commas are used elsewhere in the sentence for amplification or explanation—here within the dashes.

(Average)

6. Which of the following sentences contains a capitalization error?

   A. The commander of the English navy was Admiral Nelson.

   B. Napoleon was the president of the French First Republic.

   C. Queen Elizabeth II is the Monarch of the British Empire.

   D. William the Conqueror led the Normans to victory over the British.

The answer is C.

Words that represent titles and offices are not capitalized unless used with a proper name. This is not the case here.

COMPETENCY 10
UNDERSTAND WRITING AS A PROCESS

NCTE beliefs about the teaching of writing:

1. Everyone has the capacity to write, writing can be taught, and teachers can help students become better writers

2. People learn to write by writing

3. Writing is a process

4. Writing is a tool for thinking

5. Writing grows out of many different purposes

6. Conventions of finished and edited texts are important to readers and therefore to writers

7. Writing and reading are related

8. Writing has a complex relationship to talk

9. Literate practices are embedded in complicated social relationships

10. Composing occurs in different modalities and technologies

11. Assessment of writing involves complex, informed, human judgment

—Writing Study Group of the NCTE Executive Committee November 2004

> **SKILL** Recognizing techniques for generating and organizing ideas prior
> **10.1** to writing

As you instruct your students in composition, you should explain that, like all skills, writing is a skill that improves with practice. What follows is a way for you to address your students. You can use this same process as you prepare for your teacher certification essays.

What to Tell the Students

Even before you select a topic, determine what each prompt is asking you to discuss. This first decision is crucial. If you pick a topic, you don't really understand or about which you have little to say, you'll have difficulty developing your essay. Take a few moments to analyze each topic carefully *before* you begin to write.

> Topic A: A modern invention that can be considered a wonder of the world

In general, the topic prompts have two parts: the subject of the topic and an assertion about the subject.

The subject is a *modern invention*. In this prompt, the word *modern* indicates you should discuss something invented recently, at least in this century. The word *invention* indicates you're to write about something created by humans (not natural phenomena such as mountains or volcanoes). You may discuss an invention that has potential for harm, such as chemical warfare or the atomic bomb, or you may discuss an invention that has the potential for good: the computer, DNA testing, television, antibiotics, and so on.

The assertion (a statement of point of view) is that *the invention has such powerful or amazing qualities that it should be considered a wonder of the world*. The assertion potentially it limits the range for discussion. In other words, you would discuss particular qualities or uses of the invention, not just discuss how it was invented or whether it should have been invented at all.

Note also that this particular topic encourages you to use examples to show the reader that a particular invention is a modern wonder. Some topic prompts lend themselves to essays with an argumentative edge, in which you take a stand on a particular issue and persuasively prove your point. Here, you could offer examples or illustrations of the many "wonders" and uses of the particular invention you chose.

Be aware that misreading or misinterpreting the topic prompt can lead to serious problems. Papers that do not address the topic occur when one reads too quickly or only half-understands the topic. Misreading can also lead to a paper that addresses only part of the topic prompt rather than the entire topic.

To develop a complete essay, spend a few minutes planning. Jot down your ideas and quickly sketch an outline. Although you may feel under pressure to begin writing, you will write more effectively if you plan out your major points.

Prewriting

Before actually writing, you'll need to generate content and to develop a writing plan. Three prewriting techniques that can be helpful are brainstorming, questioning, and clustering.

Brainstorming

When brainstorming, quickly create a list of words and ideas that are connected to the topic. Let your mind roam free to generate as many relevant ideas as possible in a few minutes. For example, on the topic of computers you may write:

> computer—modern invention
>
> types—personal computers, microchips in calculators and watches
>
> wonder —acts like an electronic brain
>
> uses—science, medicine, offices, homes, schools
>
> problems—too much reliance; the machines aren't perfect

This list could help you focus on the topic and states the points you could develop in the body paragraphs. The brainstorming list keeps you on track and is well worth the few minutes it takes to jot down the ideas. Although you haven't ordered the ideas, seeing them on paper is an important step.

Questioning

Questioning helps you focus as you mentally ask a series of exploratory questions about the topic. You may use the most basic questions: who, what, where, when, why, and how.

> *"**What** is my subject?"*
> *[computers]*
>
> *"**What** types of computers are there?"*
> *[personal computers, microchip computers]*
>
> *"**Why** have computers been a positive invention?"*
> *[act like electronic brains in machinery and equipment; help solve complex scientific problems]*
>
> *"**How** have computers been a positive invention?"*
> *[used to make improvements in:*
> *science (space exploration, moon landings)*
> *medicine (MRIs, CAT scans, surgical tools, research models)*
> *business (PCs, FAX, telephone equipment)*
> *education (computer programs for math, languages, science, social (studies),*
> *personal use (family budgets, tax programs, healthy diet plans)]*
>
> *"**How** can I show that computers are good?"*
> *[citing numerous examples]*
>
> *"**What** problems do I see with computers?"*
> *[too much reliance; not yet perfect]*
>
> *"**What** personal experiences would help me develop examples to respond to this topic?"*
> *[my own experiences using computers]*

Of course, you may not have time to write out the questions completely. You might just write the words *who, what, where, when, why, how* and the major points next to each. An abbreviated list might look as follows:

> ***What**—computers/modern wonder/making life better*
> ***How**—through technological improvements: lasers, calculators, CAT scans.*
> ***Where**—in science and space exploration, medicine, schools, offices*

In a few moments, your questions should help you to focus on the topic and to generate interesting ideas and points to make in the essay. Later in the writing process, you can look back at the list to be sure you've made the key points you intended.

Clustering

Some visual thinkers find clustering an effective prewriting method. When clustering, you draw a box in the center of your paper and write your topic within that box. Then you draw lines from the center box and connect it to small satellite boxes that contain related ideas. Note the cluster below on computers:

Sample Cluster

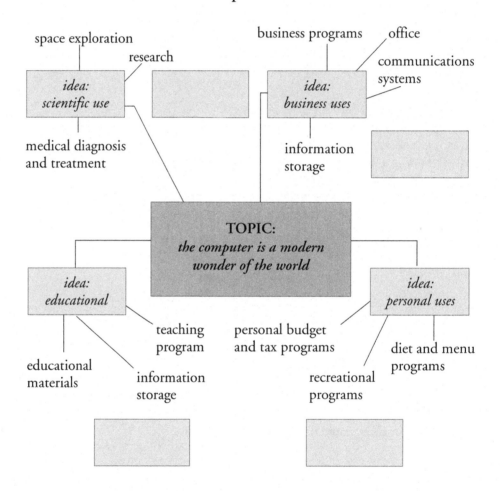

Writing the Thesis

After focusing on the topic and generating your ideas, form your thesis, which is the controlling idea of your essay. The thesis expresses your point of view and guides your essay's purpose and scope. The thesis should allow you either to explain your subject or to take an arguable position about it. A strong thesis statement is neither too narrow nor too broad.

Subject and assertion of the thesis

From the analysis of the general topic, you saw the topic in terms of its two parts, the subject and the assertion.

The subject of the thesis relates directly to the topic prompt but expresses the specific area you have chosen to discuss. (Remember that the exam topic will be general and will allow you to choose a particular subject related to the topic). For example, the computer is one modern invention.

The assertion of the thesis is your viewpoint, or opinion, about the subject. The assertion provides the motive or purpose for your essay, and it may be an arguable point or one that explains or illustrates a point of view.

For example, you may present an argument for or against a particular issue. You may contrast two people, objects, or methods to show that one is better than the other. You may analyze a situation in all aspects and make recommendations for improvement. You may assert that a law or policy should be adopted, changed or abandoned. You may also, as in the computer example, explain to your reader that a situation or condition exists; rather than argue a viewpoint, you would use examples to illustrate your assertion about the essay's subject.

Specifically, the subject of Topic A is *the computer*. The assertion is that *it is a modern wonder that we rely on and that has improved our lives*. Now you quickly have created a workable thesis in a few moments:

> *The computer is a modern wonder of the world that we have come to rely on and that has improved our lives.*

Guidelines for writing thesis statements

The following guidelines are not a formula for writing thesis statements but rather are general strategies for making your thesis statement clearer and more effective.

1. State a *particular point of view* about the topic with both a *subject* and an *assertion*. The thesis should give the essay purpose and scope and thus provide a guide for the reader. If the thesis is vague, your essay may be undeveloped because you do not have an idea to assert or a point to explain. Weak thesis statements are often framed as facts, questions, or announcements:

   A. Avoid a fact statement as a thesis. While a fact statement may provide a subject, it generally does not include a point of view about the subject that provides the basis for an extended discussion.

   > Recycling saved our community over $10,000 last year. *This fact statement provides a detail, not a point of view. Such a detail might be found within an essay, but it does not state a point of view.*

B. Avoid framing the thesis as a vague question. In many cases, rhetorical questions do not provide a clear point of view for an extended essay.

> How do people recycle? *This question neither asserts a point of view nor helps the reader to understand the essay's purpose and scope.*

C. Avoid the "announcer" topic sentence that merely states the topic you will discuss.

> I will discuss ways to recycle. *This sentence states the subject, but the scope of the essay is only suggested. Again, this statement does not assert a viewpoint that guides the essay's purpose. It merely "announces" that the writer will write about the topic.*

2. Start with a *workable thesis*. You might revise your thesis as you begin writing and discover your own point of view.

3. If feasible and appropriate, state the thesis in multipoint form to outline the scope of the essay. By stating the points in parallel form, you clearly lay out the essay's plan for the reader.

> To improve the environment, we can recycle our trash, elect politicians who see the environment as a priority, and support lobbying groups who work for environmental protection.

4. Because of the exam time limit, place your thesis in the first paragraph to key the reader to the essay's main idea.

Creating a Working Outline

A good thesis gives structure to your essay and helps focus your thoughts. When forming your thesis, look at your prewriting strategy—clustering, questioning, or brainstorming. Then, decide quickly which two or three major areas you will discuss. Remember, you must limit the scope of the paper because of the time factor.

OUTLINE: lists the main points of a thesis that will be used as topics for each paragraph

The **OUTLINE** lists the main points as topics for each paragraph. Looking at the prewriting cluster on computers, you might choose several areas in which computers help us; for example, in science and medicine, business, and education. You might also consider people's reliance on this "wonder" and include at least one paragraph about this reliance. A formal outline for this essay might look like the one below:

I. Introduction and thesis

II. Computers used in science and medicine

III. Computers used in business

IV. Computers used in education

V. People's reliance on computers

VI. Conclusion

Under time pressure, however, you may use a shorter organizational plan, such as abbreviated key words in a list. For example:

1. intro: wonders of the computer -OR-	a. intro: wonders of computers—science
2. science	b. in the space industry
3. med	c. in medical technology
4. schools	d. conclusion
5. business	
6. conclusion	

Developing the Essay

With a working thesis and an outline, you can begin writing the essay. The essay should be divided into three main sections:

I. The introduction sets up the essay and leads to the thesis statement

II. The body paragraphs are developed with concrete information leading from the topic sentences

III. The conclusion ties the essay together

Introduction

Put your thesis statement into a clear, coherent opening paragraph. One effective device is to use a funnel approach, in which you begin with a brief description of the broader issue and then move to a clearly focused, specific thesis statement.

Consider the following possible introductions to the essay on computers. The length of each is obviously different. Read each, and consider the other differences.

Does each introduce the subject generally?

Does each lead to a stated thesis?

Does each relate to the topic prompt?

Introduction 1: *Computers are used every day. They have many uses. Some people who use them are workers, teachers, and doctors.*

Analysis: This introduction does give the general topic—computers are used every day—but it does not explain what those uses are. This introduction does not offer a point of view in a clearly stated thesis, nor does it convey the idea that computers are a modern wonder.

Introduction 2: *Computers are used just about everywhere these days. I don't think there's an office around that doesn't use computers, and we use them a lot in all kinds of jobs. Computers are great for making life easier and work better. I don't think we'd get along without the computer.*

Analysis: This introduction gives the general topic as computers and mentions one area that uses computers. The thesis states that people could not get along without computers, but it does not state the specific areas the essay will discuss. Note, too, that the meaning is not helped by vague diction, such as *a lot* and *great*.

Introduction 3: *Each day, we either use computers or see them being used around us. We wake to the sound of a digital alarm operated by a microchip. Our cars run by computerized machinery. We use computers to help us learn. We receive phone calls and letters transferred from computers across continents. Our astronauts walked on the moon and returned safely, all because of computer technology. The computer is a wonderful electronic brain that we have come to rely on, and it has changed our world through advances in science, business, and education.*

Analysis: This introduction is the most thorough and fluent because it provides interest in the general topic and offers specific information about computers as a modern wonder. It also leads to a thesis that directs the reader to the scope of the discussion—advances in science, business, and education.

Topic sentences

Just as the essay must have an overall focus reflected in the thesis statement, each paragraph must have a central idea reflected in the topic sentence. A good topic sentence provides transition from the previous paragraph and relates to the essay's thesis. Good topic sentences, therefore, provide unity throughout the essay.

Consider the following potential topic sentences. Determine whether each provides transition and clearly states the subject of the paragraph.

Topic Sentence 1: *Computers are used in science.*

Analysis: This sentence simply states the topic: Computers are used in science. It does not relate to the thesis nor provide transition from the introduction. The reader still does not know how computers are used in science.

Topic Sentence 2: *Now I will talk about computers used in science.*

Analysis: Like the faulty "announcer" thesis statement, this "announcer" topic sentence is vague and merely names the topic.

Topic Sentence 3: *First, computers used in science have improved our lives.*

Analysis: The transition word *First* helps link the introduction and this paragraph. It adds unity to the essay. It does not, however, give specifics about the improvements computers have made in our lives.

Topic Sentence 4: *First used in scientific research and spaceflights, computers are now used extensively in the diagnosis and treatment of disease.*

Analysis: This sentence is the most thorough and fluent. It provides specific areas that will be discussed in the paragraph and it offers more than an announcement of the topic. The writer gives concrete information about the content of the paragraph that will follow.

SUMMARY GUIDELINES FOR WRITING TOPIC SENTENCES
Specifically relate the topic to the thesis statement
State clearly and concretely the subject of the paragraph
Provide some transition from the previous paragraph
Avoid topic sentences that are facts, questions, or announcements

Sample Test Questions and Rationale

(Easy)

1. Writing ideas quickly without interruption of the flow of thoughts or attention to conventions is called:

    A. Brainstorming

    B. Mapping

    C. Listing

    D. Free writing

The answer is D.

Free writing for ten or fifteen minutes allows students to write out their thoughts about a subject. This technique allows students to develop ideas that they are conscious of, but it also helps them develop ideas that are lurking in the subconscious. It is important to let the flow of ideas run through the hand. If students get stuck, they can write the last sentence over again until inspiration returns.

(Rigorous)

2. In preparing a report about William Shakespeare, students are asked to develop a set of interpretive questions to guide their research. Which of the following would not be classified as an interpretive question?

    A. What would be different today if Shakespeare had not written his plays?

    B. How will the plays of Shakespeare affect future generations?

    C. How does Shakespeare view nature in A Midsummer's Night Dream and Much Ado About Nothing?

    D. During the Elizabethan age, what roles did young boys take in dramatizing Shakespeare's plays?

The answer is D.

This question requires research into the historical facts; the movie Shakespeare in Love notwithstanding, women did not act in Shakespeare's plays, and their parts were taken by young boys. Answers A and B are hypothetical questions requiring students to provide original thinking and interpretation. Answer C requires comparison and contrast, which are interpretive skills.

SKILL 10.2 Demonstrating knowledge of techniques for selecting and presenting detailed evidence as support for ideas

Check out ten steps to writing an essay:

http://www.aucegypt.edu/academic/writers/

If you have a good thesis and a good outline, you should be able to construct a complete essay. Your paragraphs should contain concrete, interesting information and supporting details to support your point of view. As often as possible, create images in your reader's mind. Fact statements also add weight to your opinions, especially when you are trying to convince the reader of your viewpoint.

Supporting Details

Because every good thesis has an assertion, you should offer specifics, facts, data, anecdotes, expert opinion, and other details to prove that assertion. While you know what you mean, your reader does not. On the exam, you must explain and develop ideas as fully as possible in the time allowed.

In the following paragraph, the sentences in bold print provide a *skeleton of a paragraph that discusses the benefits of recycling.* The sentences in bold are generalizations that by themselves do not explain the need to recycle. The sentences in italics *add details to support the general points in bold.* Notice how the supporting details help you understand the necessity for recycling.

> **While one day recycling may become mandatory in all states, right now it is voluntary in many communities.** *Those of us who participate in recycling are amazed by how much material is recycled.* **For many communities, the blue-box recycling program has had an immediate effect.** *By just recycling glass, aluminum cans, and plastic bottles, we have reduced the volume of disposable trash by one-third, thus extending the useful life of local landfills by over a decade. Imagine the difference if those dramatic results were achieved nationwide.* **The number of reusable items we thoughtlessly dispose of is staggering.** *For example, Americans dispose of enough steel every day to supply Detroit car manufacturers for three months. Additionally, we dispose of enough aluminum annually to rebuild the nation's air fleet. These statistics, available from the Environmental Protection Agency (EPA), should encourage all of us to watch what we throw away.* **Clearly, recycling in our homes and in our communities directly improves the environment.**

Notice how the author's supporting examples enhance the message of the paragraph and relate to the author's thesis noted above. If you only read the boldface sentences, you have a glimpse of the topic. This paragraph of illustration, however, is developed through numerous details creating specific images: *reduced the volume of disposable trash by one-third; extended the useful life of local landfills by over a decade; enough steel every day to supply Detroit car manufacturers for three months; enough aluminum to rebuild the nation's air fleet.* If the writer had merely written a few general sentences, as those shown in bold, you would not fully understand the vast amount of trash involved in recycling or the positive results of current recycling efforts.

Conclusion

End your essay with a brief, straightforward concluding paragraph that ties together the essay's content and leaves the reader with a sense of its completion. The conclusion should reinforce the main points, offer some insight into the topic, provide a sense of unity for the essay by relating it to the thesis, and signal clear closure of the essay.

Sample Test Questions and Rationale

(Rigorous)

1. In this paragraph from a student essay, identify the sentence that provides a detail.

   (1) The poem concerns two different personality types and the human relation between them. (2) Their approach to life is totally different. (3) The neighbor is a very conservative person who follows routines. (4) He follows the traditional wisdom of his father and his father's father. (5) The purpose in fixing the wall and keeping their relationship separate is only because it is all he knows.

   A. Sentence 1

   B. Sentence 3

   C. Sentence 4

   D. Sentence 5

   The answer is C.

   Sentence 4 provides a detail to sentence 3 by explaining how the neighbor follows routine. Sentence 1 is the thesis sentence, which is the main idea of the paragraph. Sentence 3 provides an example to develop that thesis. Sentence 5 is a reason that explains why.

(Easy)

2. Which of the following should not be included in the opening paragraph of an informative essay?

   A. Thesis sentence

   B. Details and examples supporting the main idea

   C. Broad general introduction to the topic

   D. A style and tone that grabs the reader's attention

   The answer is B.

   The introductory paragraph should introduce the topic, capture the reader's interest, state the thesis, and prepare the reader for the main points in the essay. Details and examples, however, should be given in the second part of the essay, so as to help develop the thesis presented at the end of the introductory paragraph, following the inverted triangle method consisting of a broad general statement followed by some information, and then the thesis at the end of the paragraph.

(Average)

3. Middle and high school students are more receptive to studying grammar and syntax:

   A. Through worksheets and end- of- lessons practices in textbooks

   B. Through independent homework assignments

   C. Through analytical examination of the writings of famous authors

   D. Through application to their own writing

   The answer is D.

   At this age, students learn grammatical concepts best through practical application in their own writing.

Sample Test Questions and Rationale (cont.)

(Average)

4. **In general, the most serious drawback of using a computer in writing is that:**

    A. The copy looks so good that students tend to overlook major mistakes

    B. The spell check and grammar programs discourage students from learning proper spelling and mechanics

    C. The speed with which corrections can be made detracts from the exploration and contemplation of composing

    D. The writer loses focus by concentrating on the final product rather than the details

The answer is C.

Because the process of revising is very quick with the computer, it can discourage contemplation, exploring, and examination, which are very important in the process of writing.

SKILL 10.3 **Recognizing methods for developing ideas into a well-organized composition that is cohesive and coherent**

Enhancing Interest

- Start with an attention-grabbing introduction. Doing so sets an engaging tone for the entire piece and will be more likely to pull in readers.

- Use dynamic vocabulary and varied sentence beginnings. Keep the readers on their toes. If they can predict what you are going to say next, they will lose interest quickly.

- Avoid using clichés (as cold as ice, the best thing since sliced bread, nip it in the bud). These are easy shortcuts, but they are not interesting, memorable, or convincing.

Ensuring Understanding

- Avoid using the words clearly, obviously, and undoubtedly. Often, what is clear or obvious to the author is not as apparent to the readers. Instead of using these words, make your point so strongly that it is clear on its own.

- Use the word that best fits the meaning you intend, even if it is longer or a little less common. Try to find a balance, and go with a familiar, yet precise, word.

- When in doubt, explain further.

With strong research skills, you will find more information than you could possibly use. Your task now becomes eliminating irrelevant or unimportant information. The key is to focus on your thesis statement. What evidence will support your main point?

Techniques to Maintain Focus

- Focus on a main point. The point should be clear to readers, and all sentences in the paragraph should relate to it.

- Start the paragraph with a topic sentence. This should be a general, one-sentence summary of the paragraph's main point, relating back to the thesis and forward to the content of the paragraph. (A topic sentence is sometimes unnecessary if the paragraph continues a developing idea clearly introduced in a preceding paragraph, or if the paragraph appears in a narrative of events where generalizations might interrupt the flow of the story.)

- Stick to the point. Eliminate sentences that do not support the topic sentence.

- Be flexible. If you do not have enough evidence to support the claim of your topic sentence, do not fall into the trap of wandering or introducing new ideas within the paragraph. Either find more evidence, or adjust the topic sentence to corroborate with the evidence that is available.

SKILL 10.4 **Demonstrating knowledge of revision, editing, and proofreading methods and standards**

Learn more about editing and proofreading strategies for revision:

http://owl.english.purdue. edu/handouts/ general/gl_edit.html

You want to employ various techniques that will help you revise text to achieve clarity and economy of expression.

Revising Sentences to Eliminate Wordiness, Ambiguity, and Redundancy

You may think this exercise simply catches errors in spelling or word use, but you should reframe your thinking about revising and editing. Revision is an extremely important step that often is ignored. Some questions you should ask are:

- Is the reasoning coherent?

- Is the point established?

- Does the introduction make the reader want to read this discourse?

- What is the thesis? Is it proven?

- What is the purpose? Is it clear? Is it useful, valuable, and interesting?

- Is the style of writing so wordy that it exhausts the reader and interferes with engagement?

- Is the writing so spare that it is boring?

- Are the sentences too uniform in structure?

- Are there too many simple sentences?

- Are too many of the complex sentences the same structure?

- Are the compound sentences truly compound, or are they unbalanced?

- Are parallel structures truly parallel?

- If there are characters, are they believable?

- If there is dialogue, is it natural or stilted?

- Is the title appropriate?

- Does the writing show creativity, or is it boring?

- Is the language appropriate? Is it too formal? Too informal? If jargon is used, is it appropriate?

Studies have clearly demonstrated that the most fertile area in teaching writing is revision. If students can learn to revise their own work effectively, they are well on their way to becoming effective, mature writers. Word processing is an important tool for teaching this stage in the writing process. Microsoft Word has tracking features that make the revision exchanges between teachers and students more effective than ever before.

COMPETENCY 11

UNDERSTAND THE USE OF RESEARCH AND TECHNOLOGY IN WRITING

> ### SKILL Recognizing the differences between primary and secondary
> ### 11.1 sources

The resources used to support a piece of writing can be divided into two major groups: primary sources and *secondary sources*.

Primary sources are works, records, and the like that were created during the period being studied or immediately after it. Secondary sources are works written significantly after the period being studied and based upon primary sources. PRIMARY SOURCES are the basic materials that provide raw data and information. SECONDARY SOURCES are the works that contain the explications of, and judgments on, this primary material.

Primary sources include the following kinds of materials:

PRIMARY SOURCES:
the basic materials that provide raw data and information

SECONDARY SOURCES:
works that contain explications of and judgments on primary material

- Documents that reflect the immediate, everyday concerns of people: memoranda, bills, deeds, charters, newspaper reports, pamphlets, graffiti, popular writings, journals or diaries, records of decision-making bodies, letters, receipts, snapshots, and others.

- Theoretical writings that reflect care and consideration in composition and an attempt to convince or persuade. The topic will generally be deeper than is the case with "immediate" documents. These may include newspaper or magazine editorials, sermons, political speeches, or philosophical writings.

- Narrative accounts of events, ideas, and trends written with intentionally by someone contemporary with the events described.

- Statistical data, although statistics may be misleading.

- Literature and nonverbal materials, novels, stories, poetry and essays from the period, as well as coins, archaeological artifacts, and art produced during the period.

Secondary sources include the following kinds of materials:

- Books written on the basis of primary materials about the time period.

- Books written on the basis of primary materials about persons who played a major role in the events under consideration.

- Books and articles written on the basis of primary materials about the culture, the social norms, the language, and the values of the period.

- Quotations from primary sources.

- Statistical data on the period.

- The conclusions and inferences of other historians.

- Multiple interpretations of the ethos of the time.

Questions for Analyzing Sources

To determine the authenticity or credibility of your sources, consider these questions:

- Who created the source and why? Was it created through a spur-of-the-moment act, a routine transaction, or a thoughtful, deliberate process?

- Did the recorder have firsthand knowledge of the event? Did the recorder report what others saw and heard?

- Was the recorder a neutral party, or did the recorder have opinions or interests that might have influenced what was recorded?
  Did the recorder produce the source for personal use, for one or more individuals, or for a large audience?

- Was the source meant to be public or private?

- Did the recorder wish to inform or persuade others? (Check the words in the source. The words may tell you whether the recorder was trying to be objective or persuasive.) Did the recorder have reasons to be honest or dishonest?

- Was the information recorded during the event, immediately after the event, or after some lapse of time?

Learn more about assessing the credibility of online sources:

http://www.webcredible. co.uk/user-friendly-resources/web-credibility/ assessing-credibility-online-sources.shtml

Sample Test Question and Rationale

(Average)

1. **Which of the following are secondary research materials?**

   A. The conclusions and inferences of other historians

   B. Literature and nonverbal materials, novels, stories, poetry, and essays from the period, as well as coins, archaeological artifacts, and art produced during the period

   C. Interviews and surveys conducted by the researcher

   D. Statistics gathered as the result of the research's experiments

The answer is A.

Secondary sources are works written significantly after the period being studied and based upon primary sources. In this case, historians have studied artifacts of the time and drawn their conclusions and inferences. Primary sources are the basic materials that provide raw data and information. Students or researchers may use literature and other data they have collected to draw their own conclusions or inferences.

SKILL 11.2 **Identifying the advantages and disadvantages of various sources of information** *(e.g., interviews, autobiographies, textbooks, newspapers, journals, the Internet, popular nonfiction books)* **and of using technology in research** *(e.g., ability to search widely, danger of plagiarism)*

Whether researching for your own purposes or teaching students research skills, the best place to start is usually at a library. Not only do libraries have numerous books, videos, and periodicals to use, but also librarians are always a valuable resource for information and can help retrieve information. In spite of the abundance of online sources, researchers still need librarians.

> *"Those who declared librarians obsolete when the Internet rage first appeared are now red-faced. We need them more than ever. The Internet is full of 'stuff' but its value and readability is often questionable. 'Stuff' doesn't give you a competitive edge, high-quality related information does."*
>
> —*Patricia Schroeder, President of the Association of American Publishers*

The Internet is a multifaceted goldmine of information, but you must be careful to discriminate between reliable and unreliable sources. Use sites that are associated with an academic institution, such as a university or a scholarly organization. Typical domain names end in "edu" or "org."

Keep *content* and *context* in mind when researching. Don't be so wrapped up with how you are going to apply your resource to your project that you miss the author's entire purpose or message. Remember that there are multiple ways to get the information you need. Read an encyclopedia article about your topic to get a general overview, and then focus from there. Note names of important people associated with your subject, time periods, and geographic areas. Make a list of key words and their synonyms to use while searching for information. And finally, don't forget about articles in magazines and newspapers, or even personal interviews with experts related to your field of interest.

Sample Test Question and Rationale

(Rigorous)

1. **For their research paper on the effects of the Civil War on American literature, students have brainstormed a list of potential online sources and are seeking your authorization. Which of these represent the strongest source?**

   A. *http://www.wikipedia.org/*

   B. *http://www.google.com*

   C. *http://www.nytimes.com*

   D. *http://docsouth.unc.edu/southlit/civilwar.html*

The answer is D.

Sites with an "edu" domain are associated with educational institutions and tend to be more trustworthy for research information. Wikipedia has an "org" domain, which means it is a nonprofit. Although Wikipedia may be appropriate for background reading, its credibility as a research site is questionable. Both Google and the New York Times are "com" sites, which are for profit. Even though this does not discredit their information, each site is problematic for researchers. With Google, students will get overwhelmed with hits and may not choose the most reputable sites for their information. As a newspaper, the New York Times would not be a strong source for historical information.

SKILL 11.3 Recognizing methods for verifying accuracy *(e.g., cross-checking sources)*

To be sure you are using credible resources, review these guidelines for the use of secondary sources:

- Do not rely upon only a single secondary source.

- Check facts and interpretations against primary sources whenever possible.

- Do not accept the conclusions of other historians uncritically.

- Place greatest reliance on secondary sources created by the best and most respected scholars.

- Do not use the inferences of other scholars as if they were facts.

- Ensure that you recognize any bias the writer brings to his or her interpretation of history.

- Understand the primary point of the book as a basis for evaluating the relevance of the material presented in it to your questions.

Cross-checking or comparing sources not only helps you to test their validity, but also helps you to understand your sources in context. One observer of the 1939 invasion of Poland is good; two (or three or four) are even better. Each source will contribute something new to your understanding of the event and to your sense of how you might best represent or analyze it.

Sample Test Question and Rationale

(Easy)

1. **In preparing your high school freshmen to write a research paper about a social problem, what recommendation can you make so they can determine the credibility of their information?**

    A. Assure them that information on the Internet has been peer reviewed and verified for accuracy

    B. Find one solid source and use that exclusively

    C. Use only primary sources

    D. Cross-check your information with another credible source

The answer is D.

When researchers find the same information in multiple reputable sources, the information is considered credible. Using the Internet for research requires strong critical evaluation of the source. Nothing from the Internet should be taken without careful scrutiny of the source. To rely on only one source is dangerous and short-sighted. Most high school freshmen would have limited skills to conduct primary research for a paper about a social problem.

SKILL 11.4 Assessing the credibility, objectivity, and reliability of a source of information

While bias cannot be eliminated, writers should carefully examine their resources and their own writings to avoid negative one-sidedness.

When evaluating sources, first go through this checklist to make sure the source is worth reading:

- Title (How relevant is it to your topic?)
- Date (How current is the source?)
- Organization (What institution produced this source?)
- Length (How in depth is the source?)

Check for signs of bias:

- Does the author or publisher have political ties or religious views that could affect his or her objectivity?
- Is the author or publisher associated with any special-interest groups that might only see one side of an issue, such as Greenpeace or the National Rifle Association?
- How fairly does the author treat opposing views?
- Does the language of the piece show signs of bias?

Keep an open mind while reading, and don't let opposing viewpoints prevent you from absorbing the text. Remember that you are not judging the author's work; you are examining its assumptions, assessing its evidence, and weighing its conclusions.

Further, review your own writing carefully to eliminate any conscious bias. Are you so convinced of your own viewpoint that you ignore valid opposing arguments? Have you backed every assertion with credible and reliable information?

Before accepting as gospel anything that is printed in a newspaper or presented on radio, television, or the Internet, you should consider the source. Even though news reporters and editors claim to be unbiased in the presentation of news, they usually take an editorial point of view. A newspaper may avow that it is liberal or conservative and may even make recommendations at election time, but it may still claim to present the news without bias. Sometimes this is true, and sometimes it is not. For example, Fox News declares itself to be conservative and to support the Republican Party. Its presentation of news often reveals that bias.

On the other hand, CBS has tended to favor more liberal politicians although it avows that it is even-handed in its coverage. Dan Rather presented a story critical of President Bush's military service that was based on a document that could not be validated. His failure to play by the rules of certification of evidence cost him his job and his career. Even if authenticated, such a story would not have gotten past the editors of a conservative-leaning news system.

Even politicians usually play by the rules of fairness in the choices they make about going public. They usually try to be even-handed when selecting news outlets. However, some channels and networks show deference to one politician over another.

Sample Test Question and Rationale

(Rigorous)

1. **To determine the credibility of information, researchers should do all of the following except**

   A. Establish the authority of the document

   B. Disregard documents with bias

   C. Evaluate the currency and reputation of the source

   D. Use a variety of research sources and methods

The answer is B.

Keep an open mind. Researchers should examine the assertions, facts, and reliability of the information. Bias does not automatically invalidate information. Being completely objective is an ideal not often realized. The researcher has to analyze this information with more scrutiny to determine its reliability.

SKILL 11.5 Synthesizing information from multiple sources and perspectives

Learn more about the art of asking good questions:

http://www.youthlearn.org/learning/teaching/questions.asp

Synthesizing involves developing new understanding about a topic by gathering and studying information from multiple sources and perspectives, inferring significant new understanding from that study, and giving expression to the inferences. More simply, this skill captures the heart and soul of research: to yield new insights about some topic.

This skill implies an awareness of the spectrum of sources available to a modern student and an ability to assign appropriate weight to information from any given source.

Modern students should be aware, for instance, of print resources such as encyclopedias, journals, magazines, books, newspapers, legal documents, letters, and the like. In addition, they need to be able to use the Internet to access information not only for electronic versions of print resources but also for information stored in multimedia formats. Similarly, they need to be aware that they can gather information through interviewing people who hold positions or who have life experiences related to the particular topic.

Students need to be aware of the perspective underlying the information that they gather. Variations in perspective are legion, but common ones to consider would be based on age, gender, experience, education, nationality, political agenda, geographical location, economic status, and position in an organization or business. It would be important to consider, for instance, whether information on a collective bargaining issue comes from the CFO or from a union representative. Familiarity with the concepts of bias and credibility provides an important foundation for making the most sense of various perspectives.

Mastery of this skill involves developing a matrix or paradigm that does justice to the dynamic relationships existing among the various sources of information and perspectives gathered in the attempt to understand something new about a given topic. Then, through careful study of the matrix or paradigm, a student should be able to identify trends, connections, or insights that comprise the goal of the research—the new understanding, the synthesis. The final stage of this skill is to communicate the synthesis effectively. This skill includes having the know-how to craft a multimedia presentation that incorporates print, audio, and visual sources.

SKILL 11.6 Applying knowledge of ethical principles and appropriate formats for quoting material, citing sources, and creating bibliographies

This skill pertains to recognizing that stealing intellectual property is an academic and, in some cases, a legal crime; because it is so, students need to learn how to give credit where credit is due.

Students need to be aware of the rules that apply to borrowing ideas from various sources. Increasingly, consequences for violations of these rules (plagiarism) are becoming more severe, and students are expected to be aware of how to avoid such problems. Such consequences include failing a particular assignment, losing credit for an entire course, expulsion from a learning environment, and civil penalties.

Software exists that enables teachers and other interested individuals to determine quickly whether a given paper includes plagiarized material. As members of society in the information age, students are expected to recognize the basic justice of intellectual honesty and to conform to the systems meant to ensure it. Pleading ignorance is less and less of a defense.

There are several style guides for documenting sources. Each guide has its own particular ways of signaling that information has been directly borrowed or paraphrased; familiarity with where to find the relevant details of the major style guides is an essential for students. Many libraries publish overviews of the major style guides for students to consult, most bookstores carry full guides for the major systems, and relevant information is readily available on the Web as well.

Documentation of sources takes two main forms. The first form applies to citing sources in the text of the document or as footnotes or endnotes. In-text documentation is sometimes called parenthetical documentation and requires specific information within parentheses placed immediately after borrowed material. Footnotes or endnotes are placed either at the bottom of relevant pages or at the end of the document.

Beyond citing sources in the text, style guides also require a bibliography, a references section, or a works cited section at the end of the document. Sources for any borrowed material are to be listed according to the rules of the particular guide. In some cases, including a works consulted listing may be required even though no material is directly cited or paraphrased to the extent that an in-text citation would be required.

Learn more about MLA works cited documentation:

http://www.studyguide.org/ MLAdocumentation.htm

The major style guides to be familiar with include the *Modern Language Association Handbook (MLA)*, the *Manual of the American Psychological Association (APA)*, the *Chicago Manual of Style, Turabian,* and *Scientific Style and Format: The CBE Manual.*

Documentation of sources from the Internet is particularly involved and continues to evolve at a pace such that writers should visit the latest online update available for a particular style guide.

Sample Test Question and Rationale

(Rigorous)

1. **Which of the following situations is not an ethical violation of intellectual property?**

   A. A student visits ten different Web sites and writes a report to compare the costs of downloading music. He uses the names of the Web sites without their permission.

   B. A student copies and pastes a chart verbatim from the Internet but does not document it because it is available on a public site.

   C. From an online article found in a subscription database, a student paraphrases a section on the problems of music piracy. She includes the source in her Works Cited but does not provide an in-text citation.

   D. A student uses a comment from M. Night Shyamalan without attribution, claiming the information is common knowledge.

The answer is A.

In this scenario, the student is conducting primary research by gathering the data and using it for his own purposes. He or she is not violating any principle by using the names of the Web sites. In Answer B, students who copy and paste from the Internet without documenting the sources of their information are committing plagiarism, a serious violation of intellectual property. Even when a student puts information in his or her own words by paraphrasing or summarizing, as in Answer C, the information is still secondary and must be documented. Although dedicated movie buffs might consider anything that M. Night Shyamalan says to be common knowledge in Situation D, his comments are not necessarily known in numerous places or known by many people.

SKILL 11.7 **Recognizing how the medium of presentation can affect a reader's construction of meaning from a text**

In general, readers will attempt to construct meaning from a text if they believe the text has something important to convey to them. Establishing a general frame of relevance and conveying enthusiasm about it, then, are important considerations when deciding how to present a text.

The purpose of any given text is to communicate some type of information. For a communication to occur, there has to be an interaction between a sender (the text) and a receiver (the audience). The best-case scenario would be for the text to be internally well-suited to convey its meaning and equally well-suited to the receptive capacities of the audience.

Current learning theory establishes that students have distinct learning styles: Some learn better through auditory input; others learn through visuals; still others learn kinesthetically. With this audience learning-style variability in mind, a text

Learn about learning styles at:

http://www.learning-styles-online.com/overview/

incorporating material accessible to students with different learning styles has a better chance of being generally understood than a text presented in one medium only. Pictures, charts, audio clips, and video clips incorporated into print documents enhance the outcome for the most students possible.

Aside from considerations of learning style, a text that is presented in a medium that suits the cultural or experiential background of a given audience has a better chance of having its meaning conveyed than one presented without consideration of such audience-background characteristics. For instance, presenting a well-known fairy tale in a rap medium might well result in enhanced communication for an audience of inner-city children.

Beyond these issues, a text has a better chance of conveying its message if it is presented in an engaging manner. For instance, if a story is read in a monotone, the outcome is surely less positive than if the same story is read with prosody. Furthermore, today's students are used to much more media stimulation than the adults who typically teach them and present texts to them. Without sufficient stimulation, students may have difficulty maintaining a viable attention span.

> *For more information about the reader's construction of meaning, read "The Construction of Meaning and Identity in the Composition and Reading of an Architectural Text":*
>
> *http://www.reading.org/*

Still another way in which medium of text presentation can affect a reader's construction of meaning involves whether the processing routines include opportunities for students to participate. Such routines include opportunities for various types of role playing, for discussing ethical dilemmas in pairs with time constraints and role expectations (one person talks, the other listens and then paraphrases), and for dramatizing scenes or issues within the target text.

Clearly, presenting a drama as a script to be read silently and individually by students will not convey meaning to the same degree as would be likely if the same students were to view an actual performance of the drama. Reading the score of a piece of music is not the same as actually hearing the music played.

DOMAIN IV

WRITING FOR VARIOUS PURPOSES

PERSONALIZED STUDY PLAN

X
KNOWN MATERIAL/ SKIP IT

X

COMPETENCY 12

UNDERSTAND TECHNIQUES FOR DEVELOPING ORGANIZED, FOCUSED NARRATIVE WRITING

Narrative writing presents ordered events to inform or to entertain. Both in fiction and in nonfiction, the goal of narrative writing is to portray a series of events that occurred to a person or people. Narrative writing can be used in the following writing tasks:

- Anecdotes

- Personal writing or memoirs

- Creative writing

- Fiction

An important element for good narrative writing is theme. Typically more important than most plot elements, the theme of the story represents the underlying message, moral, ideal, or lesson that the writer wants to communicate to the readers. Common literary themes include love, money, good versus evil, and jealousy. Literature does not openly state its theme. Instead, the theme is conveyed through settings, plots, and characters. Good writing will suggest the theme without directly mentioning it.

Generating ideas for themes or ideas for narratives is the first step of the writing process, but it can be a daunting task for student writers. Successful authors often offer the following advice when helping other writers to generate good ideas for their writing:

- Freewriting: Write nonstop for ten minutes. When you are brainstorming, just write what comes to your mind. Do not evaluate your ideas at this time. Jot down notes, thoughts, descriptions, names, events, themes … anything that comes to mind.

- Keep a journal: Journals help writers record, express, organize, and explore their thoughts and ideas. Any one journal entry or event from your life could spark an idea later on for a good narrative piece. A journal also allows students to consider their own experiences and how they may play into a future character or plot.

> *Learn more about teaching literature using narratives:*
>
> *http://www. teachingliterature.org/ teachingliterature/chapter7/ activities.htm*

> *Learn more about journal writing:*
>
> *http://www.education-world.com/a_curr/curr144. shtml*

- Read: Read as much as you can. Ideas, characters, or storylines from other writers may produce ideas within a student's head for his or her own story. A character or storyline might remind students of something in their lives or inspire an original idea. Reading also provides students with examples of what makes a good story.

- Collaborate with peers: Two minds are sometimes better than one, and working with peers may provide students with that one idea or memory that may be just what the writer needs to get started.

- Short stories: Sometimes when the pressure of writing an entire, detailed story is removed, a good short story may evolve. Students and/or teachers can analyze several short stories to determine which might have the potential to be developed into a more detailed piece. Then, a more thorough story is more likely to emerge naturally during the revision process.

- Self or peer questioning: When questioned about their experiences, young writers may trigger ideas for stories that can be used or adapted as a plot for a good narrative.

- Webbing/word associations: Webbing allows students to write down their ideas in a somewhat organized way. Students are asked during both webbing and word associations to write down words that are connected, triggered from one another, or linked in some way. This quick-thinking exercise may produce ideas or thoughts that can be developed into themes or ideas for writing.

Learn more about student centered learning:

http://www.wcer.wisc. edu/step/ep301/Fall2000/ Tochonites/stu_cen.html

Sample Test Question and Rationale

(Average)

1. **Modeling is a practice that requires students to:**

   A. Create a style unique to their own language capabilities

   B. Emulate the writing of professionals

   C. Paraphrase passages from good literature

   D. Peer evaluate the writings of other students

The answer is B.

Modeling has students analyze the writing of a professional writer and try to reach the same level of syntactical, grammatical, and stylistic mastery as the author whom they are studying.

SKILL 12.2 Applying knowledge of techniques for engaging and maintaining readers' interest

Typically, the purpose of writing narratives is to entertain, and maintaining a reader's interest is often an important goal of a writer. What good is a book, a short story, or a newspaper article that doesn't get read?

Developing creative and unique storylines is a good way to maintain readers' interest, and this factor should be addressed in the planning/brainstorming process with students. Teachers should help students develop good plots for their narrative pieces. Stories with high levels of human interest often maintain readers' interest well. When a story relates to events that most people experience or face, the chance that the reader will remain interested in the story increases.

However, most teachers will tell you that after reading the fourth story about a lost pet or a move to a new state, their own interest begins to wane. That is not to say that these stories are not of human interest and should not be written, but students need to be guided towards finding unique ways to tell their stories by changing the perspective or thickening the plot. Suspense, adventure, mystery, love, and humor are just some of the good plot elements to keep readers reading.

Creating interesting characters is one way to maintain reader interest. Characters who seem real will help readers connect with or feel for that character. Once the readers are interested in what will happen to the character, their interest will compel them to read the story. Well-developed and thoroughly researched settings also make a story unique and interesting.

Technical elements can help maintain readers' interest, too. For example, dialogue not only helps to develop good characters, but it also helps with the pace and flow of the story. Another technical way to maintain readers' interest is by varying points of view. Sometimes, authors change the writing perspective by chapters or sections of the book to keep the reader interested in how the story will be presented. Finally, varying sentence styles and structures as well as using unique transitions and chapter openings help maintain readers' interest in the narrative.

See also Skill 12.3 for more information about effective plots, characters, and settings.

Sample Test Question and Rationale

(Average)

1. The English department is developing strategies to encourage all students to become a community of readers. From the list of suggestions below, which would be the least effective way for teachers to foster independent reading?

    A. Each teacher sets aside a weekly, 30-minute, in-class reading session during which the teacher and students read a magazine or book for enjoyment

    B. The teacher and the students develop a list of favorite books to share with each other

    C. The teacher assigns at least one book report each grading period to ensure that students are reading from the established class list

    D. The students gather books for a classroom library so that books can be shared with each other

The answer is C.

Teacher-directed assignments such as book reports appear routine and unexciting. Students will be more excited about reading when they can actively participate. In Answer A, the teacher is modeling reading behavior and providing students with a dedicated time during which time they can read independently and still be surrounded by a community of readers. In Answers B and D, students share and make available their reading choices.

SKILL 12.3 Identifying the characteristics of effective plots, characters, settings, and points of view in narrative writing

Students will improve their narrative writing skills by recognizing the elements of a good story.

Plots

Effective plots are essential to narrative writing and are complemented by the narrative's characters, settings, and points of view. The best plots are driven by the characters. To develop an effective plot, the writer must incorporate and balance meaningful dialogue, necessary interior thoughts, and characters' actions and reactions.

Characters

Describing a character's physical features is only the beginning of character development. Students often feel that they develop good characters by describing the physical features, but excellent character development takes more. Physical features need to be balanced with actions, thoughts, temperament, mannerisms, and other traits. A character's action and motives are essential to the plot of the story and lead to a more well-rounded character.

Students should be given opportunities to practice developing different types of characters. One activity involves having the teacher "act out" specific traits while the students identify these traits based on the teacher's pantomime. Sad, happy, and shy are easy traits to start with, and then the teacher can encourage students to suggest more difficult traits (such as jealous, lazy, cruel, witty) to portray.

Devising a list of possible character traits is the easy part. Bringing those traits alive through writing in the narrative, though, is the challenging part. To help bridge this gap, writing classes often use an exercise called "Show, Don't Tell." The objective of this exercise and style of writing is to have students describe the character's traits without coming straight out and telling the reader what those traits are.

For example, a student should be encouraged to change a statement such as:

> William was shy about speaking in front of the class.

This sentence simply tells the reader that the character is shy. A more descriptive characterization would be:

> William slowly walked to the podium at the front of the room. He lowered his eyes to his papers as he turned to face the class. A fluttering sensation filled his stomach as he inhaled to begin his speech.

Use of more descriptive language leads to more interesting characters and a more effective plot line. In addition, such phrasing builds suspense and makes the experience more realistic to the reader—all elements that help maintain readers' interest in the story.

Settings

Effective settings enhance quality narrative pieces. When authors are thorough in their descriptions of unique settings, the reader feels more connected to the story, perhaps almost as if they are there. Even the simplest setting with which many readers would be familiar (i.e., modern-day suburbia) warrants clear description of the area, time of day, time of year, and so on. Like with character development, "Show, Don't Tell" is an excellent exercise to create an effective setting.

For example, instead of:

> *Sarah walked to the park in late autumn.*
>
> *A crisp breeze cooled Sarah's cheeks as she quickened her pace, hurrying along the path littered with golden leaves.*

Again, these details help the reader feel as a part of the story.

Unique settings, however, require much more detailed descriptions. Research is often needed to depict accurate historical settings or settings in another country or region. For example, writers might research traditional language or slang in a region with which they are not familiar. Science fiction and fantasy require extremely in-depth description if the reader is to visualize a world that is only known in the author's mind.

Points of View

In narrative writing, the point of view is the voice of the story. A story's point of view is not necessarily that of the author. An effective point of view encourages the reader to connect with the narrator (usually the main character), not the author, of the story. The ability to use viewpoints effectively is a mark of a good writer.

Most narrative pieces are written in the first-person or the third-person point of view. In the first-person point of view, sentences are written as though the character is speaking or telling the story. The following is an example of first-person point of view:

> *I woke up suddenly. Realizing I was late, I grabbed my tote bag and ran out of the door.*

The benefit of writing in the first person is that all the opinions and thoughts of that one character's mind are accessible to the reader. However, the limit of this style is just the same—that this character is the only viewpoint the reader has, and we are limited to what this character knows.

Stories can also be written two ways in the third person: the third-person omniscient or the third-person limited point of view. The third-person omniscient can move among different characters' viewpoints with knowledge of everyone's thoughts, actions, and experience. The third-person limited follows one character throughout the book and does not pretend to understand everything about every character.

To maintain interest and/or to create a different reading experience, some authors switch a story's point of view among characters as they go through chapters or sections of the book. With this method, characters can take turns being read in first person or third-person limited, and the reader is eventually exposed to the thoughts and minds of more than one character.

Sample Test Questions and Rationale

(Easy)

1. The following passage is written from which point of view?

   As she mused, the pitiful vision of her mother's life laid its spell on the very quick of her being—that life of commonplace sacrifices closing in final craziness. She trembled as she heard again her mother's voice saying constantly with foolish insistence: **Dearevaun Seraun! Dearevaun Seraun!***

   * "The end of pleasure is pain!" (Gaelic)

   A. First-person narrator

   B. Second-person direct address

   C. Third-person omniscient

   D. First-person omniscient

   The answer is C.

   The passage is clearly in the third person (the subject is "she"), and it is omniscient since it gives the characters' inner thoughts.

(Rigorous)

2. For students to prepare for a their roles in a dramatic performance:

   A. They should analyze their characters to develop a deeper understanding of the character's attitudes and motivations

   B. They should attend local plays to study settings and stage design

   C. They should read articles and books on acting methodology

   D. They should practice the way other actors have performed in these roles

   The answer is A.

   By examining how their characters feel and think, students will understand the characters' attitudes and motivation.

SKILL
12.4 **Recognizing effective use of details and concrete language**

Details play an important role in any narrative piece. Without details, readers would likely find a story confusing, hard to follow, tedious, and flat. Keeping in mind that the purpose of most narrative pieces is to entertain, the writer uses details to keep the reader interested in the story.

Attention to details and use of concrete language that connect the reader to the world of the story are the foundation of excellent writing. Details can take the form of facts (especially for historical fiction), imagery, conversations, basic descriptions, and more. Effective use of details means the author includes the particulars that matter so that the actions, characters and plot of the story seem concrete to the reader. In addition, effective details have been used appropriately, not just for the sake of throwing in information.

Below are two strategies to help students develop detail in their stories:

- **Peer questioning:** Have students sit with a partner and review each other's stories. Have the students ask questions such as "What color was his hat? How did Jake feel after having that dream? Why was Mary so excited about that car ride?" The answers to these questions will add details that describe, inform, and enhance the depth of the story.

- **Observe and record:** Watching the world around them will help students notice the sounds, character traits, physical traits, smells, scenes, and conflicts of life around them they may not notice otherwise. Have students maintain a notebook or folder of observations, for possible use in a story later.

When the writer chooses to use details effectively, those details give the story its life and are the key to connecting the reader to the story.

Sample Test Question and Rationale

(Average)

1. **Which of the following is the least effective procedure for promoting consciousness of audience?**

   A. Pairing students during the writing process

   B. Reading all rough drafts before the students write the final copies

   C. Having students compose stories or articles for publication in school literary magazines or newspapers

   D. Having students write letters to friends or relatives

The answer is B.

Reading all rough drafts will not encourage students to take control of their text and might even inhibit their creativity. On the contrary, pairing students will foster their sense of responsibility, and having them compose stories for literary magazines will boost their self-esteem as well as their organization skills.

> **SKILL 12.5** **Analyzing how audience, purpose, and context affect narrative writing**

When writing a narrative piece, the writer must consider the audience, the purpose, and the context.

Audience

Audience is a key consideration for any writer. The writer must be aware of the intended audience of a narrative piece before beginning, since knowledge of audience will affect the piece's tone, vocabulary and other choice of words, level of formality, subject, and sentence structure. For example, a story written to entertain sixth graders will be quite different from a historical fiction piece for high school seniors.

Since a writer must anticipate the readers' questions or needs, the author must be knowledgeable of his or her audience in order to anticipate these needs and to see the story through the readers' eyes. This task is challenging, as the author has to balance what the readers expect and need while also fulfilling the piece's purpose.

Learn more about audience analysis:

http://www.ljlseminars.com/audience.htm

Purpose

When we attempt to communicate, we are usually prompted by a purpose for our communication. We may want to:

- Express feelings
- Persuade
- Explore an idea
- Argue
- Entertain
- Explain
- Inform

For most narrative writing, the purpose is to explain or entertain. When beginning a narrative piece or brainstorming session, a writer should always ask, "Why am I writing?" For many students, the answer to this appears to be, "I have an assignment due" or "To get a good grade." An effective teacher, however, will move students past this response and help them realize that being cognizant of a piece's purpose helps focus the writing so that the main theme, point, idea, or reason is clearly communicated to the reader.

Context

A writer must be aware of a narrative piece's context as well. Context also provides an outline to the expectations of a narrative piece. Selection of the form of writing (a report, essay, memoir, or story) helps the writer achieve the purpose by determining the style, organization, and tone that is associated with the selected context.

> **SKILL 12.6 Demonstrating knowledge of narrative techniques and tools used to tell stories** *(e.g., transitions, flashbacks, suspense, dialogue, mood, foreshadowing, in medias res)*

Authors have many techniques for creating effective narrative plots, settings and characters. Teachers should expose students to a variety of these techniques within the writing process as formal or mini-lessons so that students can begin to practice and use these methods in their written work.

Transitions

Technical transitions are important elements that add to a piece of the writing's flow. However, these transitions aid more in the flow of sentences and paragraphs than in the flow of the entire narrative.

The following are examples of transitions:

"another reason"	*"in addition"*	*"first of all"*	*"besides that"*
"furthermore"	*"also"*	*"moreover"*	*"for example"*

Beside these words and phrases, transitions can be sentences or paragraphs that act as two-way indicators. They show the relationship of ideas to each other and move the reader from one point to another. Narrative transitions are transitions that provide logical and smooth connections between events in the story. These transitions are often used between chapters, sections of chapters, and as the character moves through various settings. Effective transitions are essential to keeping the flow of the story straightforward so that the reader can follow the story easily.

Flashbacks

Another device authors can use to add depth to their plots is the flashback. Flashbacks provide information about the past during the course of the current action of a story. Flashbacks can provide the reader with background information, but writers need to be sure to "lead" the reader with an effective transition. An example of a simple transition is: "Heather recalled that morning at work." After a flashback, the author must link the reader back to the current action so that it can be continued.

Suspense

Suspense is the feeling of uncertainty or that something is about to happen. Authors use suspense to maintain readers' interest, and they do so by using descriptive language, foreshadowing, and other techniques to keep the reader reading. The use of suspense/tension adds another level to the plot and compels the reader to see what the outcome will be. Suspense is an effective technique to use in thrillers, mysteries, and other dramatic narrative pieces.

Dialogue

Dialogue is an important aspect of most narrative pieces. Without conversations, readers can easily become bored with a story. Narration can become long, tedious, and uninteresting without dialogue.

When used properly, dialogue can accomplish any or all of the following:

- Keep the story moving

- Display characters' thoughts and personalities

- Create a "hook" for the opening of the story

- Condense or replace large amounts of background

- "Show, Don't Tell"

- Add humor

Some elements to remember when writing dialogue are:

- Dialogue should read like natural speech: For example, an elderly doctor would not use the term "awesome," just as an average tenth grader is unlikely to use the word "succinctly."

- Use dialogue that serves a purpose: Dialogue should move the story while making the characters seem real. If the dialogue doesn't accomplish this, take it out and use narration instead.

- Keep dialogue short: Generally, three or fewer sentences is adequate for one character to say at a time. You don't have to say everything at once; readers will recall the details.

- **Mix dialogue and action:** Physical details help to break up dialogue while keeping the story going. For example, "I can't believe it!" exclaimed Beth. She crumpled her test paper between her fists until it resembled a snowball. "I studied for three hours for that test!"

- **Vary taglines:** But don't overdo it! Writers do not need to consult a thesaurus for every version of "said," but they should be encouraged to select a tagline that adds to the purpose of the conversation.

- **Avoid stereotypes, profanity, and slang:** Seek to be objective rather than shocking or too cool.

- **Punctuate dialogue correctly:** Without correct punctuation, meaning could be misconstrued.

Some stories by Ernest Hemingway rest completely on dialogue. In "A Clean Well-Lighted Place," the taglines are not always clear, and the punctuation can be confusing. Understanding the meaning can be challenging.

Mood

The mood of a narrative is an important element in keeping the structure and purpose of a piece held together without being blatantly obvious. When writing a narrative, authors automatically develop a mood with their choices of words, plot, characters, and more. Moods can include the satirical, determined, hopeful, confused, reflective, remorseful, light, or serious. However, mood is also the essence of what the reader takes away from the piece.

Foreshadowing

Foreshadowing is a literary device authors employ to provide hints for events to come in the plot (and therefore maintain reader interest and add dimension to the narrative piece). Foreshadowing aids the author in creating suspense/tension, providing necessary information (for a future event), and more. Foreshadowing can appear anywhere in a story, but it is exceptionally useful at the end of chapters or sections, acting as a cliffhanger to keep the reader engaged. When reading novels with their classes, teachers should help students recognize foreshadowing so they may later use the same device in their own writing.

In Medias Res

Latin for "into the middle of things," *in medias res* is a literary technique authors use when they want to start the action in the middle of the story rather than at the beginning. Authors then use flashbacks and dialogue to introduce the characters, setting, and conflict to the reader.

Sample Test Question and Rationale

(Average)

1. The new teaching intern is developing a unit on creative writing and is trying to encourage her freshman high school students to write poetry. Which of the following would not be an effective technique?

    A. In groups, students draw pictures to illustrate "The Love Song of J. Alfred Prufrock" by T.S. Eliot

    B. Either individually or in groups, students compose a song, writing lyrics that try to use poetic devices

    C. Students bring to class the lyrics of a popular song and discuss the imagery and figurative language

    D. Students read aloud their favorite poems and share their opinions of and responses to the poems

The answer is A.

Although drawing is creative, it will not accomplish as much as the other activities to encourage students to write their own poetry. Furthermore, "The Love Song of J. Alfred Prufrock" is not a freshman-level poem. The other activities involve students in music and their own favorites, which will be more appealing

COMPETENCY 13

UNDERSTAND TECHNIQUES FOR DEVELOPING ORGANIZED, FOCUSED EXPOSITORY OR TECHNICAL WRITING

> ### SKILL 13.1 Selecting an organizational pattern appropriate for providing information

The first decision a writer makes is the purpose for a particular writing project. If the purpose is expository—providing information about a particular topic—then the next question regards how to organize the information to communicate what the writer has in mind. Students need a tool kit for developing expository essays; the following tools should be in that kit.

Citing Particulars, Instances, Examples, and Illustrations

Citing examples is probably the easiest and often the best way to clarify a general statement. For example, if the point of an expository essay is, "The houses in our block represent the worst characteristics of modern tract-house architecture," then citing examples and explaining in the negative aspects of tract- house architecture by referring to particular houses is the most obvious way to develop it. This is an important form of development for students to master; it will be useful for many writing situations, including writing essay answers on exams.

Incident and Extended Illustration

Instead of providing a series of instances, the writer might make a point by telling a story or describing a single illustration in some detail. If the point of the essay is that "running for the U.S. presidency today requires extraordinary fundraising skills," the development might include an extended account of George W. Bush or Bill Clinton, with a focus on how they raised the funds to finance their campaigns. This extended illustration will require some research, of course. However, students might also choose a topic with which they are familiar and develop it by using an incident or extended illustration from their own experience.

Check here for eleven graphic organizers to teach cause and effect:

http://www.greece.k12. ny.us/instruction/ela/6-12/ Tools/cause%20and%20 effect.pdf

Cause and Effect

We use cause-and-effect reasoning regularly in our daily lives and conversations. The statement, "The beekeeping business is declining in America because the use of insecticides is killing off the bees," can be developed by exploring the causes of the excessive use of insecticides and the ways in which they are killing off bees. Students need help learning to use cause-and-effect reasoning because of the tendency to fall into the post-hoc-ergo-propter-hoc fallacy. Just because one event occurred after another does not necessarily mean that one caused the other. The connection between the two events must be established before the reasoning can be considered valid.

Analogy

Helping students develop skills to make comparisons between the unknown and the familiar will be useful in all their writing exercises. Analogy is the most common tool for this skill. In analogy, the writer draws a parallel between the point being made and an illustration that is familiar. Victor Hugo described the Battle of Waterloo as a giant letter A. Aldous Huxley said that life is like a game of chess. The similarities must be clear, or the analogy will not work.

Comparison and Contrast

Comparison-and-contrast technique is similar to analogy, but in this case, the two examples are compared example by example. A proposition like "Boston is not a small New York" calls for side-by-side comparisons of the two cities showing ways in which they are alike and ways in which they are not. Students might compare their grade school experiences with their high school experiences, or where they live now with where they lived previously.

Restatement and Amplification

Sometimes an extended restatement of the topic with amplifications makes the point clear.

Sample Test Questions and Rationale

(Easy)

1. Which of the following is most true of expository writing?

   A. It is mutually exclusive of other forms of discourse

   B. It can incorporate other forms of discourse in the process of providing supporting details

   C. It should never employ informal expression

   D. It should only be scored with a summative evaluation

   The answer is B.

   Expository writing sets forth an explanation or an argument about any subject.

(Average)

2. Explanatory or informative discourse is

   A. Exposition

   B. Narration

   C. Persuasion

   D. Description

   The answer is A.

   Exposition sets forth a systematic explanation of any subject. It can also introduce the characters of a literary work and their situations in the story.

(Rigorous)

3. Which of the following is an example of the post hoc fallacy?

   A. When the new principal was hired, student-reading scores improved; therefore, the principal caused the increase in scores.

   B. Why are we spending money on the space program when our students don't have current textbooks?

   C. You can't give your class a 10-minute break. Once you do that, we'll all have to give our students a 10-minute break.

   D. You can never believe anything he says because he's not from the same country as we are.

   The correct answer is A.

   A *post hoc* fallacy assumes that because one event preceded another, the first event caused the second event. In this case, student scores could have increased for other reasons. Answer B is a red herring fallacy, in which one raises an irrelevant topic to side track from the first topic. In this case, the space budget and the textbook budget have little effect on each other. Response C is an example of a slippery slope, in which one event is followed precipitously by another event. Response D is an ad hominem ("to the man") fallacy, in which a person is attacked rather than the concept or interpretation he or she puts forth.

SKILL 13.2 **Demonstrating knowledge of techniques for developing and sustaining a controlling idea that conveys a perspective on a subject**

The formal outline has lost favor in recent years as a way of controlling thesis statement development, but helping students develop a working sentence outline will improve their ability to write coherently. If the essay conveys a particular perspective on a subject, the form will be persuasive discourse.

The thesis will be arguable and will have two possible sides. Take the example "The best way to control illegal immigration is to build a fence." This is only one perspective on the immigration issue. Another perspective might be "The best way to control illegal immigration is to penalize companies that hire illegal immigrants." In either case, the supporting arguments should be determined ahead of time. A useful tool for students when developing this kind of essay is to ask the questions "Why?" and "How?" of the topic sentence, then use the answers as topic sentences in the development of the essay. This technique will keep the argument's development on track.

For example, if you ask why "the best way to control illegal immigration is to build a fence along the border," you have several possible answers: (1) "An adequate physical barrier will prevent the individuals and groups who are now crossing over from coming into the United States." (2) "Border guards are not sufficient to stop individuals and groups." (3) "Penalizing companies that hire illegal workers is too difficult and doesn't work." If you ask "how," then you can answer, "Instead of spending the money on more border guards, that money can be used to pay for the fence."

It's best to develop at least three points. This will not produce a formal outline, but it will provide a working outline that can be changed as each section of the essay is developed.

SKILL Identifying extraneous details and inappropriate information
13.3

You should continually assess whether sentences contribute to the overall task of supporting the main idea. When a sentence is deemed irrelevant, either omit it from the passage or make it relevant by using one of the following strategies:

- **Adding detail:** Sometimes a sentence can seem out of place if it does not contain enough information to link it to the topic. Adding specific information can show how the sentence is related to the main idea.

- **Adding an example:** This strategy is especially important in passages in which information is being argued or compared and contrasted. Examples can support the main idea and give the document overall credibility.

- **Using diction effectively:** It is important to understand connotation, avoid ambiguity, and steer clear of too much repetition when selecting words.

- Adding transitions: Transitions are extremely helpful for making sentences relevant because they are specifically designed to connect one idea to another. They can also reduce a paragraph's choppiness.

The following passage contains several irrelevant sentences that are highlighted in bold.

> The New City Planning Committee is proposing a new capitol building to represent the multicultural face of New City. **The current mayor is a Democrat.** The new capitol building will be on 10th Street across from the grocery store and next to the recreational Center. It will be within walking distance to the subway and bus depot, as the designers want to emphasize the importance of public transportation. Aesthetically, the building will have a contemporary design featuring a brushed-steel exterior and large, floor-to-ceiling windows. **It is important for employees to have a connection with the outside world even when they are in their offices.** Inside the building, the walls will be moveable. This will not only facilitate a multitude of creative floor plans, but it will also create a focus on open communication and flow of information. **It sounds a bit gimmicky to me.** Finally, the capitol will feature a large outdoor courtyard full of lush greenery and serene fountains. **Work will now seem like Club Med to those who work at the New City capitol!**

Sample Test Question and Rationale

(Easy)

1. In the paragraph below, which sentence does not contribute to the overall task of supporting the main idea?

   (1) The Springfield City Council met Friday to discuss new zoning restrictions for the land to be developed south of the city. (2) Residents who opposed the new restrictions were granted 15 minutes to present their case. (3) Their argument focused on the dangers that increased traffic would bring to the area. (4) It seemed to me that the Mayor Simpson listened intently. (5) The council agreed to table the new zoning until studies would be performed.

   A. Sentence 2

   B. Sentence 3

   C. Sentence 4

   D. Sentence 5

The answer is C.

The other sentences provide detail to the main idea of the new zoning restrictions. Because sentence 4 provides no example or relevant detail, it should be omitted.

SKILL 13.4 Recognizing effective uses of transitions

Even if the sentences that make up a given paragraph or passage are arranged in logical order, the document as a whole can still seem choppy or disconnected. **TRANSITIONS**, words that signal relationships between ideas, can help improve the flow of a document.

> **TRANSITIONS:** words that signal relationships between ideas

Transitions achieve clear and effective presentation of information by establishing connections between sentences, paragraphs, and sections of a document. With transitions, each sentence builds on the ideas in the previous sentence, and each paragraph has clear links to the preceding one. As a result, the reader receives clear directions on how to piece together the writer's ideas in a logically coherent argument. By signaling how to organize, interpret, and react to information, transitions allow a writer to explain his or her ideas effectively and elegantly.

The effective use of transitional devices at all levels is a mark of maturity in writing. For example, a topic sentence can be used to establish continuity, especially if it is positioned at the beginning of a paragraph. The most common use of an effective transition would be to refer to what has preceded, repeat preceding information, or summarize it and then introduce a new topic.

An essay by W. H. Hudson uses this device: "Although the potato was very much to me in those early years, it grew to be more when I heard its history." It summarizes what has preceded, makes a comment on the author's interest, and introduces a new topic: the history of the potato.

Another example of a transitional sentence could be: "Not all matters end so happily." This sentence refers to the previous information and prepares the reader for the next paragraph, which will be about matters that do not end happily. This transitional sentence is a little more forthright: "The increase in drug use in our community leads us to another general question."

An entire paragraph may be transitional in purpose and form. In "Darwiniana," Thomas Huxley uses a transitional paragraph:

> So much, then, by way of proof that the method of establishing laws in science is exactly the same as that pursued in common life. Let us now turn to another matter (though really it is but another phase of the same question), and that is, the method by which, from the relations of certain phenomena, we prove that some stand in the position of causes toward the others.

COMMON TRANSITIONS	
LOGICAL RELATIONSHIP	**TRANSITIONAL EXPRESSION**
Similarity	also, in the same way, just as . . . so too, likewise, similarly
Exception/Contrast	but, however, in spite of, on the one hand . . . on the other hand, nevertheless, nonetheless, notwithstanding, in contrast, on the contrary, still, yet, although
Sequence/Order	first, second, third, next, then, finally, until
Time	after, afterward, at last, before, currently, during, earlier, immediately, later, meanwhile, now, presently, recently, simultaneously, since, subsequently, then
Example	for example, for instance, namely, specifically, to illustrate
Emphasis	even, indeed, in fact, of course, truly
Place/Position	above, adjacent, below, beyond, here, in front, in back, nearby, there
Cause and Effect	accordingly, consequently, hence, so, therefore, thus, as a result, because, consequently, hence, if...then, in short
Additional Support or Evidence	additionally, again, also, and, as well, besides, equally important, further, furthermore, in addition, moreover, then
Conclusion/Summary	finally, in a word, in brief, in conclusion, in the end, in the final analysis, on the whole, thus, to conclude, to summarize, in sum, in summary
Statement support	most important, more significant, primarily, most essential
Addition	again, also, and, besides, equally important, finally, furthermore, in addition, last, likewise, moreover, too
Clarification	actually, clearly, evidently, in fact, in other words, obviously, of course, indeed

The following example shows good logical order and transitions:

> *No one really knows how Valentine's Day started. There are several legends, however, which are often told. The first attributes Valentine's Day to a Christian priest who lived in Rome during the third century, under the rule of Emperor Claudius. Rome was at war, and apparently Claudius felt that married men didn't fight as well as bachelors. Consequently, Claudius banned marriage for the duration of the war. But Valentinus, the priest, risked his life to secretly marry couples in violation of Claudius' law. The second legend is even more romantic. In this story, Valentinus is a prisoner, having been condemned to death for refusing to worship pagan deities. While in jail, he fell in love with his jailer's daughter, who happened to be blind. Daily he prayed for her sight to return, and miraculously it did. On February 14, the day that he was condemned to die, he was allowed to write the young woman a note. In this farewell letter he promised eternal love and signed at the bottom of the page the now famous words, "Your Valentine."*

Sample Test Question and Rationale

(Average)

1. **Which transition word would show contrast between these two ideas?**

   We are confident in our skills to teach English. We welcome new ideas on this subject.

   A. We are confident in our skills to teach English, and we welcome new ideas on this subject.

   B. Because we are confident in our skills to teach English, we welcome new ideas on the subject.

   C. When we are confident in our skills to teach English, we welcome new ideas on the subject.

   D. We are confident in our skills to teach English; however, we welcome new ideas on the subject.

The answer is D.

Transitional words, phrases and sentences help clarify meanings. In Answer A, the transition word and introduces another equal idea. In Answer B, the transition word because indicates cause and effect. In Answer C, the transition word when indicates order or chronology. In Answer D, however shows that these two ideas contrast with each other.

SKILL 13.5 Applying knowledge of effective expository techniques and tools

News reporters generally become excellent writers because they practice frequently, which is a principle most writing teachers try to employ with their students. Also, news writing can teach skills for writing clearly and coherently. Reporters generally write in two modes: straight reporting and feature writing. In both modes, they must be concerned with accuracy and objectivity. Reporters do not write their opinions or persuasive discourse. The topic is typically assigned, although some experienced reporters have the opportunity to develop their own stories.

Investigative reporting is sometimes seen as a distinct genre, although technically all reporters are "investigative." They research the background of the story they're reporting, using as many means as are available.

For example, the wife of a conservative, model minister murders her husband with premeditation and in cold blood. The reporter reports the murder and the arrest of the wife, but the story is far from complete until some questions are answered, the most obvious one being "Why?" The reporter is obligated to try to answer that question and will interview as many people as will talk about the lives of the minister and his wife, their parents, the members of the church, their neighbors, and others. The reporter will also look at newspaper archives in the town where the murder took place as well as at newspapers in any town the husband and/or wife have lived in previously. High school yearbooks are sources that are often explored in these cases.

When the *Washington Post* reporters Bob Woodward and Carl Bernstein broke the Watergate story in 1972 and 1973, they set new standards for investigative reporting and had a strong influence on journalistic writing. Most reporters wanted to be Woodward and Bernstein and became more aggressive than reporters had been in the past. Even so, the basic techniques and principles of reporting still applied. The reporting of these two talented journalists demonstrated that while newspapers keep communities aware of what's going on, they also have the power to influence the news.

A good news story is written as an "inverted pyramid," using deductive reasoning. The thesis or point of the story is stated first and is supported with details. The story reasons from general to specific. The lead sentence might be: "The body of John Smith was found in the street in front of his home with a bullet wound through his skull." The headline will be a trimmed-down version of that sentence and shaped to grab attention. It might read: "Murdered man found on Spruce Street."

The news article might fill several columns: the first part detailing the finding of the body; the next examining the role of the police; the third broadening to include details about the victim's life, then the story highlight providing details about his family, friends, and neighbors. If John Smith held a position of prominence in the community, those details would broaden further and include information about his relationships to fellow workers and his day-to-day contacts in the community.

The successful reporter's skills include the ability to conduct thorough research, maintain an objective stance (not to become involved personally in the story), and write an effective "inverted pyramid."

Feature writing is more like an informative essay, although it may also follow the inverted pyramid model. This form of reporting focuses on a topic designed to be interesting to at least one segment of the readership—possibly sports enthusiasts, travelers, vacationers, families, women, food lovers, and so on. The article would focus on one aspect of the area of interest, such as a particular experience for the vacationing family. The first sentence might read something like this: "Lake Lure offers a close-to-home relaxing weekend getaway for families in East Tennessee." The story development might include an ever-widening pyramid of details focused particularly on what the family can experience at Lake Lure. Directions to get there might be included, too.

Although the headline should encapsulate the point that an article makes, the reporter rarely writes it. This phenomenon can sometimes result in a disconnection between headline and article. Well-written headlines provide a guide for the reader; they are also attention grabbers. Effective headlines require a special kind of writing, quite different from the inverted pyramid used by the investigative or feature reporter.

SKILL 13.6 **Demonstrating knowledge of rhetorical devices used to reinforce information and sustain interest** *(e.g., parallelism, analogy, humor, repetition, illustrations, varied language)*

PARALLELISM: a literary device that gives two or more parts of a sentence a similar form

Writers and speakers use important rhetorical techniques to clarify their main ideas and to keep their audiences involved.

Parallelism

PARALLELISM gives two or more parts of a sentence a similar form so as to give the whole a definite pattern. Coordinated ideas are arranged in phrases, sentences, and paragraphs that balance one element with another of equal

Learn more about parallel structure vs. faulty parallelism:

http://jerz.setonhill.edu/ writing/grammar/parallel. html

importance and similar wording. The repetition of sounds, meanings, and structures serves to order, emphasize, and highlight relationships. In its simplest form, parallelism consists of single words that have a slight variation in meaning: "ordain and establish" or "overtake and surpass." Sometimes three or more units are parallel, such as "Reading maketh a full man, conference a ready man, and writing an exact man" (Francis Bacon, "Of Studies").

Lacking parallelism:
She likes cooking, jogging, and to **read.**

Parallel:
She likes cooking, jogging, and **reading**.

Lacking parallelism:
The dog ran across the yard, jumped over the fence, and **down the alley he sprinted**.

Parallel:
The dog ran across the yard, jumped over the fence, and **sprinted down the alley**.

Analogy

ANALOGY: a literary device used to clarify an unfamiliar point by referring to the familiar

ANALOGIES are used to clarify an unfamiliar point by referring to the familiar. When employing the method of analogy, it should always be possible to show that the resemblances noted are relevant on the point to be established, whereas the differences are irrelevant. In many cases, it is difficult to be sure of this distinction; arguments from analogy are therefore precarious unless supported by independently establishable considerations.

Writing a book of poetry is like dropping a rose petal down the Grand Canyon and waiting for the echo. (Don Marquis)

Humor

HUMOR: a literary device used to evoke feelings of amusement in others

HUMOR is the ability or quality of people, objects, or situations to evoke feelings of amusement in others. The term encompasses a form of entertainment or human communication that evokes such feelings, or which makes people laugh or feel happy. As such, humor applies to writing that makes people laugh or that amuses them. Many famous writers, such as Mark Twain, have been defined by their use of humor. Writing comedy for the stage or television has developed as an entirely new subcategory for writers.

Humor may be achieved through the use of exaggeration, understatement, irony, words that sound funny, jokes, stereotyping, and word play, to name a few. Humor is difficult to write successfully. More often than not, student attempts fall flat because it is a writing form that simply requires more maturity than most students have achieved. Student attempts to be funny should be dealt with gently.

Even if the attempt may be ridiculous or even ludicrous, approval on the part of the teacher might lead to improvement.

> Example of student humor:
> *What did the people say when they hung the vassal?*
> *Serf's up.*

Repetition

Studied repetition can be an effective rhetorical device if used skillfully. However, with students, repetition is often careless and leads to wordy and amateurish writing. Students should develop the ability to find synonyms for often-used terms in an essay that will not seem pretentious or obvious. Sometimes, a sentence needs to be rewritten to eliminate a careless repetition.

> Example
> *"Users of the library often use little care in handling books" can become "Users of the library are often careless in handling books."*

Illustrations

Carefully used illustrations can bring a dull piece of writing alive and make a cloudy point clear. It's wise to promote in students the tendency to illustrate. They will become better writers if they develop this tendency and skill.

Varied Language

There is always the tendency on the part of a reader, even a serious one who desires to glean the meaning of a particular written piece, to experience glazed-over eyes and drooping eyelids. There are many things a writer can do to avoid this reader reaction, and the most important one is to vary the language. There are many ways to do this.

Notice how the three sentences in the above paragraph begin with the same empty subject-verb construction (There is…There are…There are). Did your eyes glaze over? Did you have to reread the paragraph to understand it clearly? What exactly are "things" and "ways"?

The following are some proven techniques for varying your writing style:

- Avoid writing only long or only short paragraphs

- Write a variety of sentence patterns

    - Avoid writing only simple sentences, even if they are embellished with phrases and modifiers

- Avoid writing only one form of a complex sentence

- Having the adverbial clause appear at the beginning of a sentence frequently can become boring

- Move the adverbial clause to the middle of the sentence sometimes and to the end sometimes

- Avoid writing only compound sentences or only compound sentences in one form

- Using "therefore" over and over becomes monotonous

• Paragraphs should be written in a variety of forms—topic sentence first, in the middle, or at the end, for instance

Sample Test Question and Rationale

(Rigorous)

1. What syntactic device is most evident from Abraham Lincoln's "Gettysburg Address"?

It is rather for us to be here dedicated to the great task remaining before us—that from these honored dead we take increased devotion to that cause for which they gave the last full measure of devotion—that we here highly resolve that these dead shall not have died in vain—that this nation, under God, shall have a new birth of freedom—and that government of the people, by the people, for the people, shall not perish from the earth.

A. Affective connotation

B. Informative denotations

C. Allusion

D. Parallelism

The answer is D.

Parallelism is the repetition of grammatical structure. In speeches such as this as well as in speeches of Martin Luther King, Jr., parallel structure creates a rhythm and balance of related ideas. Lincoln's repetition of clauses beginning with "that" ties four examples back to "the great task." Connotation is the emotional attachment of words; denotation is the literal meaning of words. Allusion is a reference to a historic event, person, or place.

COMPETENCY 14
UNDERSTAND TECHNIQUES FOR DEVELOPING ORGANIZED, FOCUSED PERSUASIVE WRITING

SKILL 14.1 Recognizing effective techniques for establishing a context for an issue or controversy

In classical rhetoric, the Greek term translated "introduction" means "a leading into." The Latin term means "beginning a web" by mounting a woof or laying a warp. The basic function of the introduction, then, is to fill in the background and lead the reader into the discourse. Introductions inform the readers of the purpose of the discourse and dispose them to being receptive to what is written.

One way to elicit reader interest is to show that the subject is important, curious, or interesting. An introduction may show that although the points may seem improbable, they are, in fact, true. Also, the introduction may show that the subject has been neglected, misunderstood, or misrepresented. It may explain an unusual mode of development or forestall some misconception of the purpose. The introduction may also rouse interest with an anecdotal lead-in.

An important function of the beginning section of a persuasive discourse is the statement of fact, where the essential facts of the piece are presented. This can be seen easily in a court trial where the accusing lawyer, usually the prosecutor, lays out the facts in the case. A good example of statement of fact can be seen in the trial *State of Tennessee v. John Thomas Scopes* in Rhea County, Tennessee:

> That John Thomas Scopes, heretofore on the 24th of April 1925, in the county aforesaid, then and there, unlawfully did willfully teach in the public schools of Rhea County, Tennessee, which said public schools are supported in part and in whole by the public school fund of the state, a certain theory and theories that deny the story of the divine creation of man as taught in the Bible, and did teach instead thereof that man has descended from a lower order of animals, he, the said John Thomas Scopes, being at the time, and prior thereto, a teacher in the public schools of Rhea County, Tennessee, aforesaid, against the peace and dignity of the State.

SKILL 14.2 Demonstrating knowledge of techniques for stating and developing a controlling idea or arguable thesis

You should differentiate between "subject" and "thesis" for your students. The subject is the topic of the discourse. For example, it is not enough to decide that "democracy" is the subject or topic one is going to write about. First, something must be predicated of the subject. The subject must be converted into a proposition. For example:

> *Democracy functions best when people are educated.*

Now we have a thesis. Many aspects of the subject "democracy" could be developed in an essay, and many have been, but the burden lies with the writer to decide which aspect to address in this particular piece. Once that aspect has been determined, the writer must develop a thesis sentence.

For students, a cardinal principle when writing a thesis statement is that it must be stated in a single declarative sentence. As soon as the student writer launches into the second sentence, he or she has wandered off into development and does not clarify the thesis statement. However, experienced writers can depart from this expected formula.

The importance of having a declarative thesis statement cannot be overstated. For example, a hortatory sentence like, "Let us fight to preserve the integrity of our democracy" or interrogatory sentences like, "Is democracy a feasible form of government?" leave the subject cloudy, uncertain, and tentative, and are very difficult to develop. Therefore, the thesis will be clearly and firmly stated if the predicate asserts or denies something about the subject: "The integrity of our democracy can be preserved only if we fight to maintain it"; or " "Democracy is (is not) a feasible form of government." Both of these statements lend themselves to clear supporting development.

The thesis statement forces the writers to determine at the outset what exactly they want to say about the chosen subject. It also lays the foundation for a unified, coherent discourse. The thesis statement often suggests some of the supporting statements that will occur in the body, too.

Prewriting facilitates a thesis statement. The writing teacher does well to require that students prewrite ideas about the subject before attempting to write a thesis statement. Prewriting should yield several possible thesis statements; these help students determine which one will be developed in this particular essay. Remember—the beginning of all good writing is a sharply defined thesis.

SKILL 14.3 Demonstrating knowledge of techniques for defending positions with evidence and support

Once you put forth a thesis, you can support it in various ways. The most obvious way to do so involves using reasons, which will answer the question "Why?" Another technique is to give examples. You can also give details.

The presentation made by a prosecutor in a court trial is a good example of an argument that uses all of these techniques. Let's look at two examples.

Example 1

The thesis of the prosecutor may be:

> John O'Hara stole construction materials from a house being built at 223 Hudson Ave. by the Jones Construction Company.

As a reason, he might cite the following: He is building his own home on Green Street and needs materials and tools. This statement will answer the question "Why?"

He might give examples: Twenty bags of concrete disappeared the night before Mr. O'Hara poured the basement for his house on Green Street. The electronic nail-setter disappeared from the building site on Hudson Ave. the day before Mr. O'Hara began to erect the frame of his house on Green Street.

He might fill in the details: Mr. O'Hara's truck was observed by a witness on Hudson Ave. in the vicinity of the Jones Construction Company site the night the concrete disappeared. A witness observed Mr. O'Hara's truck again on that street the night the nail-setter disappeared.

Example 2

Another example of a thesis in a trial might be:

> Adam Andrews murdered Joan Rogers in cold blood on the night of December 20.

Reason #1: She was about to reveal their affair to his wife.

Reason #2: Andrews's wife would inherit half of his sizeable estate in case of a divorce, since they signed no prenuptial agreement.

Read more about thesis statements:

http://www.unc.edu/depts/wcweb/handouts/thesis.html

Example #1: Rogers has demonstrated that he is capable of violence during an incident with a partner in his firm.

Example #2: Rogers has had previous affairs in which he was accused of violence.

Detail #1: Andrews' wife once called the police and signed a warrant.

Detail #2: A previous lover sought police protection from Andrews.

An opinion can be a thesis, but it requires support. Opinions can also use reasons, examples, and details.

> *Our borders must be protected.*

Reason #1: Terrorists can get into the country undetected.

Example #1: An Iranian national was able to cross the Mexican border and live in this country for years before being detected.

Detail: The Iranian national came through Central America to Mexico, then followed the route that Mexican illegal immigrants regularly take.

Example #2: A group of Middle Eastern terrorists was arrested in Oregon after they had crossed the Canadian border.

Detail: No screening took place at that border.

Reason #2: Illegal aliens are an enormous drain on resources such as health care.

Example: The states of California and Texas bear enormous burdens for health care and education for illegal immigrants.

Detail: Legal citizens are often denied care in those states because resources are stretched so thin.

SKILL 14.4 Recognizing effective techniques for expanding arguments with logic, credibility, and emotion

The three appeals are *rational, ethical* (defined as establishing credibility), and emotional, according to the original Greek rhetoricians; these appeals have stood the tests of time. Today, even with all the multimedia tools available, there are three possibilities for persuading another person to accept a position or to take some action. How do politicians persuade large groups of people to accept their points of view? How do they persuade those people to take action? They use these three means of persuasion.

Rational Appeal

Rational appeal involves logical reasoning. If an essay is going to change anyone's mind, it must make sense. Once the thesis is established, asking the questions "How?" or "Why?" leads to possible reasons the writer can use to persuade.

For example:

> Building a strong fence on the border will solve the immigration crisis.

Why? (1) "It will stop those border crossings that the scattered border patrol officers have not been able to stop up till now." (2) "It will give the border patrol officers the tool they need to stop those who try to cross the border illegally." How? "The cost of the fence can be covered by a decrease in the number of officers now guarding the border." Any thesis should have at least three supporting points.

> *Any thesis should have at least three supporting points.*

Ethical Appeal

The rhetoricians defined ethical appeal as establishing credibility. Some people will accept a speaker's point of view just because of who he or she is. A veteran border patrol officer has credibility regarding protection of the border because that officer knows more about the issues than others do. The governor of a border state usually has credibility, too. When Governor Schwarzenegger of California addresses border issues, people listen.

There are many ways to establish credibility. The background discussion that begins an essay or speech is a good place to demonstrate that the writer/speaker knows the issue well enough to take a position on it. The credentials of the writer/speaker may persuade the audience that this person is credible.

Emotional Appeal

Most people like to think that they make decisions on the basis of logic or reasoning, but the truth is that few change their minds or take action unless they have been moved emotionally. An argument that relies too heavily on emotion, though, will destroy credibility.

There are two major ways to create emotional appeal. The first way involves describing an experience in such way that the reader/listener can participate in the experience. An argument against returning illegal immigrants to Mexico often relies on heart-rending stories of families, especially children, who will suffer if they are sent back. Descriptive language is the tool to use to make an experience available through one of the senses, as in describing a scene of suffering children in such a way that the reader/listener can "see" the children in his or her mind's eye or "hear" them crying.

The second way to move a reader/listener emotionally is by using "charged" words—words that carry emotional overtones themselves such as "cruel" or "callous" or "unfeeling." Others are "murderers," "liars," and "prejudice."

Sample Test Question and Rationale

(Rigorous)

1. Identify the type of appeal used by Molly Ivins in this excerpt from her essay "Get a Knife, Get a Dog, But Get Rid of Guns."

   As a civil libertarian, I, of course, support the Second Amendment. And I believe it means exactly what it says: A well-regulated militia being necessary to the security of a free state, the right of the people to keep and bear arms shall not be infringed.

   A. Ethical

   B. Emotional

   C. Rational

   D. Literary

The answer is A.

An ethical appeal is using the credentials of a reliable and trustworthy authority. In this case, Ivins cites the Constitution.

SKILL 14.5 Applying knowledge of persuasive techniques and rhetorical devices used to develop and support arguments effectively

The two forms of reasoning used to support an argument are inductive and deductive. Inductive reasoning goes from the particular to the general. For example, I observe that all the green apples I have ever tasted are sour: (1) I have tasted some from my grandfather's orchard; (2) I have tasted the Granny Smiths that my mother buys in the grocery store and uses to make pies; (3) I tasted the green apples in my friend's kitchen. All are sour (conclusion). Then I can *generalize* that all green apples are sour. This is inductive reasoning, a prevalent aspect of the way we think and deal with each other and an essential aspect to persuasive discourse.

Deductive reasoning, on the other hand, reverses the order by going from general to particular. The generalization drawn in the previous illustration, "All green apples are sour," can be used to make a statement about a particular apple. A new variety of green apples has appeared in the grocery store. Arguing from the generalization that all green apples are sour, I may reject this new variety because I am sure that they are going to be sour. Deductive reasoning is based on the syllogism:

> *All green apples are sour.*
>
> *This apple is green.*
>
> *Therefore, this apple is sour.*

Learn more about deductive and inductive argument:

http://www.iep.utm.edu/d/ded-ind.htm

When a prosecutor presents a trial in a courtroom, he typically puts forth the statement of fact: On November 2 in an alley between Smith and Jones Street at the 400 block, Stacy Highsmith was brutally raped and murdered. The coroner has concluded that she was bludgeoned with a blunt instrument at or around midnight, and her body was found by a shopkeeper the next morning. (There may be other "knowns" presented in the statement of fact.)

Following the laying out of the facts of the case, the prosecutor will use inductive reasoning to accuse the person on trial for the crime. For example: (1) Terry Large, the accused, was seen in the neighborhood at 11:30 PM on November 2; (2) He was carrying a carpenter's toolkit, which was later recovered; (3) A hammer with evidence of blood on it was found in that toolkit; and (4) The blood was tested, and it matched the victim's DNA. Ultimately, the prosecutor will reach the generalization: Terry Large murdered Stacy Highsmith in the alley in the middle of the night on November 2.

Sample Test Question and Rationale

(Rigorous)

1. What type of reasoning does Henry David Thoreau use in the following excerpt from "Civil Disobedience"?

   Unjust laws exist; shall we be content to obey them, or shall we endeavor to amend them, and obey them until we have succeeded, or shall we transgress them at once? Men generally, under such a government as this, think that they ought to wait until they have persuaded the majority to alter them. They think that, if they should resist, the remedy would be worse than the evil. But it is the fault of the government itself that the remedy is worse than the evil. … Why does it always crucify Christ, excommunicate Copernicus and Luther, and pronounce Washington and Franklin rebels?

   A. Ethical reasoning

   B. Inductive reasoning

   C. Deductive reasoning

   D. Intellectual reasoning

The answer is C.

Deductive reasoning begins with a general statement that leads to the particulars. In this essay, Thoreau begins with the general question about what should be done about unjust laws. His argument leads to the government's role in suppressing dissent.

COMPETENCY 15

UNDERSTAND TECHNIQUES FOR DEVELOPING ORGANIZED, FOCUSED WRITING FOR THE ANALYSIS OF LITERARY AND INFORMATIONAL TEXTS

SKILL 15.1 Analyzing the structure, organization, themes, and ideas of a literary or informational work

Essential terminology and literary devices germane to literary analysis include alliteration, allusion, antithesis, aphorism, apostrophe, assonance, blank verse, caesura, conceit, connotation, consonance, couplet, denotation, diction, epiphany, exposition, figurative language, free verse, hyperbole, iambic pentameter, inversion, irony, kenning, metaphor, metaphysical poetry, metonymy, motif, onomatopoeia, ottavo rima, oxymoron, paradox, parallelism, personification, quatrain, scansion, simile, soliloquy, Spenserian stanza, sprung rhythm, stream of consciousness, synecdoche, terza rima, tone, and wit. Some of these devices are further defined below.

For more information, consult glossary of poetry terms:

http://www.infoplease.com/spot/pmglossary1.html

Share this Web site with your students— Newshour extra: poetry:

http://www.pbs.org/newshour/extra/poetry/#

LITERARY DEVICES	
Antithesis	Balanced writing about conflicting ideas, usually expressed in sentence form. Some examples are "expanding from the center," "shedding old habits," and "searching never finding."
Aphorism	A focused, succinct expression about life from a sagacious viewpoint. Writings by Ben Franklin, Sir Francis Bacon, and Alexander Pope contain many aphorisms. "Whatever is begun in anger ends in shame" is an aphorism.
Apostrophe	Literary device addressing an absent or dead person, an abstract idea, or an inanimate object. Sonneteers, such as Sir Thomas Wyatt, John Keats, and William Wordsworth, address the moon, stars, and the dead Milton. For example, in William Shakespeare's *Julius Caesar*, Mark Antony addresses the corpse of Caesar in the speech that begins: "O, pardon me, thou bleeding piece of earth / That I am meek and gentle with these butchers! / Thou art the ruins of the noblest man / That ever lived in the tide of times."

Table continued on next page

Blank Verse	Poetry written in unrhymed iambic pentameter. Works by Shakespeare and Milton are epitomes of blank verse. Milton's *Paradise Lost* states, "Illumine, what is low raise and support, / That to the highth of this great argument/ I may assert Eternal Providence / And justify the ways of God to men."
Caesura	A pause, usually signaled by punctuation, in a line of poetry. The earliest usage occurs in *Beowulf*, the first English epic dating from the Anglo-Saxon era. Pope uses a caesura in the line, "To err is human, // to forgive, divine."
Conceit	A comparison, usually in verse, between seemingly disparate objects or concepts. John Donne's metaphysical poetry contains many clever conceits. "The Flea" (1633), for example, compares a flea bite to the act of love.
Connotation	The ripple effect surrounding the implications and associations of a given word, distinct from the denotative or literal meaning. For example, the word "rest" in "Good night, sweet prince, and flights of angels sing thee to thy rest," refers to a burial.
Consonance	The repeated usage of similar consonant sounds, most often used in poetry. "Sally sat sifting seashells by the seashore" is a familiar example.
Couplet	Two rhyming lines of poetry. Shakespeare's sonnets end in heroic couplets, written in iambic pentameter. Pope is also a master of the couplet. His *The Rape of the Lock* is written entirely in heroic couplets.
Denotation	What a word literally means, as opposed to its connotative meaning.
Diction	The right word in the right place for the right purpose. The hallmark of a great writer is precise, unusual, and memorable diction.
Epiphany	The moment of realization and comprehension. James Joyce used this device in his short story collection *The Dubliners*.
Exposition	Background information about characters meant to clarify and add to the narrative; the initial plot element that precedes the buildup of conflict.
Figurative Language	Language that is not literal but is meant to be interpreted through symbolism. Figurative language is made up of such literary devices as hyperbole, metonymy, synecdoche, and oxymoron. A synecdoche is a figure of speech in which the word for part of something is used to mean the whole; for example, "sail" for "boat," or vice versa.
Free Verse	Poetry that does not have any predictable meter or rhyme. Margaret Atwood, e.e. cummings, and Ted Hughes write in this form.

Table continued on next page

Hyperbole	Exaggeration for a specific effect. For example, "I'm so hungry that I could eat a million of these."
Iambic Pentameter	The two elements in a set five-foot line of poetry. An iamb has two syllables, unaccented and accented, per foot or measure. Pentameter means that five feet appear in each line of poetry.
Inversion	An atypical sentence order to create a given effect or interest. Bacon and Milton's work use inversion successfully. Emily Dickinson also was fond of arranging words outside of their familiar order. In "Chartless," for example, she writes "Yet know I how the heather looks" and "Yet certain am I of the spot." Instead of saying "Yet I know" and "Yet I am certain," she reverses the usual order and shifts the emphasis to the more important words.
Irony	An unexpected disparity between what is written or stated and what is really meant or implied by the author. Verbal, dramatic and situational are the three literary ironies. Verbal irony occurs when an author says one thing and means something else. Dramatic irony occurs when an audience perceives something that a character in the literature does not know. Situational irony is a discrepancy between expected results and actual results. Shakespeare's plays contain numerous and highly effective uses of irony. O. Henry's short stories frequently have ironic endings.
Kenning	Another way to describe a person, place, or thing so as to avoid prosaic repetition. The earliest examples can be found in Anglo-Saxon literature such as *Beowulf* and "The Seafarer." Instead of writing King Hrothgar, the anonymous monk wrote "great Ring-Giver," or "Father of his people." A lake becomes the swans' way, and the ocean or sea becomes the great whale's way. In ancient Greek literature, this device was called an "epithet."
Metaphysical Poetry	Verse characterization by ingenious wit, unparalleled imagery, and clever conceits. The greatest metaphysical poet is John Donne. Henry Vaughn and other seventeenth-century British poets contributed to this movement as in Words: "I saw eternity the other night, like a great being of pure and endless light."
Metonymy	Use of an object or idea closely identified with another object or idea to represent the second. Washington, D.C. refers to the U.S. government, and the White House means the U.S. president.
Motif	A key, oft-repeated phrase, name, or idea in a literary work. Dorset/Wessex in Hardy's novels and the moors and the harsh weather in the Bronte sisters' novels are effective use of motifs. Shakespeare's *Romeo and Juliet* represents the ill-fated young lovers' motif.
Onomatopoeia	Word used to evoke the sound in its meaning. The early Batman series used "pow," "zap," "whop," "zonk," and "eek" in an onomatopoetic way.
Ottavo Rima	An eight-line stanza of poetry whose rhyme scheme is abababcc. Lord Byron's mock epic, Don Juan, is written in this form.
Oxymoron	A contradictory form of speech, such as jumbo shrimp, unkindly kind, or singer John Mellencamp's "It hurts so good."

Table continued on next page

Paradox	Seemingly untrue statement which, when examined more closely, proves to be true. John Donne's sonnet "Death Be Not Proud" postulates that death shall die and humans will triumph over death. At first thought not true, Donne's sonnet ultimately explains and proves this paradox.
Parallelism	A type of close repetition of clauses or phrases that emphasize key topics or ideas in writing. The psalms in the King James Version of the Bible contain many examples.
Personification	Giving human characteristics to inanimate objects or concepts. Great writers, with few exceptions, are masters of this literary device.
Quatrain	A poetic stanza composed of four lines. A Shakespearean or Elizabethan sonnet is made up of three quatrains and a heroic couplet.
Scansion	The analysis of a poetic line. Count the number of syllables per line and determine where the accents fall. Divide the line into metric feet. Name the meter by the type and number of feet. Much is written about scanning poetry. Try not to inundate your students with this jargon; rather allow them to feel the power of the poets' words, ideas, and images.
Soliloquy	A highlighted speech in drama, usually delivered by a major character and expounding on the author's philosophy or expressing universal truths. Soliloquies are delivered with the character alone on the stage, as in Hamlet's famous "To be or not to be" soliloquy.
Spenserian Stanza	Stanza invented by Sir Edmund Spenser for use in *The Faerie Queene*, his epic poem honoring Queen Elizabeth I. Each stanza consists of nine lines, eight of which are in iambic parameter. The ninth line, called an "alexandrine," has two extra syllables or one additional foot.
Sprung Rhythm	Invented and used extensively by the poet Gerard Manley Hopkins. Sprung rhythm consists of variable meter, which combines stressed and unstressed syllables fashioned by the author. See "Pied Beauty" or "God's Grandeur."
Stream of Consciousness	A style of writing which reflects the mental processes of the characters, and expressing, at times, jumbled memories, feelings, and dreams. James Joyce, Virginia Woolf, and William Faulkner use stream of consciousness in their writings.
Terza Rima	A series of poetic stanzas that use the recurrent rhyme scheme of aba, bcb, cdc, ded, and so forth. The second-generation Romantic poets—Keats, Byron, Shelley, and, to a lesser degree, Yeats—used this Italian verse form, especially in their odes. Dante used this stanza in The Divine Comedy.
Tone	The discernible attitude inherent in an author's work regarding the subject, readership, or characters. Swift or Pope's tone is satirical. Boswell's tone toward Johnson is admiring.
Wit	Writing of genius, keenness, and sagacity expressed through clever use of language. Alexander Pope and the Augustans wrote about and were said to possess wit.

Sample Test Questions and Rationale

(Average)

1. **Which of the following is a characteristic of blank verse?**

   A. Meter in iambic pentameter

   B. Clearly specified rhyme scheme

   C. Lack of figurative language

   D. Unspecified rhythm

   The answer is A.

   An iamb is a metrical unit of verse having one unstressed syllable followed by one stressed syllable. This is the most commonly used metrical verse in English and American poetry. An iambic pentameter is a ten-syllable verse made of five of these metrical units, either rhymed as in sonnets or unrhymed as in free or blank verse.

(Average)

2. **Which is an untrue statement about a theme in literature?**

   A. The theme is always stated directly somewhere in the text

   B. The theme is the central idea in a literary work

   C. All parts of the work (plot, setting, mood) should contribute to the theme in some way

   D. By analyzing the various elements of the work, the reader should be able to arrive at an indirectly stated theme

   The answer is A.

   The theme may be stated directly, but it can also be implicit in various aspects of the work, such as the interaction between characters, symbolism, or description.

(Average)

3. **In the following quotation, addressing the dead body of Caesar as though he were still a living being is to employ an:**

   O, pardon me, though
   Bleeding piece of earth
   That I am meek and gentle with
   These butchers.
   —Marc Antony, from *Julius Caesar*

   A. Apostrophe

   B. Allusion

   C. Antithesis

   D. Anachronism

   The answer is A.

   This rhetorical figure addresses personified things, absent people, or gods. An allusion, on the other hand, is a quick reference to a character or event known to the public. An antithesis is a contrast between two opposing viewpoints, ideas, or presentations of characters. An anachronism is the placing of an object or person out of its time with the time of the text. The best-known example is the clock in Shakespeare's *Julius Caesar*.

Sample Test Questions and Rationale (cont.)

(Rigorous)

4. In the sentence, "The Cabinet conferred with the president," "Cabinet" is an example of a/an:

   A. Metonym

   B. Synecdoche

   C. Metaphor

   D. Allusion

The answer is B.

In a synecdoche, a whole is referred to by naming a part of it. Also, a synecdoche can stand for a whole of which it is a part, as in this example.

SKILL 15.2 Evaluating a writer's use of stylistic devices and other elements of literary or informational writing

Style can be thought of as those characteristics of writing that reveal the voice or individuality of the writer. Voice is part of what might be called the rhetorical stance a writer assumes as he or she undertakes a creative project. Aspects of style seldom can be separated from one another. Sentence structure, paragraph patterns, and diction are all elements of style; style is the particular combination of choices among these elements made by a writer. The choices are governed especially by what has been called the writer's "stance," the position taken for a particular writing task. The writer moves out of himself or herself, communicating through a voice, adopting a tone and a point of view.

Vocabulary

The vocabulary peculiar to an author is often the writer's most identifiable characteristic. Mark Twain, who was a master at rendering colloquial speech, is a case in point. His early life on the Mississippi River furnished him with a unique vocabulary that distinguishes his writings from that of others. A writer's vocabulary usually reflects his or her experiences, particularly early ones. While an author may alter the vocabulary that has emerged from earlier experiences to achieve a particular purpose, traces can usually be identified by a careful observer.

Sentence Structure

Another characteristic of style that may distinguish a particular writer is the patterning of sentences. Ernest Hemingway is well known for the short, clipped speech of many of his characters. Meanwhile, William Faulkner's long sentences are a distinguishing feature of *his* style. If a writer typically writes in a particular sentence pattern, e.g., complex sentences that open with an adverbial clause, then his work will be recognizable for that characteristic.

Imagery

A writer's use of imagery also may be the author's most identifiable characteristic. Flannery O' Connor's writing is characterized by her images of the South, where she lived out her short life. She created characters that could have emerged from no other place on earth than the southern United States of America.

Symbolism

Another feature that often distinguishes a writer is the use of symbols. Defining symbolism as a literary device that allows for the broader applicability of prose to meanings beyond what may be literally described, many writers—in fact, most or all authors of fiction—make the symbolic use of concepts and objects central to the meaning of their works. Joseph Conrad and James Joyce, for example, use symbolism extensively to represent themes that applied to greater contexts in their contemporary politics and society.

Allusion

Writers of fiction rely very heavily on allusions to achieve overtones of meaning, to wring the most meaning possible out of as few words as possible. The most common kind of allusion is biblical. Because most Western writers have grown up in a milieu steeped in Christianity and because most writers know that they can count on readers to have a similar background, biblical allusions occur frequently in English and American literature.

The modern American author who usually comes to mind with regard to biblical allusion is William Faulkner. His novel *Absalom, Absalom* is a retelling of the story of King David and his son. Even so, the story has impact on the literal level without the strongly biblical tint of the story as told by Faulkner. Knowing the biblical story adds depth and understanding to Faulkner's novel.

Learn more about teaching imagery—from the brain to the paper:

http://students.ed.uiuc.edu/vallicel/Teaching_imagery.html

SKILL 15.3 Comparing the descriptions, motivations, and actions of characters in different literary texts or across literary and nonliterary contexts

Students should learn that characters in literature, fiction and nonfiction, reveal themselves in many ways. Authors populate their writing with a variety of personalities as a way to explore our relationships with the world.

Characterization

The choice the writer makes about the devices used to reveal character requires an understanding of human nature and the artistic skill to convey a personality to the reader. Characterization usually is accomplished subtly through dialogue, interior monologue, description, and the character's behavior. In some successful stories, the writer tells the reader directly what this character is like. However, sometimes there will be discrepancies between what the narrator tells the reader about the character and what is revealed through the character's actions. In this case, the narrator is unreliable, and that unreliability becomes an important and significant device for understanding the story.

Archetype

Read complete books and articles on archetypes in literature:

http://www.questia.com/
library/literature/literary-
themes-and-topics/
archetypes-in-literature.jsp

An archetype is an idealized model of a person, object, or concept from which similar instances are derived, copied, patterned, or emulated. In psychology, an archetype is a model of a person, personality, or behavior. Archetypes often appear in literature. An image, character, or pattern of circumstances that recurs frequently in literature can be considered an archetype William Shakespeare, for example, is known for popularizing many archetypal characters. Although he based many of his characters on existing archetypes from fables and myths, Shakespeare's characters stand out against a complex, social literary landscape.

For example, Iago in *Othello* is the villain who masterminds plots; Polonius in Hamlet is the trusted adviser and doting father; Romeo and Juliet are the archetypical star-crossed lovers.

In Greek drama, *Oedipus Rex* has a structure that appears to be repeated in the lives of all men in the sense that all sons are replacements for their fathers. Faulkner, in "Barn Burning," provides an original example that calls forth this archetype.

There are many archetypes, and skillful and creative writers often rely on them to create successful literary contexts.

Examples of action archetypes:

- The search for the killer
- The search for salvation (or the Holy Grail)
- The search for the hero
- The descent into hell

Examples of character archetypes:

- The double

- The scapegoat

- The prodigal son

- The Madonna and the Magdalene

The family has often been used as a recurring archetypal theme in literature, including Greek literature such as the *Medea*. Many of Shakespeare's plays also used this archetype: *Hamlet, Romeo and Juliet,* and *King Lear*, for example. Modern writers also use the family archetype, such as *Desire Under the Elms* by Eugene O'Neill and *A Streetcar Named Desire* by Tennessee Williams.

Toni Morrison, in her popular novel *Beloved*, uses the archetype of family by chronicling the difficulties the protagonist Sethe and her family face before , during, and after the Civil War. The result is a compelling picture of a family's response to the devastation brought on by slavery.

SKILL 15.4 Analyzing a writer's use of language to achieve a desired purpose

Just as you talk to different people in different ways, so do you write in different styles and levels of formality. Students should learn that writers use different writing styles to accomplish their purposes and to reach their different audiences.

Is a business letter outdated? Although much business-letter writing has been relegated to e-mail communications, letters are still a valuable form of communication. A carefully written letter can be powerful. It can convince, persuade, alienate, entice, motivate, and/or create good will.

As with any other communication, you need to know information about your receiver. If there will be more than one receiver of the message, write for the largest or most important group of readers without "writing down" to any of those who will read and be affected or influenced by the letter. Sending more than one form of the letter to the various receivers may be appropriate in some cases.

Purpose is the most powerful factor in writing a business letter. What is the letter expected to accomplish? Is it intended to motivate the receiver to act or to act in a specific manner? If so, you should clearly define the letter's purpose for yourself before beginning. To avoid procrastination, include a time deadline for the

Learn more about writing a cover letter:

http://www.womenwork.
org/career/careercenter/
Getting_Hired/coverletter.
htm

response.

Why should you choose a letter format as your channel of communication?

- It's easy to keep a record of the transaction.

- The message can be edited and perfected before it is transmitted.

- It facilitates the handling of details.

- It's ideal for communicating complex information.

- It's a good way to disseminate mass messages at a relatively low cost.

Because letters have external readers, they typically use formal language. They should be straightforward and courteous. The writing should be concise and complete; otherwise, more than one exchange of letters or phone calls to get the message across may be necessary.

A complaint is a different kind of business letter. Complaints can come under the classification of a "bad news" business letter, and guidelines are helpful when writing this kind of letter. A positive writing style can overcome much of the inherent negativity of a letter of complaint. No matter how right you may be, maintaining self-control and courtesy and avoiding demeaning or blaming language is more likely to be effective. Abruptness, condescension, or harshness of tone will not help achieve your purpose, particularly if you are requesting a positive response such as reimbursement for a bad product or some help in righting a wrong that may have been done to you. The goal is to solve the specific problem and to retain the good will of the receiver whenever possible.

Induction is better than deduction for this type of communication. Beginning with the details and building to the statement of the problem generally has the effect of softening the bad news. Beginning with an opening that will serve as a buffer can be useful. The same is true for the closing. Leave the reader with a favorable impression by writing a closing paragraph that will generate good will rather than bad.

E-mail has revolutionized business communications. It has most of the advantages of business letters and the added ones of immediacy, lower costs, and convenience. Even very long reports can be attached to an e-mail. At the same time, a two-line message can be sent and a response received immediately, bringing together the features of a postal system and the telephone.

E-mail has an unwritten code of behavior that includes restrictions on how informal the writing can be. The level of accepted business conversation is usually also acceptable in e-mails. Capital letters and bolding are considered shouting and are usually frowned on.

Remind students that e-mail messages, even if intended for just one reader, may eventually reach a much wider audience. In recent years, a number of e-mail writers have found themselves in embarrassing situations or legal troubles because of the circulation of their personal e-mails on the Internet. When writers need to address a sensitive, unpleasant or controversial matter, they should consult state laws to determine whether personal privacy laws protect the correspondence. If the law does protect such correspondence from being circulated by the addressee, then the writers may wish to mention this in their messages to forestall publication. Otherwise, clarity, concision, and civility in written works will protect writers.

Personal Letters

When writing personal notes or letters, the writer needs to keep the following key matters in mind:

- Once the topic is determined, the writer must determine the appropriate tone to introduce and express it. Is humor appropriate? Seriousness? Bluntness or subtlety? Does the situation call for formal or informal language? The answers to these questions will depend, in good part, on the writer's relationship to the reader. Plan appropriately for the situation and audience.

- Does the writer's introduction clearly explain the topic/situation to a reader who doesn't know or feel what the reader knows or feels? Don't assume that the writer and reader are of the same mindset. Use a checklist to make sure all key information is clearly and concisely expressed.

- If a note or letter involves a request, what type of response/result does the writer desire? Devise a strategy or strategies for achieving a desired outcome.

- If a note or letter involves a complaint about the reader, the writer needs to decide whether to ask for particular amends or to let the reader decide what, if anything, to do. If no amends are requested, the writer may wish to suggest ideas that would help avoid similar conflicts in the future. Asking the reader for his or her opinions is also a possibility.

- If a timely response to any note or letter is needed, the writer must mention this.

Provide students in-class opportunities to write a variety of personal notes and letters, whether involving real- life or hypothetical situations. Invitations, thank-you notes, complaints, requests for favors, or personal updates represent a few of the options available. Have students experiment with a variety of tones and strategies in a particular piece of personal correspondence. Structure in-class activities to allow for peer feedback.

Sample Test Questions and Rationale

(Easy)

1. In "inverted triangle" introductory paragraphs, the thesis sentence occurs:

   A. At the beginning of the paragraph

   B. In the middle of the paragraph

   C. At the end of the paragraph

   D. In the second paragraph

The answer is C.

The introduction to an essay should begin with a broad general statement, followed by one or more sentences adding interest and information to the topic. The thesis should be written at the end of the introduction.

(Average)

2. If a student uses slang and expletives, what is the best course of action to take to improve the student's formal communication skills?

   A. Ask the student to paraphrase his writing—that is, to translate it into language appropriate for the school principal to read

   B. Refuse to read the student's papers until he conforms to a more literate style

   C. Ask the student to read his work aloud to the class for peer evaluation.

   D. Rewrite the flagrant passages to show the student the right form of expression

The answer is A.

Asking the student to write for a specific audience will help him become more involved in his writing. If he continues writing to the same audience—the teacher—he will continue seeing writing as just another assignment and will not apply grammar, vocabulary, and syntax the way they should be. By rephrasing his own writing, the student will learn to write for a different public.

(Rigorous)

3. Which sentence below best minimizes the impact of bad news?

   A. We have denied you permission to attend the event

   B. Although permission to attend the event cannot be given, you are encouraged to buy the video

   C. Although you cannot attend the event, we encourage you to buy the video

   D. Although attending the event is not possible, watching the video is an option

The answer is B.

Subordinating the bad news and using passive voice minimizes the impact of the bad news. In Answer A, the sentence is in active voice and thus too direct. The word "denied" sets a negative tone. In Answer C, the bad news is subordinated, but it is still in active voice with negative wording. In Answer D, the sentence is too unclear.

SKILL **Comparing the genre-driven features of texts**
15.5

A **GENRE** is a division of a particular form of art according to criteria particular to that form. Genres are formed by sets of conventions, and many works cross into multiple genres by way of borrowing and recombining these conventions. All works are recognized as either reflecting on or participating in the conventions of a particular genre. The major literary genres include poetry, fiction, and drama. However, each of these major genres may be broken down into several subgenres.

> **GENRE:** a division of a particular form of art according to criteria particular to that form

Poetry

Early attempts to define poetry focused on the uses of speech in rhetoric, drama, song, and comedy. Later, the concentration shifted to features such as repetition and rhyme and emphasized the aesthetics that distinguish poetry from prose. Since the mid-twentieth century, poetry has come to be more loosely defined as a fundamental creative act using language. Clearly, poetry is not a simple phenomenon to define, especially given the existence of numerous examples of poetic prose and of prosaic poetry. Nowadays, saying what poetry is not seems easier than saying what it is.

Poetry often uses particular forms and conventions to expand the literal meaning of words or to evoke emotional or sensual responses. Literary devices such as assonance, alliteration, and rhythm are sometimes used to achieve musical or incantatory effects. Poetry's use of ambiguity, symbolism, irony, and other stylistic elements often leaves a poem open to multiple interpretations. Similarly, metaphor and simile create a resonance between otherwise disparate images—a layering of meanings, forming connections previously not perceived.

Fiction

R. F. Dietrich and Roger H. Sundell, in *The Art of Fiction*, write the following:

> *In its broadest sense, a fiction is any imaginative recreation or reconstruction of life. In this sense, not only are your daydreams fiction, but also the myths you daily create about yourself and others to help you explain life.*

However, the term *fiction* is generally synonymous with literature. Fiction refers only to novels or short stories and is often divided into two categories: popular fiction (e.g., science fiction or mystery fiction) and literary fiction (e.g., works by Marcel Proust or William Faulkner). Typically, a work of fiction has a plot that eventually yields a climax, characters that carry the conflicts that lead to climax or resolution, and a discernible theme.

Drama

Drama is a literary form involving parts written for actors to perform. The term comes from the Greek word meaning "action." Dramas can be performed in various media: live performance, radio, film, or television. Drama is also often combined with music and dance, such as in opera, which is sung throughout; musicals, which include spoken dialogue and songs; or plays that have musical accompaniment, such as the Japanese Noh drama.

DOMAIN V
ORAL AND VISUAL COMMUNICATIONS

PERSONALIZED STUDY PLAN

PAGE	COMPETENCY AND SKILL	KNOWN MATERIAL/ SKIP IT
267	**16: Understand principles and techniques for preparing and delivering oral and visual communication**	☐
	16.1: Analyzing elements of effective listening and speaking	☐
	16.2: Demonstrating knowledge of techniques for promoting an atmosphere of tolerance and support	☐
	16.3: Recognizing effective techniques for questioning, summarizing, paraphrasing, extending, redirecting ideas and comments, and achieving closure	☐
	16.4: Recognizing appropriate rhetorical strategies	☐
	16.5: Analyzing characteristics and effects of different presentation techniques	☐
	16.6: Recognizing principles of graphic communications, oral communications, and audiovisual communications	
280	**17: Understand techniques for the critical analysis of oral and visual messages delivered through various media**	☐
	17.1: Evaluating strategies used by the media	☐
	17.2: Analyzing media messages	☐
	17.3: Comparing messages across media	☐
	17.4: Analyzing the relationship between the media and the democratic process	☐
	17.5: Analyzing the relationship between the media and personal and societal values, opinions, and behaviors	☐
	17.6: Distinguishing techniques used by visual and oral media	☐
	17.7: Distinguishing between classical and contemporary logical arguments	☐

COMPETENCY 16

UNDERSTAND PRINCIPLES AND TECHNIQUES FOR PREPARING AND DELIVERING ORAL AND VISUAL COMMUNICATION

SKILL 16.1 Analyzing elements of effective listening and speaking in conversation and in small- and large-group situations

The art of debate, discussion, and conversation are different from the basic writing forms of discourse. The ability to use language and logic to convince an audience to accept your reasoning and to side with you truly is an art. This form of writing and speaking is extremely structured and logically sequenced with supporting reasons and evidence. At its best, it is the highest form of propaganda. A position statement, evidence, reason, evaluation, and refutation are integral parts of this writing schema.

Interviewing provides opportunities for students to apply expository and informative communication techniques. It teaches them how to structure questions to evoke fact-filled responses. Compiling the information from an interview into a biographical essay or speech helps students to list, sort, and arrange details in an orderly fashion.

Speeches that encourage students to describe persons, places, or events in their own lives or oral interpretations of literature help them sense the creativity and effort used by professional writers.

Learn more about oral communication skills:

http://www.glencoe. com/sec/teachingtoday/ weeklytips.phtml/88

Listening

Communication skills are crucial in a collaborative society. A person cannot be a successful communicator, though, without being an active listener.

Focus on what others say, rather than planning what to say next. By listening to everything another person says, you may pick up on natural cues that lead the conversation without so much added effort.

Facilitating

Using standard opening lines to facilitate a conversation is acceptable. Don't agonize over coming up with witty "one-liners," as the main obstacle in initiating conversation lies in making the first statement. After that, the real substance begins. A useful technique may be to make a comment or ask a question about a shared situation. Use an opener with which you are comfortable, because then your partner in conversation will be comfortable with it as well.

Stimulating Higher-Level Critical Thinking Through Inquiry

People often rely on questions to communicate with others. However, most people fall back on simple clarifying questions rather than open-ended inquiries. For example, if you paraphrase a response by asking, "Did you mean this…" you may receive merely a "yes" or "no" answer. In an open-ended inquiry, one would ask, "What did you mean when you said…?"

Try to ask open-ended, deeper-level questions, since those tend to have the greatest reward and lead to greater understanding. With answers to those questions, you can make more complex connections and achieve more significant information.

The successful conversationalist is a person who:

- Keeps up with and ponders the meanings of events and developments
- Reads about interesting topics, both in print and online
- Has probed certain topics in some depth
- Usually has a passionate interest in human behavior
- Is interested in and concerned about social issues, both in the immediate community and on a wider scale, and has ideas for solving some of those problems

With all of this information in mind, the most important habit you can develop as a good conversationalist is to *listen*, not just wait until the other person quits speaking so you can take the floor again. By actually listening to what the other person has to say, you can also learn more about that person. Following a gathering, you will be remembered as the person who was interested enough to listen and respond to others' ideas and opinions. You will be the person who will be remembered with the most regard.

Although you can be passionate about your convictions in polite conversation, you should not be overbearing or unwilling to consider another's point of view. Keeping your emotions under control in these circumstances is important, even if the other person does not.

Political correctness is a concept tossed around frequently in the twenty-first century. It has always existed, of course. The successful speaker of the nineteenth century understood and was sensitive to audiences. However, that person was typically a man, and the only audience that was important was a male audience, and more often than not, the only important audience was a white one.

Much has changed in discourse since the nineteenth and twentieth centuries, just as the society the speaker lives in and addresses has changed, and the speaker who disregards the existing conventions for political correctness usually finds trouble.

Rap music makes a point of ignoring those conventions, particularly with regard to gender, and is often the target of hostile attacks. On the other hand, rap performers often intend to be revolutionary and have developed their own audiences and have become outrageously wealthy by exploiting those newly developed audiences based primarily on thumbing their noses at establishment conventions.

Even so, the successful speaker must understand and be sensitive to what is current in political correctness. The "n word" is a case in point. There was a time when that term was thrown about at will by politicians and other public speakers, but no more. Nothing could spell the end of a politician's career more certainly than using that term in his or her campaign or public addresses.

Terms such as these are called *pejorative*—a word or phrase that expresses contempt or disapproval. Such terms as "redneck," "queer," or "cripple" may be considered pejorative only if used by a nonmember of the group to which they apply.

References to gender have become particularly sensitive in the twentieth century as a result of the women's rights movement, and speakers who disregard these sensitivities do so at their peril. The generic "he" is no longer acceptable; this development requires that you have a strategy to deal with pronominal references without the repetitive use of "he/she," "his/her," and so on.

You can approach this situation in several ways:

- Switch to a passive construction that does not require a subject

- Switch back and forth, using the male pronoun in one reference and the female pronoun in another one, making sure to sprinkle them reasonably evenly

- Switch to the plural

The last alternative is the one most often chosen. This situation requires some care, and the speaker should spend time developing these skills before stepping in front of an audience.

Debates and panel discussions fall under the umbrella of formal speaking. The rules for formal speaking should apply, although lapsing into conversational language is acceptable. Swear words should be avoided in these situations.

A debate presents two sides of a contested thesis—pro and con. Each side posits a hypothesis, proves it, and defends it. A formal debate is much like a formal dance, with each side following a strictly defined format. However, within those guidelines, debaters are free to develop their arguments and rebuttals as they choose. The successful debater prepares by thoroughly developing both sides of the thesis: "Mexico's border with the United States must be closed" and "Mexico's border with the United States must remain open," for example. Debaters must be thoroughly prepared to argue their own side, but they must also have a strategy for rebutting the opposing side's arguments.

One successful way to win an argument is to rebut the opposing side, so debaters must be prepared for opposing arguments and listen for the opportunity to counter the opponent's claims.

All aspects of critical thinking and logical argument are employed during a debate, and successful debaters use ethical appeal (their own credibility) and emotional appeal to persuade the judges who will determine the winner—that is, the side that best establishes its thesis, proves it logically, but also persuades the audience to come over to its position.

A panel is typically composed of experts who explain and defend a particular topic. Often, panels include representatives from more than one field of study and more than one position on the topic. Typically, each expert has a limited amount of time to make an opening statement that either presents explanatory material or argues a point of view. Then, the meeting is opened up to the audience for questions.

A moderator keeps order and controls the time limits on the opening statements and responses. The moderator may sometimes intervene to ask a panel member who was not the target of a particular question to elaborate or rebut the answer of the panel member who was questioned. Panels are usually limited to four or five people, although in special cases, they may be much larger.

Sample Test Questions and Rationale

(Average)

1. What is the best course of action when a child refuses to complete a reading/literature assignment on the grounds that it is morally objectionable?

   A. Speak with the parents and explain the necessity of studying this work

   B. Encourage the child to sample some of the text before making a judgment

   C. Place the child in another teacher's class where they are studying an acceptable work

   D. Provide the student with alternative selections that cover the same performance standards that the rest of the class is learning

The answer is D.

In the case of a student finding a reading offensive, it is the responsibility of the teacher to assign another title. As a rule, it is always advisable to notify parents if a particularly sensitive piece is to be studied.

(Average)

2. Oral debate is most closely associated with which form of discourse?

   A. Description

   B. Exposition

   C. Narration

   D. Persuasion

The answer is D.

It is extremely important to be convincing while having an oral debate. This is why persuasion is so important—because this is the way that you can influence your audience.

(Rigorous)

3. Which of the following types of question will not stimulate higher-level critical thinking?

   A. A hypothetical question

   B. An open-ended question

   C. A close-ended question

   D. A judgment question

The answer is C.

A close-ended question requires a simple answer, like "yes" or "no." An open-ended question can generate an extended response that would require critical thinking. Both a hypothetical question and a judgment question require deeper thinking skills.

(Rigorous)

4. In preparing a speech for a contest, your student has encountered problems with gender-specific language. Not wishing to offend either women or men, she seeks your guidance. Which of the following is not an effective strategy?

   A. Use the generic "he" and explain that people will understand and accept the male pronoun as all-inclusive

   B. Switch to plural nouns and use "they" as the gender-neutral pronoun

   C. Use passive voice so that the subject is not required

   D. Use male pronouns for one part of the speech, and then use female pronouns for the other part of the speech

The answer is A.

No longer is the male pronoun considered the universal pronoun. Speakers and writers should choose gender-neutral words and avoid nouns and pronouns that inaccurately exclude one gender or another.

SKILL 16.2 Demonstrating knowledge of techniques for encouraging risk taking and promoting an atmosphere of tolerance and support

See Skills 6.1, 6.3–6.6

SKILL 16.3 Recognizing effective techniques for questioning, summarizing, paraphrasing, extending, redirecting ideas and comments, and achieving closure

Preparing to speak on a topic should be seen as a process that has stages: discovery, organization, and editing.

Discovery

Many possible sources for information can be used to create an oral presentation.

> Learn more about designing effective oral presentations:
>
> http://www.ruf.rice. edu/~riceowl/oral_ presentations.htm

1. The first step in the discovery process is to settle on a topic or subject. For example, the topic or subject could be immigration. In the discovery stage, one's own knowledge, experience, and beliefs should be the first source, and notes should be taken as the speaker probes this source.

2. The second source can be interviews with friends and experts.

3. The third source is research: what has been written or said publicly on the topic. This stage can get out of hand very quickly, so a plan for collecting source information should be well organized, with time limits set for each part.

Organization

At this point, several decisions need to be made. The first is to determine the *purpose* of the speech. Does the speaker want to persuade the audience to believe something or to act on something, or does the speaker simply want to present information that the audience might not have?

Once that decision is made, a *thesis* should be developed. What point does the speaker want to make? What information will support that point? In what order will that information be arranged?

Introductions and *conclusions* should be written last. The introduction draws the audience into the topic. The conclusion polishes off the speech, making sure the thesis is clear, reinforcing the thesis, or summarizing the points that have been made.

Editing

Editing is the most important stage in speech preparation. Once decisions have been made in the discovery and organization stages, allow time to let the speech rest for a while before going back to it with "fresh eyes." Objectivity is extremely important, and the speaker should be willing to make drastic changes if they are needed. Turning loose of one's own composition can be difficult, but good speechmakers are able to do so. However, this can also get out of hand, so outside comments should be limited. The speaker must recognize that at some point a commitment to the speech as it stands must be made if he or she is to deliver the message with conviction.

The concept of *recursiveness* is very useful when writing speeches. Everything must be written at the outset with full knowledge that it can be changed. The willingness to go backward, even to the discovery stage, is what makes a good speechwriter.

The content to be presented orally plays a big role in organization and delivery. For example, a literary analysis or a book report will be organized inductively, laying out the details and then presenting a conclusion. If the analysis focuses on multiple layers in a story, such a discussion will probably follow the preliminary conclusion. Keeping in mind that the speaker wants to keep the audience's attention, if the content has to do with difficult-to-follow facts and statistics, slides (or PowerPoint presentations) may be used as a guide to the presentation. The speaker can also intersperse interesting anecdotes, jokes, or humor from time to time so that the listeners don't fall asleep.

SKILL **Recognizing rhetorical strategies appropriate for various kinds of**
16.4 **oral and visual messages**

A logical argument consists of three stages.

1. State the premises of the argument. These are the propositions which are necessary for the argument to continue. They are the evidence or reasons for accepting the argument and its conclusions. Premises (or assertions) are often indicated by phrases such as "because," "since," "obviously," and so on. (The phrase "obviously" is often viewed with suspicion, as it can be used to intimidate others into accepting suspicious premises. If something doesn't seem obvious to you, don't be afraid to question it. You can always say, "Oh, yes, you're right, it is obvious" when you've heard the explanation.)

2. **Use the premises to derive further propositions by a process known as inference.** In inference, one proposition is arrived at based on one or more already-accepted propositions. There are various forms of valid inference. The propositions arrived at by inference may then be used in further inference. Inference is often denoted by phrases such as "implies that" or "therefore."

3. **Conclude the argument with the proposition that is affirmed on the basis of the premises and inference.** Conclusions are often indicated by phrases such as "therefore," "it follows that," "we conclude," and so on. The conclusion is often stated as the final stage of inference.

Delivery Techniques

Instruct your students on the ways in which nonverbal communication can affect the way a presentation is understood.

NONVERBAL COMMUNICATION TECHNIQUES	
Posture	Maintain a straight but not stiff posture. Instead of shifting weight from hip to hip, point your feet directly at the audience and distribute your weight evenly. Keep your shoulders towards the audience. If you have to turn your body to use a visual aid, turn 45 degrees and continue speaking towards the audience.
Movement	Instead of staying glued to one spot or pacing back and forth, stay within four to eight feet of the front row of your audience. Take a step or half-step to the side every once in a while. If you are using a lectern, feel free to move to the front or side of it to engage your audience more. Avoid distancing yourself from the audience; you want audience members to feel involved and connected.
Gestures	Gestures can maintain a natural atmosphere when speaking publicly. Use them just as you would when speaking to a friend. They shouldn't be exaggerated, but they should be used for added emphasis. Avoid keeping your hands in your pockets or locked behind your back, wringing your hands and fidgeting nervously, or keeping your arms crossed.
Eye Contact	Many people are intimidated by using eye contact when speaking to large groups. Interestingly, eye contact usually helps the speaker overcome speech anxiety by connecting with the attentive audience and easing feelings of isolation. Instead of looking at a spot on the back wall or at your notes, scan the room and make eye contact for one to three seconds per person.

In addition to the content of your presentation, you want to use a strong delivery. As with most skills, the key is practice, practice, practice. Record and play back your presentation to hear how you sound.

ORAL DELIVERY TECHNIQUES	
Voice	Many people fall into one of two traps when speaking: using a monotone or talking too fast. Both phenomena result from anxiety. A monotone restricts your natural inflection but can be remedied by releasing tension in upper and lower body muscles. Subtle movement will keep you loose and natural. Talking too fast, meanwhile, is not necessarily bad if you are exceptionally articulate. If you are not a strong speaker or if you are talking about very technical items, however, the audience will easily become lost. When you talk too fast and begin tripping over your words, consciously pause after every sentence you say. Don't be afraid of brief silences. The audience needs time to absorb what you are saying.
Volume	Problems with volume, whether too soft or too loud, can be overcome with practice. If you tend to speak too softly, have someone stand in the back of the room and signal you when your volume is strong enough. If possible, have someone in the front of the room as well to make sure you're not overcompensating with excessive volume. Conversely, if you have a problem with speaking too loudly, have the person in the front of the room signal you when your voice is soft enough. Check with the person in the back to make sure it is still loud enough to be heard. In both cases, note your volume level for future reference. Don't be shy about asking your audience, "Can you hear me in the back?" Suitable volume is beneficial for both you and the audience.
Pitch	Pitch refers to the length, tension, and thickness of your vocal bands. As your voice gets higher, the pitch gets higher. In oral performance, pitch reflects the emotional arousal level. More variation in pitch typically corresponds to more emotional arousal, but it can also be used to convey sarcasm or highlight specific words.

Although these skills are essential for you to be an effective teacher, you want your students to develop these techniques as well. By encouraging the development of proper techniques for oral presentations, you are enabling your students to develop self-confidence for higher levels of communication.

Learn more about using your voice:

http://www.longview. k12.wa.us/mmhs/wyatt/ pathway/voice.html

Sample Test Question and Rationale

(Average)

1. **In preparing students for their oral presentations, the instructor provided all of these guidelines, except one. Which is not an effective guideline?**

   A. Even if you are using a lectern, feel free to move about; this will connect you to the audience

   B. Your posture should be natural, not stiff; keep your shoulders toward the audience

   C. Gestures can help communicate as long as you don't overuse them or make them distracting

   D. You can avoid eye contact if you focus on your notes; this will make you appear more knowledgeable

The answer is D.

Although many people are nervous about making eye contact, they should focus on two or three people at a time. Body language, such as movement, posture, and gestures, helps the speaker connect to the audience.

SKILL 16.5 Analyzing the characteristics and evaluating the effects of different methods of various presentation techniques

Just as writing styles are unique, so are presentation skills. As teachers, you will help your students recognize those basic skills to effective public speaking.

Language Skills to Evaluate:

- The ability to talk at length with few pauses and fill time with speech

- The ability to call up appropriate things to say in a wide range of contexts

- The size and range of a student's vocabulary and syntax skills

- The coherence of sentences; the ability to speak in reasoned and semantically dense sentences

Learn more about designing effective oral presentations:

http://www.ruf.rice. edu/~riceowl/oral_ presentations.htm

- Knowledge of the various forms of interaction and conversation for various situations

- Knowledge of the standard rules of conversation

- The ability to be creative and imaginative with language, and to express oneself in original ways

- The ability to invent and entertain, and to take risks in linguistic expression

Methods of Evaluation:

- Commercially designed language assessment products

- Instructor observation using a rating scale from 1 to 5 (where 1 = limited proficiency and 5 = native-speaker equivalency)

- Informal observation of students' behaviors

Uses of Language Assessment:

- Diagnosis of language strengths and weaknesses

- Detection of patterns of systematic errors

- Appropriate bilingual/ESL program placement if necessary

Common Language Errors:

- Application of rules that apply in a student's first language but not in the second

- Using pronunciation that applies to a student's first language but not in the second

- Applying a general rule to all cases even when there are exceptions

- Trying to cut corners by using an incorrect word or syntactic form

- Avoiding use of precise vocabulary or idiomatic expressions

- Using incorrect verb tenses

> *Check out this oral presentation rubric:*
>
> *http://www.tcet.unt.edu/ START/instruct /general/ oral.htm*

Sample Test Questions and Rationale

(Rigorous)

1. Mr. Ledbetter has instructed his students to prepare a slide presentation that illustrates an event in history. Students are to include pictures, graphics, media clips, and links to resources. What competencies will students exhibit at the completion of this project?

   A. Analyzing the impact of society on media

   B. Recognizing the media's strategies to inform and persuade

   C. Demonstrating strategies and creative techniques to prepare presentations using a variety of media

   D. Identifying the aesthetic effects of a media presentation

   The answer is B.

   Students will have learned how to use various media to convey a unified message. By employing multimedia in their presentations, students will be telling a story with more than words.

(Rigorous)

2. In a class of nonnative speakers of English, which type of activity will help students the most?

   A. Have students make oral presentations so that they can develop a phonological awareness of sounds

   B. Provide students more writing opportunities to develop their written communication skills

   C. Encourage students to listen to the new language on television and radio

   D. Provide a variety of methods to develop speaking, writing, and reading skills

   The answer is A.

   Research indicates that nonnative speakers of English develop stronger second-language skills by understanding the phonological differences in spoken words.

SKILL 16.6 Recognizing principles of graphic communications, oral communications, and audiovisual communications

Visual graphics include a spectrum of artifacts. Pictures, graphs, charts, tables, and drawings are all useful to a greater or lesser degree in a wide variety of educational communications.

Keep in mind several principles regarding these graphic communications. One principle addresses aesthetics: Effective graphics should be pleasing to the eye. This is especially true if the graphic is some type of picture: It should be strategically placed; its colors should be well chosen; and the size of the graphic should be suited to its intended purpose. Within the graphic itself, design features should enhance the intended communication. At the very least, the graphic needs to be large enough to view easily. Legends associated with a given graphic should be clear and thorough. The graphic, to be most effective, should be presented in a context that allows students to understand its function and importance.

Oral communication as it applies in the classroom includes formal and informal speaking and listening by both teachers and students. Principles of oral communication include attention to such issues as vocabulary levels, appropriate volume, repetition of key points, prosody, and active listening. Students today, in general, have significantly fewer words in their vocabularies than did those of prior generations. Attention must be paid to developing clear definitions for key terms and to expressing ideas in terms accessible to the given student audience.

Speaking clearly and at volumes appropriate for given contexts is, of course, critical to any oral communication effort. When speaking to a whole room, for instance, a speaker has to project his or her voice beyond usual comfort levels in order to be effective. Repetition of key points, including whole class response routines, enhances communication of intended information. Using inflection and modulation enhances communication as well. Finally, there can be no oral communication without a receptive audience. Learning how to listen strategically is an important key.

Audiovisual communications include films and filmstrips, and the principles that apply singly to graphic and oral communications also apply to audiovisual communications. In a classroom context, present audiovisual resources in ways that ensure student engagement. Rather than simply inserting a video and playing it for the whole period, pause the video at least a few times during the period and leading the class through some type of processing routines. This exercise will build in some accountability and some engagement for the students.

Technologies that incorporate interactive dimensions of audiovisual material are especially effective in communicating information and ensuring adequate student focus, especially in the absence of dynamic, teacher-directed processing.

Learn more about presenting effective presentations with visual aids:

http://www.osha.gov/doc/outreachtraining/htmlfiles/traintec.html

COMPETENCY 17
UNDERSTAND TECHNIQUES FOR THE CRITICAL ANALYSIS OF ORAL AND VISUAL MESSAGES DELIVERED THROUGH VARIOUS MEDIA

SKILL 17.1 Evaluating strategies used by the media for a variety of purposes

More money is spent each year on advertising to children than on educating them. Thus, the media's strategies are considerably well thought-out and effective. They employ large, clear letters, bold colors, simple line drawings, and popular symbols to announce upcoming events, push ideas, and advertise products. By using attractive photographs, brightly colored cartoon characters, or instructive messages, they increase sales, win votes, or stimulate learning. The graphics are designed to communicate messages clearly, precisely, and efficiently. Some even target subconscious yearnings for sex and status.

Because so much effort is spent on influencing students through media tactics, just as much effort should be devoted to educating those students about media awareness. A teacher should explain that artists, the aspects they choose to portray, and the ways in which they portray them reflect their attitude and understanding of those aspects. Artistic choices are not entirely based on creative license—they also reflect an imbedded meaning that the artist wants to represent. Colors, shapes, and positions are meant to arouse basic instincts for food, sex, and status, and are often used to sell cars, clothing, or liquor.

To stimulate analysis of media strategies, ask students questions such as:

- Where/when do you think this picture was taken/film was shot/piece was written?
- Would you like to have lived at this time in history, or in this place?
- What objects are present?
- What do the people presented look like? Are they happy or sad?
- Who is being targeted?
- What can you learn from this piece of media?
- Is it telling you something is good or bad?
- What message is being broadcasted?

Learn more about teaching film, television, and media:

http://www.tc.umn. edu/~rbeach/ linksteachingmedia/ chapter8/16.htm

Advertising Techniques

Because students are very interested in the types of approaches advertisers use, you
can develop high-interest assignments requiring them to analyze commercial messages. What is powerful about Nike's "Just Do It" campaign? What is the appeal of
Jessica Simpson's eponymous perfume?

TYPICAL ADVERTISING TECHNIQUES	
Beauty Appeal	Beauty attracts us; we are drawn to beautiful people, places, and things.
Celebrity Endorsement	This technique associates product use with a well-known person. We are led to believe that by purchasing this product, we will attain characteristics similar to those of the celebrity.
Compliment the Consumer	Advertisers flatter the consumer who is willing to purchase their product. By purchasing the product, the consumer is recognized by the advertisers as having made a good decision with the selection.
Escape	Getting away from it all is very appealing; you can imagine adventures you cannot have; the idea of escape is pleasurable.
Independence/ Individuality	This technique associates a product with people who can think and act for themselves. Products are linked to individual decision making.
Intelligence	This technique associates a product with smart people who can't be fooled.
Lifestyle	This technique associates a product with a particular style of living/way of doing things.
Nurture	Every time you see an animal or a child, an appeal is made to your paternal or maternal instincts. This technique associates products with taking care of someone.
Peer Approval	This technique associates product use with friendship/acceptance. Advertisers can also use this technique negatively to make you worry that you'll lose friends if you don't use a certain product.
Rebel	This technique associates products with behaviors or lifestyles that oppose society's norms.
Rhetorical Question	This technique poses a question to the consumer that demands a response. A question is asked, and the consumer is supposed to answer in a way that affirms the product's goodness.
Scientific/ Statistical Claim	This technique provides some sort of scientific proof or experiment, very specific numbers, or an impressive sounding mystery ingredient.
Unfinished Comparison/Claim	This technique uses phrases such as "Works better in poor driving conditions!" Works better than what?

Sample Test Question and Rationale

(Rigorous)

1. What is the common advertising technique used by these advertising slogans?

   "It's everywhere you want to be."
   —Visa

   "Have it your way."
   —Burger King

   "When you care enough to send the very best."
   —Hallmark

   "Be all you can be."
   —U.S. Army

   A. Peer approval

   B. Rebel

   C. Individuality

   D. Escape

The answer is C.

All of these ads associate products with people who can think and act for themselves. Products are linked to individual decision making. With peer approval, the ads would associate their products with friends and acceptance. For rebelling, the ads would associate products with behaviors or lifestyles that oppose society's norms. Escape would suggest the appeal of getting away from it all.

SKILL 17.2 Analyzing media messages for logic and reasoning

To present their messages effectively, the media employ various approaches to reach their audiences. Some messages are more obvious than others, and students should be taught to analyze all of them to determine the logic and reasoning.

Posters

The power of the political poster in the twenty-first century seems trivial considering the barrage of electronic campaigning, mudslinging, and reporting that seem to take over the video and audio media in election season. Even so, the political poster is a powerful propaganda tool that has been around for a long time. For example, in the first century AD, a poster that calls for the election of a Satrius as quinquennial has survived to this day. Nowhere have political posters been used more powerfully or effectively than in Russia during the 1920s campaign to promote communism. Many of the greatest Russian writers of that era were the poster writers. Those posters would not be understood at all, except in light of what was going on in the country at the time.

Today we see political posters primarily at rallies and protests, where they are usually hand-lettered and hand-drawn. The message is rarely subtle. Understanding the messages of posters requires little thought as a rule. However, they are usually meaningless unless the context is clearly understood. For example, a poster reading "Camp Democracy" can be understood only in the context of the protests against the Iraq War near President Bush's home near Crawford, Texas. "Impeach" posters were understood in 2006 to be directed at President Bush, not a local mayor or representative.

Cartoons

The political cartoon (aka editorial) presents a message or point of view concerning people, events, or situations using caricature and symbolism to convey the cartoonist's ideas, sometimes subtly, sometimes brashly, but always quickly. A good political cartoon

- Has wit and humor, usually obtained by exaggeration that is slick and not used merely for comic effect

- Has a foundation in truth; that is, the characters are recognizable to the viewer

- Has some basis in fact (even if it has a philosophical bias)

- Has a moral purpose

> Check out the teaching guide for the professional cartoonist index:
>
> http://www.cagle.com/teacher/

Using political cartoons as a teaching tool enlivens lectures, prompts classroom discussion, promotes critical thinking, develops multiple talents and learning styles, and helps prepare students for standardized tests. It also provides humor. However, political cartoons may be the most difficult form of literature to teach. Many teachers who choose to include them in their social studies curricula caution that, although students may enjoy them, it's doubtful whether they are actually getting the cartoonists' messages.

The best strategy for teaching such a unit uses a subskills approach that leads students step-by-step to higher orders of critical thinking. For example, the teacher can introduce caricature and use cartoons to illustrate the principles. Students can identify and interpret symbols if they are given the principles for doing so and get plenty of practice, and cartoons are excellent teaching tools. Using this approach can cut down the time it takes for students to develop these skills, and many of the students who might otherwise lose the struggle to learn to identify symbols may overcome the roadblocks through the analysis of political cartoons. Many political cartoons exist for the teacher to use in the classroom, and they are more readily available than ever before.

A popular example of an editorial cartoon that provides a way to analyze current events in politics is the comic strip "Doonesbury" by Gary Trudeau. For example, prior to the 2004 presidential election, the media-savvy teenager Alex does her best to participate in the political process. In January, she rallies her middle school classmates to the phones for a Deanathon; by August, she is luring Ralph Nader supporters into discussions on Internet chat rooms. Knowledgeable about government, active in the political process, and willing to enlist others, Alex has many traits that educators seek to develop in their students.

Sample Test Question and Rationale

(Easy)

1. **What is not a characteristic of an effective editorial cartoon?**

    A. It presents a message or point of view concerning people, events, or situations using caricature and symbolism to convey the cartoonist's ideas

    B. It has wit and humor, which is usually obtained by exaggeration that is slick and not used merely for comic effect

    C. It has a foundation in truth; that is, the characters must be recognizable to the viewer, and the point of the drawing must have some basis in fact even if it has a philosophical bias

    D. It seeks to reflect the editorial opinion of the newspaper that carries it

The answer is D.

An editorial cartoon does not necessarily reflect the opinion of the newspaper that publishes it.

SKILL 17.3 Comparing messages across different media

Check out the language of media literacy—a glossary of terms:

http://www.medialit.org/reading_room/article565.html

A common classroom assignment that applies to this skill is to view the movie version of a book studied by a particular class, to compare and contrast the two media, and to argue which did the better job of conveying the intended message(s).

Conveying the same message across different media is difficult because of the dynamics specific to those media. The degree of difficulty increases as the complexity of the message does. Nonetheless, certain general observations inform the discussion.

A print message has two kinds of unique features. Some seem to be positive. For instance, print messages have longevity; they are also easily portable. Print messages appeal almost exclusively to the mind and allow students to recursively read sections that warrant more thought. Other features of print seem potentially negative. For instance, a print message requires an active reader; without such a reader, print messages are not very effective. Print messages are not accessible to nonreaders.

A graphic message in the hands of an artistic genius can produce images that seem to be Jungian archetypes. More commonly, a graphic message gives a quick overview of some quantifiable situation. Some learners find that graphic information works for them better than print, and many struggling readers find graphic messages more helpful, too. However, compared to print, graphic messages convey a much shorter range of information. If a particular graphic is inspiring, the inspirations conveyed are subject to the descriptions of the various readers who view it. With print, the inspired scripts are already there for the reader, provided the reader is applying active reading skills.

An audio message allows for messages delivered with attention to prosody. Students who can't read can access the material. Audio messages invite the listener to form mental images consistent with the topic of the audio. Audio messages also allow the learners to close their eyes for better mental focus. Listening to an audio message is a more passive modality than reading a print message, though. As a rule, people read faster than normal speech patterns, so print conveys more information in a given time span.

An audiovisual message offers the easiest accessibility for learners. It has the advantages of each medium, the graphic and the audio. Learners' eyes and ears are engaged. Nonreaders get significant access to content. Viewing an audiovisual presentation is an even more passive activity than listening to an audio message, however, because information is coming to learners effortlessly through two senses. Activities to foster a critical perspective on an audiovisual presentation serve as valuable safeguards against any overall and unwelcome passivity.

> Check out more strategies for developing listening skills:
>
> *http://www.nclrc.org/ essentials/listening/ stratlisten.htm*

SKILL 17.4 Analyzing the relationship between the media and the democratic process

Ideally, the relationship between the media (primarily news and documentary programs) and the democratic process would be for the media to convey critical information to the people so that the people could cast more intelligent votes than they would without the input. In this ideal scenario, media objectivity is assumed; the reality is, however, that media objectivity is widely assumed to be missing. Various media broadcasting organizations report information in ways that suggest a bias, a slant, favoring one or another political ideology.

As educators, you should help students evaluate more critically information coming from the major news networks and associated channels. Educators can help students recognize bias and can suggest strategies for approaching media input in ways that result in more comprehensive and objective views of issues and situations. For instance, educators can suggest that students gather information on an issue from several media organizations in order to get a better perspective on it.

The media are extremely effective in spreading information quickly. Therefore, the media itself influence the process by the very fact that if candidates for office know of an event with media coverage, they try to make an appearance and an impression. Since time is limited in most media formats, candidates attempt to focus on broadcasting a few power points. This phenomenon results in little more than propaganda. Questions posed by newscasters meet with various deflections. Few candidates tip their hands any more than absolutely necessary. One downside of the relationship between the media and candidates is that substance seems to take a back seat to slogans.

Access to the media involves expense, and that creates a problem for the democratic process; being wealthy becomes a prerequisite for candidacy. Certainly, this emphasis on money creates all kinds of complications for the democratic process. Candidates are in danger of being beholden to sponsors. Instead of following their own consciences, they follow the dictates of the contributors.

Exit polling by the media influences the democratic process by projecting outcomes based on a small percentage of actual votes. Potential voters may alter their choices based on this information, or they may decide not to vote at all. The time differences from the East Coast to the West Coast provide an environment for this distortion. With the advent of mail-in ballots, media speculation based on polling has the potential to exert even more influence on voting patterns.

The media play an extremely important role in the democratic process, and this role is bound to expand as technology evolves. If we are to have a strong democracy, we must become increasingly sophisticated in our evaluation of media input.

SKILL 17.5 Analyzing the relationship between the media and personal and societal values, opinions, and behaviors

The media exert a profound influence on personal and societal values, opinions, and behaviors. One of the main avenues of this influence is advertising. The media depends upon advertising for its economic viability. The advertising industry devotes tremendous resources to the study of how to influence values, opinions, and behaviors.

It should come as no surprise that the techniques used by advertisers to promote their products often have little to do with the pros and cons of the products themselves. Rather, advertisers frequently appeal to sex and status to peddle their wares. In this sense, the media helps foster conspicuous and often mindless consumption.

Educators can help students become more aware of how advertising operates by leading them through analysis of various advertisements to identify the basis of their appeal.

The media directly attempt to influence societal values, opinions, and behaviors through news and documentary programming. The power and scope of the media in disseminating information is not only pivotal, but also is becoming more so as technology continues to make such information instantly available. Alerting students to the need for developing a critical perspective with regard to sources of broadcasting news and information is an important goal of educators.

Behavior models available through dramas, sitcoms, and cartoons comprise another profound influence of the media on personal and societal values, opinions, and behaviors. Young people, in particular, are exposed to a wide spectrum of such models. Increasingly, material that would have been considered too vulgar and risqué is available to them through the media. Since the young are experimenting with various identity models, it is not surprising that they adopt these media models and exhibit values, opinions, and behaviors that seem vulgar, rude, and risqué. An educator should be aware of this development in order to avoid being unduly reactive to such student behaviors.

Body image is also profoundly influenced by the media. Trying to meet impossible standards of beauty presented by the media has resulted in suffering and disease for many young people, particularly young women. Countering this trend is another worthy educational goal.

In general, an analysis of the media's influence on personal and societal values leads to the conclusion that educators must be proactive in addressing the negative aspects of this pervasive influence. Helping students develop a critical perspective with regard to all these aspects of media consumption is an essential educational goal.

Distinguishing techniques used by visual (*i.e., still and moving*) **and oral media**

Teach your students how to create a graph:

http://nces.ed.gov/ nceskids/createagraph/ default.aspx

Still visual media include pictures, drawings, photographs, tables, charts, maps, and diagrams. Techniques employed by still visual media include choosing colors appropriate to the purpose, placing important information in strategic locations within the still, sequencing stills (stages, overlays), sizing stills for optimum effect, placing stills in understandable contexts, and providing sufficient key or legend information.

Moving visual media include movies and videos. Techniques employed by visual media include most of those applicable to still media, plus determining a storyline or presentation rationale. In other words, the moving presentation needs to have an understandable beginning, development, and conclusion. Obviously, choosing effective transitions between scenes and installing a reasonable pace of image movement figure importantly in visual media. If the presentation is in slow motion or going by at warp speed for no discernable reason, the intended impact is diminished.

Oral media include songs, chants, speeches, and readings of stories, poems, and articles. Oral media can be stored on records, tapes, CDs, and an ever-evolving array of computer-like implements. Techniques employed by oral media include choosing an appropriate volume, applying principles of prosody (pace, pitch, inflection, voice modulation, or accents), employing rhythm and rhyme, and enhancing impact through musical instruments or sound effects.

Sample Test Question and Rationale

(Rigorous)

1. **In presenting a report to peers about the effects of Hurricane Katrina on New Orleans, the students wanted to use various media in their argument to persuade their peers that more needed to be done. Which of these would be the most effective?**

   A. A PowerPoint presentation showing the blueprints of the levees before the flood and redesigned now for current construction

   B. A collection of music clips made by the street performers in the French Quarter before and after the flood

   C. A recent video showing the areas devastated by the floods and the current state of rebuilding

   D. A collection of recordings of interviews made by the various government officials and local citizens affected by the flooding

The answer is C.

For maximum impact, a video would offer dramatic scenes of the devastated areas. A video by its very nature is more dynamic than a static PowerPoint presentation. Furthermore, the condition of the levees would not provide as much impetus for change as seeing the devastated areas. Oral messages, such as music clips and interviews, provide another way of supplementing the message; but again, they are not as dynamic as video.

SKILL 17.7 Distinguishing between classical and contemporary logical arguments

Learning how to frame an argument is an important writing and critical thinking skill. Students can choose from various argument styles; below are just two of many.

Classical Argument

In its simplest form, the classical argument has five main parts:

1. The introduction, which warms up the audience, establishes goodwill and rapport with the readers, and announces the general theme or thesis of the argument.

2. The narration, which summarizes relevant background material, provides any information the audience needs to know about the environment and circumstances that produce the argument, and set up the stakes—what's at risk.

3. The confirmation, which lays out in a logical order (usually strongest to weakest or most obvious to most subtle) the claims that support the thesis, providing evidence for each claim.

4. The refutation and concession, which looks at opposing viewpoints to the writer's claims, anticipates objections from the audience, and allows as many of the opposing viewpoints as possible without weakening the thesis.

5. The summation, which provides a strong conclusion, amplifies the force of the argument, and shows the readers that this solution best meets the circumstances.

Contemporary Argument

Fact

Similar to an informative speech, a persuasive speech on a question of fact seeks to find an answer where a clear one doesn't exist. The speaker evaluates evidence and attempts to convince the audience that his or her conclusion is correct. The challenge is to accept a certain carefully crafted view of the facts presented.

Value

This kind of persuasion tries to convince the audience that a certain thing is good or bad, moral or immoral, valuable or worthless. It focuses less on knowledge and more on beliefs and values.

Policy

This speech is a call to action, arguing that something should be done, improved, or changed. Its goal is action from the audience, but it also seeks passive agreement with the proposition proposed. This speech appeals to both reason and emotion, and tells listeners what they can do and how they can do it.

Sample Test Question and Rationale

(Rigorous)

1. Which part of a classical argument is illustrated in this excerpt from Caryl River's essay "What Should Be Done About Rock Lyrics?"

   But violence against women is greeted by silence. It shouldn't be. This does not mean censorship, or book (or record) burning. In a society that protects free expression, we understand a lot of stuff will float up out of the sewer. Usually, we recognize the ugly stuff that advocates violence against any group as the garbage it is, and we consider its purveyors as moral lepers. We hold our nose and tolerate it, but we speak out against the values it proffers.

   A. Narration

   B. Confirmation

   C. Refutation and concession

   D. Summation

The answer is C.

The author refutes the idea of censorship and concedes that society tolerates offensive lyrics as part of our freedom of speech. Narration provides background material to produce an argument. In confirmation, the author details the argument with claims that support the thesis. In summation, the author concludes the argument by offering the strongest solution.

Resources

Abrams, M. H. ed. *The Norton Anthology of English Literature*. 6th ed. 2 vols. New York: Norton, 1979. A comprehensive reference for English literature, containing selected works from Beowulf through the twentieth century and information about literary criticism.

Beach, Richard. "Strategic Teaching in Literature." *Strategic Teaching and Learning: Cognitive Instruction in the Content Areas*. Edited by Beau Fly Jones and others. ASCD Publications, 1987: 135–-159. A chapter dealing with a definition of and strategic teaching strategies for literature studies.

Brown, A. C. and others. *Grammar and Composition* 3rd Course. Boston: Houghton Mifflin, 1984. A standard ninth-grade grammar text covering spelling, vocabulary, reading, listening, and writing skills.

Burmeister, L. E. *Reading Strategies for Middle and Secondary School Teachers*. Reading, MA: Addison-Wesley, 1978. A resource for developing classroom strategies for reading and content area classes, using library references, and adapting reading materials to all levels of students.

Carrier, W. and B. Neumann, eds. *Literature from the World*. New York: Scribner, 1981. A comprehensive world literature text for high school students, with a section on mythology and folklore.

Cline, R. K. J. and W. G. McBride. *A Guide to Literature for Young Adults: Background, Selection, and Use*. Glenview, IL: Scott Foresman, 1983. A literature reference containing sample readings and an overview of adolescent literature and the developmental changes that affect reading.

Coater, R.B., Jr., ed. "Reading Research and Instruction." *Journal of the College Research Association*. Pittsburgh, PA: 1995. A reference tool for reading and language arts teachers, covering the latest research and instructional techniques.

Corcoran, B. and E. Evans, eds. *Readers, Texts, Teachers*. Upper Montclair, NJ: Boynton/Cook, 1987. A collection of essays concerning reader response theory, including activities that help students interpret literature and help the teacher integrate literature into the course of study.

Cutting, Brian. *Moving on in Whole Language: The Complete Guide for Every Teacher*. Bothell, WA: Wright Group, 1992. A resource of practical knowledge in whole language instruction.

Damrosch, L. and others. *Adventures in English Literature*. Orlando, FL: Harcourt, Brace, Jovanovich, 1985. One of many standard high school English literature textbooks with a solid section on the development of the English language.

Davidson, A. *Literacy 2000 Teacher's Resource*. Emergent Stages 1 & 2.1990.

Devine, T. G. *Teaching Study Skills: A Guide for Teachers*. Boston: Allyn and Bacon, 1981.

Duffy, G. G. and others. *Comprehension Instruction: Perspectives and Suggestions*. New York: Longman, 1984. Written by researchers at the Institute of Research on Teaching and the Center for the Study of Reading, this reference includes a variety of instructional techniques for different levels.

Fleming, M. ed. *Teaching the Epic*. Urbana, IL: NCTE, 1974. Methods, materials, and projects for the teaching of epics with examples of Greek, religious, national, and American epics.

Flood, J. ed. *Understanding Reading Comprehension: Cognition, Language, and the Structure of Prose*. Newark, DE: IRA, 1984. Essays by preeminent scholars dealing with comprehension for learners of all levels and abilities.

Fry, E. B. and others. *The Reading Teacher's Book of Lists*. Edgewood Cliffs, NJ: Prentice-Hall, 1984. A comprehensive list of book lists for students of various reading levels.

Garnica, Olga K. and Martha L. King. *Language, Children, and Society*. New York: Pergamon Press, 1981.

Gere, A. R. and E. Smith. *Attitude, Language, and Change*. Urbana, IL: NCTE, 1979. A discussion of the relationship between standard English and grammar and the vernacular usage, including various approaches to language instruction.

Hayakawa, S. I. *Language in Thought and Action*. 4th ed. Orlando, Fl: Harcourt, Brace, Jovanovich, 1979.

Hook, J. N. and others. *What Every English Teacher Should Know*. Champaign, IL: NCTE, 1970. Research-based text that summarizes methodologies and specific application for use with students.

Johnson, D. D. and P. D. Pearson. *Teaching Reading Vocabulary*. 2nd ed. New York: Holt, Rinehart, and Winston, 1984. A student text that stresses using vocabulary study in improving reading comprehension, with chapters on instructional components in the reading and content areas.

Kaywell, I. F. ed. *Adolescent Literature as a Complement to the Classics*. Norwood, MA: Christopher-Gordon Pub., 1993. A correlation of modern adolescent literature to classics of similar themes.

Mack, M. ed. *World Masterpieces*. 3rd ed. 2 vols. New York: Norton, 1973. A standard world literature survey, with useful introductory material on a critical approach to literature study.

McLuhan, M. *Understanding Media: The Extensions of Man*. New York: Signet, 1964. The most classic work on the effect media has on the public and the power of the media to influence thinking.

McMichael, G. ed. *Concise Anthology of American Literature*. New York: Macmillan, 1974. A standard survey of American literature text.

Moffett, J. *Teaching the Universe of Discourse*. Boston: Houghton Mifflin, 1983. A significant reference text that proposes the outline for a total language arts program, emphasizing the reinforcement of each element of the language arts curriculum to the other elements.

Moffett, James and Betty Jane Wagner. *Student-Centered Language Arts K–12*. 4th ed. Boston: Houghton Mifflin, 1992.

Nelms, B. F. ed. *Literature in the Classroom: Readers, Texts, and Contexts*. Urbana, IL: NCTE, 1988. Essays on adolescent and multicultural literature, social aspects of literature, and approaches to literature interpretation.

Nilsen, A. P. and K. L. Donelson. *Literature for Today's Young Adults*. 2nd ed. Glenview, IL: Scott, Foresman, and Co., 1985. An excellent overview of young adult literature—its history, terminologies, bibliographies, and book reviews.

Perrine, L. Literature: *Structure, Sound, and Sense*. 5th ed. Orlando, FL: Harcourt, Brace, Jovanovich, 1988. A much-revised text for teaching literature elements, genres, and interpretation.

Piercey, Dorothy. *Reading Activities in Content Areas: An Ideabook for Middle and Secondary Schools*. 2nd ed. Boston: Allyn and Bacon, 1982.

Pooley, R. C. *The Teaching of English Usage*. Urbana, IL: NCTE, 1974. A revision of the important 1946 text, which discusses the attitudes toward English usage through history and recommends specific techniques for usage instruction.

Probst, R. E. *Response and Analysis: Teaching Literature in Junior and Senior High School*. Upper Montclair, NJ: Boynton/Cook, 1988. A resource that explores reader response theory and discusses student-centered methods for interpreting literature. Contains a section on the progress of adolescent literature.

Pyles, T. and J. Alges. *The Origin and Development of the English Language*. 3rd ed. Orlando, FL: Harcourt, Brace, Jovanovich, 1982. A history of the English language; sections on social, personal, historical, and geographical influences on language usage.

Readence, J. E. and others. *Content Area Reading: An Integrated Approach*. 2nd ed. Dubuque, IA: Kendall/Hunt, 1985. A practical instruction guide for teaching reading in the content areas.

Robinson, H. Alan. *Teaching Reading and Study Strategies: The Content Areas*. Boston: Allyn and Bacon, 1978.

Roe, B. D. and others. *Secondary School Reading Instruction: The Content Areas*. 3rd ed. Boston: Houghton Mifflin, 1987. A resource of strategies for the teaching of reading for language arts teachers with little reading instruction background.

Rosenberg, D. *World Mythology: An Anthology of the Great Myths and Epics*. Lincolnwood, IL: National Textbook, 1986. Presents selections of main myths from which literary allusions are drawn. Thorough literary analysis of each selection.

Rosenblatt, L. M. *The Reader, the Text, the Poem. The Transactional Theory of the Literary Work*. Southern Illinois University Press, 1978. A discussion of reader-response theory and reader-centered methods for analyzing literature.

Santeusanio, Richard P. A *Practical Approach to Content Area Reading*. Reading, MA.: Addison-Wesley Publishing Co., 1983.

Strickland, D. S. and others. *Using Computers in the Teaching of Reading*. New York: Teachers College Press, 1987. Resource for strategies for teaching and learning language and reading with computers and recommendations for software for all grades.

Sutherland, Zena and others. *Children and Books*. 6th ed. Glenview, IL: Scott, Foresman, and Co., 1981. Thorough study of children's literature, with sections on language development theory and chapters on specific genres with synopses of specific classic works for child/adolescent readers.

Tchudi, S. and D. Mitchell. *Explorations in the Teaching of English*. 3rd ed. New York: Harper Row, 1989. A thorough source of strategies for creating a more student-centered involvement in learning.

Tompkins, Gail E. *Teaching Writing: Balancing Process and Product*. 2nd ed. New York: Macmillan, 1994. A tool to aid teachers in integrating recent research and theory about the writing process, writing/reading connections, collaborative learning, and across the curriculum writing with practices in fourth through eighth grade classrooms.

Warriners, J. E. *English Composition and Grammar*. Benchmark ed. Orlando, FL: Harcourt, Brace, Jovanovich, 1988. Standard grammar and composition textbook, with a six-book series for seventh through twelfth grades; includes vocabulary study, language history, and diverse approaches to the writing process.

SAMPLE TEST

SAMPLE TEST
WRITING

Section I: Essay Test

You will respond to several prompts intended to gauge your competence in a variety of writing skills. In most testing situations, you will have 30 minutes to respond to these prompts. Some tests may allow 60 minutes for the essay in order to incorporate more than one question or to allow for greater preparation and editing time. Read the directions carefully and organize your time wisely.

Section II: Multiple-choice Test

This section contains 125 questions. In most testing situations, you will be expected to answer 35–40 questions in about 30 minutes. If you time yourself on the entire battery, try to finish it in about 90 minutes.

Section III: Answer Key

Section I: Essay Prompts

Prompt A

Write an expository essay discussing effective teaching strategies for helping a heterogeneous class of ninth graders to appreciate literature. Select any appropriate piece(s) of world literature to use as examples in the discussion.

Prompt B

After reading the following passage from Alduous Huxley's Brave New World, discuss the types of reader responses possible with a group of eighth graders.

He hated them all—all the men who came to visit Linda. One afternoon, when he had been playing with the other children—it was cold, he remembered, and there was snow on the mountains—he came back to the house and heard angry voices in the bedroom. They were women's voices, and they were words he didn't understand; but he knew they were dreadful words. Then suddenly, crash! something was upset; he heard people moving about quickly, and there was another crash and then a noise like hitting a mule, only not so bony; then Linda screamed. 'Oh, don't, don't, don't!' she said. He ran in. There were three women in dark blankets. Linda was on the bed. One of the women was holding her wrists. Another was lying across her legs, so she couldn't kick. The third was hitting her with a whip. Once, twice, three times; and each time Linda screamed.

Prompt C

Write a persuasive letter to the editor on any contemporary topic of special interest. Employ whatever forms of discourse, stylistic devices, and audience- appeal techniques that seem appropriate to the topic.

Section II: Writing and Language Skills

Part A

Each underlined portion of sentences 1–10 contains one or more errors in grammar, usage, mechanics, or sentence structure. Circle the choice that best corrects the error without changing the meaning of the original sentence.

(Easy) (Skill 9.2)

1. There were <u>fewer pieces</u> of evidence presented during the second trial.

   A. Fewer peaces

   B. Less peaces

   C. Less pieces

   D. Fewer pieces

(Average) (Skill 9.4)

2. <u>Mixing the batter for cookies</u>, the cat licked the Crisco from the cookie sheet.

   A. While mixing the batter for cookies

   B. While the batter for cookies was mixing

   C. While I mixed the batter for cookies

   D. While I mixed the cookies

(Average) (Skill 9.4)

3. Mr. Smith <u>respectfully submitted his resignation and had</u> a new job.

   A. Respectfully submitted his resignation and has

   B. Respectfully submitted his resignation before accepting

   C. Respectfully submitted his resignation because of

   D. Respectfully submitted his resignation and had

(Average) (Skill 9.4)

4. The teacher <u>implied</u> from our angry words that there was conflict <u>between you and me</u>.

   A. implied… between you and I

   B. inferred… between you and I

   C. inferred… between you and me

   D. implied… between you and me

(Rigorous) (Skill 9.4)

5. The Taj Mahal <u>has been designated</u> one of the Seven Wonders of the World, and people <u>know it</u> for its unique architecture.

   A. The Taj Mahal has been designated one of the Seven Wonders of the World, and it is known for its unique architecture

   B. People know the Taj Mahal for its unique architecture, and it has been designated one of the Seven Wonders of the World

   C. People have known the Taj Mahal for its unique architecture, and it has been designated of the Seven Wonders of the World

   D. The Taj Mahal has designated itself one of the Seven Wonders of the World

(Rigorous) (Skill 9.4)

6. A teacher <u>must know not only her subject matter but also</u> the strategies of content teaching.

   A. must not only know her subject matter but also the strategies of content teaching

   B. not only must know her subject matter but also the strategies of content teaching

   C. must not know only her subject matter but also the strategies of content teaching

   D. must know not only her subject matter but also the strategies of content teaching

(Rigorous) (Skill 9.4)

7. Walt Whitman was famous for <u>his composition, Leaves of Grass, serving as a nurse during the Civil War, and a devoted son</u>.

   A. *Leaves of Grass*, his service as a nurse during the Civil War, and a devoted son

   B. composing *Leaves of Grass*, serving as a nurse during the Civil War, and being a devoted son

   C. his composition, *Leaves of Grass*, his nursing during the Civil War, and his devotion as a son

   D. his composition, *Leaves of Grass*, serving as a nurse during the Civil War, and a devoted son

(Easy) (Skill 9.5)

8. Joe <u>didn't hardly know</u> his cousin Fred who'd had a rhinoplasty.

   A. Hardly did know his cousin Fred

   B. Didn't know his cousin Fred hardly

   C. Hardly knew his cousin Fred

   D. Didn't know his cousin Fred

(Average) (Skill 9.5)

9. Wally <u>groaned, "Why</u> do I have to do an oral interpretation <u>of "The Raven</u>."

   A. Groaned, "Why… of 'The Raven'?"

   B. Groaned "Why… of "The Raven"?

   C. Groaned ", Why… of "The Raven?"

   D. Groaned, "Why… of "The Raven."

(Rigorous) (Skill 9.5)

10. <u>The coach offered her assistance but the athletes wanted</u> to practice on their own.

    A. The coach offered her assistance, however, the athletes wanted to practice on their own

    B. The coach offered her assistance: furthermore, the athletes wanted to practice on their own

    C. Having offered her assistance, the athletes wanted to practice on their own

    D. The coach offered her assistance; however, the athletes wanted to practice on their own

Part B

Directions: Select the best answer in each group of multiple choices.

(Average) (Skill 1.1)

11. Which is the best definition of free verse, or *vers libre*?

    A. Poetry that consists of an unaccented syllable followed by an unaccented sound

    B. Short lyrical poetry written to entertain but with an instructive purpose

    C. Poetry that does not have a uniform pattern of rhythm

    D. A poem that tells the story and has a plot

(Rigorous) (Skill 1.1)

12. Which sonnet form describes the following?

    My galley charg'd with forgetfulness,
    Through sharp seas, in winter night
        doth pass
    'Tween rock and rock; and eke mine
        enemy, alas,
    That is my lord steereth with cruelness.
    And every oar a thought with readiness,
    As though that death were light in such
        a case.
    An endless wind doth tear the sail apace
    Or forc'ed sighs and trusty fearfulness.
    A rain of tears, a cloud of dark disdain,
    Hath done the wearied cords great
        hinderance,
    Wreathed with error and eke with
        ignorance.
    The stars be hid that led me to this pain
        Drowned is reason that should me
        consort,
        And I remain despairing of the poet

    A. Petrarchan or Italian sonnet

    B. Shakespearian or Elizabethan sonnet

    C. Romantic sonnet

    D. Spenserian sonnet

(Rigorous) (Skill 1.1)

13. Which poem is typified as a villanelle?

    A. "Do not go gentle into that good night"

    B. "Dover Beach"

    C. *Sir Gawain and the Green Knight*

    D. *Pilgrim's Progress*

(Rigorous) (Skill 1.1)

14. Which term best describes the form of the following poetic excerpt?

    And more to lulle him in his slumber
        soft,
    A trickling streake from high rock
        tumbling downe,
    And ever-drizzling raine upon the loft.
    Mixt with a murmuring winde, much
        like a swowne
    No other noyse, nor peoples troubles
        cryes.
    As still we wont t'annoy the walle'd
        towne,
    Might there be heard: but careless Quiet
        lyes,
    Wrapt in eternall silence farre from
        enemyes.

    A. Ballad

    B. Elegy

    C. Spenserian stanza

    D. Ottavo rima

(Rigorous) (Skill 1.1)

15. In classic tragedy, a protagonist's defeat is brought about by a tragic flaw, which is called:

    A. Hubris

    B. Hamartia

    C. Catharsis

    D. The skene

(Rigorous) (Skill 1.1)

16. What is the salient literary feature of this excerpt from an epic?

    Hither the heroes and the nymphs resorts,
    To taste awhile the pleasures of a court;
    In various talk th'instructive hours they passed,
    Who gave the ball, or paid the visit last;
    One speaks the glory of the English Queen,
    And another describes a charming Indian screen;
    A third interprets motion, looks and eyes;
    At every word a reputation dies.

    A. Sprung rhythm

    B. Onomatopoeia

    C. Heroic couplets

    D. Motif

(Easy) (Skill 1.2)

17. A traditional, anonymous story, ostensibly having a historical basis, usually explaining some phenomenon of nature or aspect of creation, defines a/an:

    A. Proverb

    B. Idyll

    C. Myth

    D. Epic

(Easy) (Skill 1.2)

18. Which of the following is not a characteristic of a fable?

    A. Animals that feel and talk like humans

    B. Happy solutions to human dilemmas

    C. Teaches a moral or standard for behavior

    D. Illustrates specific people or groups without directly naming them

(Average) (Skill 1.2)

19. Children's literature became established in the:

    A. Seventeenth century

    B. Eighteenth century

    C. Nineteenth century

    D. Twentieth century

(Average) (Skill 1.2)

20. Latin words that entered the English language during the Elizabethan age include:

    A. Allusion, education, and esteem

    B. Vogue and mustache

    C. Ccanoe and cannibal

    D. Alligator, cocoa, and armadillo

(Easy) (Skill 1.3)

21. Among junior high school students of low-to-average readability levels, which work would most likely stir reading interest?

    A. *Elmer Gantry*, Sinclair Lewis

    B. *Smiley's People*, John Le Carre

    C. *The Outsiders*, S. E. Hinton

    D. *And Then There Were None*, Agatha Christie

(Average) (Skill 1.3)

22. **Most children's literature prior to the development of popular literature was intended to be didactic. Which of the following would not be considered didactic?**

    A. "A Visit from St. Nicholas" by Clement Moore

    B. McGuffy's Reader

    C. Any version of Cinderella

    D. Parables from the Bible

(Easy) (Skill 1.4)

23. **The substitution of "went to his rest" for "died" is an example of a:**

    A. Bowdlerism

    B. Jargon

    C. Euphemism

    D. Malapropism

(Average) (Skill 1.4)

24. **In literature, evoking feelings of pity or compassion is to create:**

    A. Colloquy

    B. Irony

    C. Pathos

    D. Paradox

(Average) (Skill 1.4)

25. **The literary device of personification is used in which example below?**

    A. "Beg me no beggary by soul or parents, whining dog!"

    B. "Happiness sped through the halls cajoling as it went."

    C. "O wind thy horn, thou proud fellow."

    D. "And that one talent which is death to hide."

(Rigorous) (Skill 1.8)

26. **The technique of starting a narrative at a significant point in the action and then developing the story through flashbacks is called**

    A. *In medias res*

    B. Ottavo rima

    C. Irony

    D. Suspension of willing disbelief

(Easy) (Skill 2.1)

27. **The tendency to emphasize and value the qualities and peculiarities of life in a particular geographic area exemplifies:**

    A. Pragmatism

    B. Regionalism

    C. Pantheism

    D. None of the above

(Easy) (Skill 2.1)

28. **Which poet was a major figure in the Harlem Renaissance?**

    A. e. e. cummings

    B. Rita Dove

    C. Margaret Atwood

    D. Langston Hughes

(Average) (Skill 2.1)

29. **Which of the writers below is a renowned African American poet?**

    A. Maya Angelou

    B. Sandra Cisneros

    C. Richard Wilbur

    D. Richard Wright

(Average) (Skill 2.1)

30. **Which of the following titles is known for its scathingly condemning tone?**

    A. Boris Pasternak's *Dr Zhivago*

    B. Albert Camus' *The Stranger*

    C. Henry David Thoreau's "On the Duty of Civil Disobedience"

    D. Benjamin Franklin's "Rules by Which a Great Empire May Be Reduced to a Small One"

(Average) (Skill 2.1)

31. **American colonial writers were primarily:**

    A. Romanticists

    B. Naturalists

    C. Realists

    D. Neoclassicists

(Average) (Skill 2.1)

32. **Which of the following writers did not win a Nobel Prize for literature?**

    A. Gabriel Garcia-Marquez of Colombia

    B. Nadine Gordimer of South Africa

    C. Pablo Neruda of Chile

    D. Alice Walker of the United States

(Rigorous) (Skill 2.1)

33. **What were two major characteristics of the first American literature?**

    A. Vengefulness and arrogance

    B. Bellicosity and derision

    C. Oral delivery and reverence for the land

    D. Maudlin and self-pitying egocentricism

(Average) (Skill 2.4)

34. **Arthur Miller wrote The Crucible as a parallel to what twentieth-century event?**

    A. Sen. McCarthy's House un-American Activities Committee hearing

    B. The Cold War

    C. The fall of the Berlin wall

    D. The Persian Gulf War

(Average) (Skill 2.4)

35. **Which of the following is not a theme of Native American writing?**

    A. Emphasis on the hardiness of the human body and soul

    B. The strength of multicultural assimilation

    C. Contrition for the genocide of native peoples

    D. Remorse for the love of the Indian way of life

(Rigorous) (Skill 2.4)

36. **Mr. Phillips is creating a unit to study *To Kill a Mockingbird* and wants to familiarize his high school freshmen with the attitudes and issues of the historical period. Which activity would familiarize students with the attitudes and issues of the Depression-era South?**

    A. Create a detailed timeline of 15–20 social, cultural, and political events that focus on race relations in the 1930s

    B. Research and report on the life of its author, Harper Lee. Compare her background with the events in the book

    C. Watch the movie version and note language and dress.

    D. Write a research report on the stock market crash of 1929 and its effects.

(Average) (Skill 2.5)

37. **Which of the following definitions best describes a parable?**

    A. A short entertaining account of some happening, usually using talking animals as characters

    B. A slow, sad song or poem, or prose work expressing lamentation

    C. An extensive narrative work expressing universal truths concerning domestic life

    D. A short, simple story of an occurrence of a familiar kind, from which a moral or religious lesson may be drawn

(Rigorous) (Skill 2.5)

38. **Which is not a biblical allusion?**

    A. The patience of Job

    B. Thirty pieces of silver

    C. "Man proposes; God disposes"

    D. "Suffer not yourself to be betrayed by a kiss"

(Easy) (Skill 3.1)

39. **Charles Dickens, Robert Browning, and Robert Louis Stevenson were:**

    A. Victorians

    B. Medievalists

    C. Elizabethans

    D. Absurdists

(Rigorous) (Skill 3.1)

40. **The following lines from Robert Browning's poem "My Last Duchess" come from an example of what form of dramatic literature?**

    That's my last Duchess painted on the wall,
    Looking as if she were alive. I call
    That piece a wonder, now: Frà Pandolf's hands
    Worked busily a day, and there she stands.
    Will 't please you sit and look at her?

    A. Tragedy

    B. Comic opera

    C. Dramatis personae

    D. Dramatic monologue

(Rigorous) (Skill 3.1)

41. **Which author did not write satire?**

    A. Joseph Addison

    B. Richard Steele

    C. Alexander Pope

    D. John Bunyan

(Rigorous) (Skill 3.1)

42. **"Every one must pass through Vanity Fair to get to the celestial city" is an allusion from a:**

    A. Chinese folk tale

    B. Norse saga

    C. British allegory

    D. German fairy tale

(Rigorous) (Skill 3.3)

43. **Which choice below best defines naturalism?**

    A. A belief that the writer or artist should apply scientific objectivity in his/her observation and treatment of life without imposing value judgments

    B. The doctrine that teaches that the existing world is the best to be hoped for

    C. The doctrine that teaches that God is not a personality but that all laws, forces, and manifestations of the universe are God-related

    D. A philosophical doctrine that professes that the truth of all knowledge must always be in question

(Easy) (Skill 4.1)

44. **Considered one of the first feminist plays, this Ibsen drama ends with a door slamming symbolizing the lead character's emancipation from traditional societal norms.**

    A. *The Wild Duck*

    B. *Hedda Gabler*

    C. *Ghosts*

    D. *The Doll's House*

(Average) (Skill 4.1)

45. **The writing of Russian naturalists is:**

    A. Optimistic

    B. Pessimistic

    C. Satirical

    D. Whimsical

(Rigorous) (Skill 4.1)

46. **Which of the following is the best definition of existentialism?**

    A. The philosophical doctrine that matter is the only reality and that everything in the world, including thought, will, and feeling, can be explained only in terms of matter

    B. A philosophy that views things as they should be or as one would wish them to be

    C. A philosophical and literary movement, variously religious and atheistic, stemming from Kierkegaard and represented by Sartre

    D. The belief that all events are determined by fate and are hence inevitable

(Rigorous) (Skill 4.5)

47. **Hoping to take advantage of the popularity of the Harry Potter series, a teacher develops a unit on mythology comparing the story and characters of Greek and Roman myths with the story and characters of the Harry Potter books. Which of these is a commonality that would link classical literature to popular fiction?**

    A. The characters are gods in human form with human-like characteristics

    B. The settings are realistic places in the world where the characters interact as humans would

    C. The themes center on the universal truths of love and hate and fear

    D. The heroes in the stories are young males and only they can overcome the opposing forces

(Average) (Skill 5.1)

48. **Factors that have caused the decline of newspaper readership include which reason below?**

A. People are now relying on the Internet for their news, causing a decline in newspaper advertising

B. Because of environmental concerns and the high cost of paper, people are turning to the radio and television to keep current with the news

C. Many people think newspapers are too biased in their coverage and seek their information from more credible sources

D. Newspaper unions have negotiated tough contracts for their workers, and the profits are being negated by high salaries

(Easy) (Skill 5.2)

49. **What is the main form of discourse in this passage?**

It would have been hard to find a passer-by more wretched in appearance. He was a man of middle height, stout and hardy, in the strength of maturity; he might have been forty-six or seven. A slouched leather cap hid half his face, bronzed by the sun and wind, and dripping with sweat.

A. Description

B. Narration

C. Exposition

D. Persuasion

(Rigorous) (Skill 5.4)

50. **Which aspect of language is innate?**

A. Biological capability to articulate sounds understood by other humans

B. Cognitive ability to create syntactical structures

C. Capacity for using semantics to convey meaning in a social environment

D. Ability to vary inflections and accents

(Rigorous) (Skill 5.6)

51. **For their research paper on the use of technology in the classroom, students have gathered data that shows a sharp increase in the number of online summer classes over the past five years. What would be the best way for them to depict this information visually?**

A. A line chart

B. A table

C. A pie chart

D. A flow chart

(Average) (Skill 6.1)

52. **Written on the sixth grade reading level, most of S. E. Hinton's novels (for instance, *The Outsiders*) have the greatest reader appeal with**

A. Sixth graders

B. Ninth graders

C. Twelfth graders

D. Adults

(Average) (Skill 6.1)

53. Which teaching method would best engage underachievers in the required senior English class?

   A. Assign use of glossary work and extensively footnoted excerpts of great works

   B. Have students take turns reading aloud the anthology selection

   C. Let students choose which readings they'll study and write about

   D. Use a chronologically arranged, traditional text, but also assign group work, panel presentations, and portfolio management

(Average) (Skill 6.1)

54. Which of the following would be the most significant factor in teaching Homer's *Iliad* and *Odyssey* to any particular group of students?

   A. Identifying a translation on the appropriate reading level

   B. Determining the students' interest level

   C. Selecting an appropriate evaluative technique

   D. Determining the scope and delivery methods of background study

(Average) (Skill 6.1)

55. The students in Mrs. Cline's seventh grade language arts class have been invited to attend a performance of *Romeo and Juliet* presented by the drama class at the high school. To best prepare, they should:

   A. Read the play as a homework exercise

   B. Read a synopsis of the plot and a biographical sketch of the author

   C. Examine a few main selections from the play to become familiar with the language and style of the author

   D. Read a condensed version of the story and practice attentive listening skills

(Rigorous) (Skill 6.1)

56. After watching a movie of a train derailment, a child exclaims, "Wow, look how many cars fell off the tracks. There's junk everywhere. The engineer must have really been asleep." Using the facts that the child is impressed by the wreckage and assigns blame to the engineer, a follower of Piaget's theories would estimate the child to be about:

   A. Ten years old

   B. Twelve years old

   C. Fourteen years old

   D. Sixteen years old

(Easy) (Skill 6.2)

57. To understand the origins of a word, one must study its

   A. Synonyms

   B. Inflections

   C. Phonetics

   D. Etymology

(Average) (Skill 6.2)

58. The synonyms "gyro," "hero," and "submarine" reflect which influence on language usage?

   A. Social

   B. Geographical

   C. Historical

   D. Personal

(Rigorous) (Skill 6.2)

59. Which word in the following sentence is a bound morpheme: "The quick brown fox jumped over the lazy dog"?

   A. The

   B. Fox

   C. Lazy

   D. Jumped

(Rigorous) (Skill 6.5)

60. Based on the excerpt below from Kate Chopin's short story "The Story of an Hour," what can students infer about the main character?

She did not stop to ask if it were or were not a monstrous joy that held her. A clear and exalted perception enabled her to dismiss the suggestion as trivial. She knew that she would weep again when she saw the kind, tender hands folded in death; the face that had never looked save with love upon her, fixed and gray and dead. But she saw beyond that bitter moment a long procession of years to come that would belong to her absolutely. And she opened and spread her arms out to them in welcome.

   A. She dreaded her life as a widow

   B. Although she loved her husband, she was glad that he was dead for he had never loved her

   C. She worried that she was too indifferent to her husband's death

   D. Although they had both loved each other, she was beginning to appreciate that opportunities had opened because of his death

(Rigorous) (Skill 6.5)

61. Recognizing empathy in literature is mostly a/an:

   A. Emotional response

   B. Interpretive response

   C. Critical response

   D. Evaluative response

(Average) (Skill 6.7)

62. If a student has a poor vocabulary, the teacher should recommend first that:

    A. The student read newspapers, magazines, and books on a regular basis

    B. The student enroll in a Latin class

    C. The student write the words repetitively after looking them up in the dictionary

    D. The student use a thesaurus to locate synonyms and incorporate them into his or her vocabulary

(Rigorous) (Skill 7.1)

63. Which of the following is not a fallacy in logic?

    A. All students in Ms. Suarez's fourth period class are bilingual.
       Beth is in Ms. Suarez's fourth period.
       Beth is bilingual.

    B. All bilingual students are in Ms. Suarez's class.
       Beth is in Ms. Suarez's fourth period.
       Beth is bilingual.

    C. Beth is bilingual.
       Beth is in Ms. Suarez's fourth period.
       All students in Ms. Suarez's fourth period are bilingual.

    D. If Beth is bilingual, then she speaks Spanish.
       Beth speaks French.
       Beth is not bilingual.

(Average) (Skill 7.2)

64. Which of the following responses to literature typically gives middle school students the most problems?

    A. Interpretive

    B. Evaluative

    C. Critical

    D. Emotional

(Average) (Skill 7.2)

65. Which of the following is not one of the four forms of discourse?

    A. Exposition

    B. Description

    C. Rhetoric

    D. Persuasion

(Rigorous) (Skill 7.2)

66. The arrangement and relationship of words in sentences or sentence structures best describes

    A. Style

    B. Discourse

    C. Thesis

    D. Syntax

(Rigorous) (Skill 7.3)

67. Students have been asked to write a research paper on automobiles and have brainstormed a number of questions they will answer based on their research findings. Which of the following is not an interpretive question to guide research?

    A. Who were the first ten automotive manufacturers in the United States?

    B. What types of vehicles will be used fifty years from now?

    C. How do automobiles manufactured in the United States compare and contrast with each other?

    D. What do you think is the best solution for the fuel shortage?

(Easy) (Skill 7.5)

68. **Which definition is the best for defining diction?**

   A. The specific word choices of an author to create a particular mood or feeling in the reader

   B. Writing that explains something thoroughly

   C. The background, or exposition, for a short story or drama

   D. Word choices that help teach a truth or moral

(Average) (Skill 7.5)

69. **Overcrowded classes prevent the individual attention needed to facilitate language development. This drawback can be best overcome by:**

   A. Dividing the class into independent study groups

   B. Assigning more study time at home

   C. Using more drill practice in class

   D. Team teaching

(Average) (Skill 7.5)

70. **Which event triggered the beginning of Modern English?**

   A. Conquest of England by the Normans in 1066

   B. Introduction of the printing press to the British Isles

   C. Publication of Samuel Johnson's lexicon

   D. American Revolution

(Average) (Skill 7.5)

71. **Which of the following is not true about the English language?**

   A. English is the easiest language to learn

   B. English is the least inflected language

   C. English has the most extensive vocabulary of any language

   D. English originated as a Germanic tongue

(Rigorous) (Skill 7.5)

72. **What was responsible for the standardizing of dialects across America in the twentieth century?**

   A. With the immigrant influx, America became a melting pot of languages and cultures

   B. Trains enabled people to meet other people of different languages and cultures

   C. Radio, and later, television, used actors and announcers who spoke without pronounced dialects

   D. Newspapers and libraries developed programs to teach people to speak English with an agreed-upon common dialect

(Rigorous) (Skill 7.5)

73. **The most significant drawback to applying learning theory research to classroom practice is that**

    A. Today's students do not acquire reading skills with the same alacrity as when greater emphasis was placed on reading classical literature

    B. Development rates are complicated by geographical and cultural factors

    C. Homogeneous grouping has contributed to faster development of some age groups

    D. Social and environmental conditions have contributed to an escalated maturity level than research done twenty or more years ago would seem to indicate

(Easy) (Skill 7.6)

74. **The Elizabethans wrote in:**

    A. Celtic

    B. Old English

    C. Middle English

    D. Modern English

(Average) (Skill 8.1)

75. **To explore the relationship of literature to modern life, which of these activities would not enable students to explore comparable themes?**

    A. After studying various world events, such as the Palestinian-Israeli conflict, students write an updated version of *Romeo and Juliet* using modern characters and settings

    B. Before studying *Romeo and Juliet*, students watch *West Side Story*

    C. Students research the major themes of *Romeo and Juliet* by studying news stories and finding modern counterparts for the story

    D. Students would explore and compare the romantic themes of *Romeo and Juliet* and *The Taming of the Shrew*

(Average) (Skill 8.3)

76. **Which of the following is a formal reading-level assessment?**

    A. A standardized reading test

    B. A teacher-made reading test

    C. An interview

    D. A reading diary

(Rigorous) (Skill 8.4)

77. How will literature help students in a science class be able to understand the following passage?

Just as was the case more than three decades ago, we are still sailing between the Scylla of deferring surgery for too long and risking irreversible left ventricular damage and sudden death, and the Charibdas of operating too early and subjecting the patient to the early risks of operation and the later risks resulting from prosthetic valves.
—E. Braunwald, *European Heart Journal*, July 2000

A. They will recognize the allusion to Scylla and Charibdas from Greek mythology and understand that the medical community has to select one of two unfavorable choices

B. They will recognize the allusion to sailing and understand its analogy to doctors as sailors navigating unknown waters

C. They will recognize that the allusion to Scylla and Charibdas refers to the two islands in Norse mythology where sailors would find themselves shipwrecked and understand how the doctors feel isolated by their choices.

D. They will recognize the metaphor of the heart and relate it to Eros, the character in Greek mythology who represents love. Eros was the love child of Scylla and Charibdas.

(Easy) (Skill 9.2)

78. "Clean as a whistle" or "easy as falling off a log" are examples of:

A. Semantics

B. Parody

C. Irony

D. Cichés

(Average) (Skill 9.3)

79. Many of the clubs in Boca Raton are noted for their _____ elegance.

A. vulgar

B. tasteful

C. ordinary

(Average) (Skill 9.3)

80. When a student is expelled from school, the parents are usually _____ in advance.

A. rewarded

B. congratulated

C. notified

(Average) (Skill 9.3)

81. Before appearing in court, the witness was _____ the papers requiring her to show up.

A. condemned

B. served

C. criticized

(Easy) (Skill 9.3)

82. The <u>expanding</u> number of television channels has <u>prompted</u> cable operators to raise their prices, <u>even though</u> many consumers do not want to pay a higher <u>increased</u> amount for their service.

    A. expanding

    B. prompted

    C. even though

    D. increased

(Average) (Skill 9.3)

83. <u>Considered by many to be</u> one of the worst <u>terrorist</u> incidents <u>on American soil</u> was the bombing of the Oklahoma City Federal Building, which will be remembered <u>for years to come</u>.

    A. Considered by many to be

    B. terrorist

    C. on American soil

    D. for years to come

(Average) (Skill 9.3)

84. The <u>flu</u> epidemic struck <u>most of</u> the <u>respected</u> faculty and students of the Woolbright School, forcing the Boynton Beach School Superintendent to close it down <u>for two weeks</u>.

    A. flu

    B. most of

    C. respected

    D. for two weeks

(Average) (Skill 9.3)

85. Because George's _____ bothering him, he apologized for crashing his father's car.

    A. feelings were

    B. conscience was

    C. guiltiness was

(Rigorous) (Skill 9.3)

86. The charity art auction _____ every year at Mizner Park has a wide selection of artists showcasing their work.

    A. attended

    B. presented

    C. displayed

(Average) (Skill 9.4)

87. Which of the following sentences contains a subject-verb agreement error?

    A. Both mother and her two sisters were married in a triple ceremony

    B. Neither the hen nor the rooster is likely to be served for dinner

    C. My boss, as well as the company's two personnel directors, have been to Spain

    D. Amanda and the twins are late again

(Easy) (Skill 9.5)

88. A punctuation mark indicating omission, interrupted thought, or an incomplete statement is a/an:

A. Ellipsis

B. Anachronism

C. Colloquy

D. Idiom

(Easy) (Skill 9.5)

89. Which of the following sentences is properly punctuated?

A. The more you eat; the more you want

B. The authors—John Steinbeck, Ernest Hemingway, and William Faulkner—are staples of modern writing in American literature textbooks.

C. Handling a wild horse, takes a great deal of skill and patience.

D. The man, who replaced our teacher, is a comedian.

(Average) (Skill 9.5)

90. Which of the following sentences contains a capitalization error?

A. The commander of the English navy was Admiral Nelson

B. Napoleon was the president of the French First Republic

C. Queen Elizabeth II is the Monarch of the British Empire

D. William the Conqueror led the Normans to victory over the British

(Easy) (Skill 10.1)

91. Writing ideas quickly without interruption of the flow of thoughts or attention to conventions is called:

A. Brainstorming

B. Mapping

C. Listing

D. Free writing

(Rigorous) (Skill 10.1)

92. In preparing a report about William Shakespeare, students are asked to develop a set of interpretive questions to guide their research. Which of the following would not be classified as an interpretive question?

A. What would be different today if Shakespeare had not written his plays?

B. How will the plays of Shakespeare affect future generations?

C. How does Shakespeare view nature in A Midsummer's Night Dream and Much Ado About Nothing?

D. During the Elizabethan age, what roles did young boys take in dramatizing Shakespeare's plays?

(Easy) (Skill 10.2)

93. Which of the following should not be included in the opening paragraph of an informative essay?

A. Thesis sentence

B. Details and examples supporting the main idea

C. Broad general introduction to the topic

D. A style and tone that grabs the reader's attention

(Average) (Skill 10.2)

94. **Middle and high school students are more receptive to studying grammar and syntax**

    A. Through worksheets and end- of- lessons practices in textbooks

    B. Through independent homework assignments

    C. Through analytical examination of the writings of famous authors

    D. Through application to their own writing

(Average) (Skill 10.2)

95. **In general, the most serious drawback of using a computer when writing is that**

    A. The copy looks so good that students tend to overlook major mistakes

    B. The spell check and grammar programs discourage students from learning proper spelling and mechanics

    C. The speed with which corrections can be made detracts from the exploration and contemplation of composing

    D. The writer loses focus by concentrating on the final product rather than the details

(Rigorous) (Skill 10.2)

96. **In this paragraph from a student essay, identify the sentence that provides a detail.**

(1) The poem concerns two different personality types and the human relation between them. (2) Their approach to life is totally different. (3) The neighbor is a very conservative person who follows routines. (4) He follows the traditional wisdom of his father and his father's father. (5) The purpose in fixing the wall and keeping their relationship separate is only because it is all he knows.

    A. Sentence 1

    B. Sentence 3

    C. Sentence 4

    D. Sentence 5

(Average) (Skill 11.1)

97. **Which of the following are secondary research materials?**

    A. The conclusions and inferences of other historians

    B. Literature and nonverbal materials, novels, stories, poetry, and essays from the period, as well as coins, archaeological artifacts, and art produced during the period

    C. Interviews and surveys conducted by the researcher

    D. Statistics gathered as the result of the research's experiments

(Rigorous) (Skill 11.2)

98. For their research paper on the effects of the Civil War on American literature, students have brainstormed a list of potential online sources and are seeking your authorization. Which of these represents the strongest source?

   A. *http://www.wikipedia.org/*

   B. *http://www.google.com*

   C. *http://www.nytimes.com*

   D. *http://docsouth.unc.edu /southlit/civil-war.html*

(Easy) (Skill 11.3)

99. In preparing your high school freshmen to write a research paper about a social problem, what recommendation can you make so they can determine the credibility of their information?

   A. Assure them that information on the Internet has been peer reviewed and verified for accuracy

   B. Find one solid source and use that exclusively

   C. Use only primary sources

   D. Cross-check your information with other credible sources

(Rigorous) (Skill 11.4)

100. To determine the credibility of information, researchers should do all of the following except

   A. Establish the authority of the document

   B. Disregard documents with bias

   C. Evaluate the currency and reputation of the source

   D. Use a variety of research sources and methods

(Rigorous) (Skill 11.6)

101. Which of the following situations is not an ethical violation of intellectual property?

   A. A student visits ten different Web sites and writes a report to compare the costs of downloading music. He uses the names of the Web sites without their permission.

   B. A student copies and pastes a chart verbatim from the Internet but does not document it because it is available on a public site.

   C. From an online article found in a subscription database, a student paraphrases a section on the problems of music piracy. She includes the source in her Works Cited but does not provide an in-text citation.

   D. A student uses a comment from M. Night Shyamalan without attribution, claiming the information is common knowledge.

(Average) (Skill 12.1)

102. Modeling is a practice that requires students to:

   A. Create a style unique to their own language capabilities

   B. Emulate the writing of professionals

   C. Paraphrase passages from good literature

   D. Peer evaluate the writings of other students

(Average) (Skill 12.2)

103. The English department is developing strategies to encourage all students to become a community of readers. From the list of suggestions below, which would be the least effective way for teachers to foster independent reading?

A. Each teacher sets aside a weekly, 30-minute, in-class reading session during which the teacher and students read a magazine or book for enjoyment

B. The teacher and the students develop a list of favorite books to share with each other

C. The teacher assigns at least one book report each grading period to ensure that students are reading from the established class list

D. The students gather books for a classroom library so that books can be shared with each other

(Easy) (Skill 12.3)

104. The following passage is written from which point of view?

As she mused the pitiful vision of her mother's life laid its spell on the very quick of her being—that life of commonplace sacrifices closing in final craziness. She trembled as she heard again her mother's voice saying constantly with foolish insistence: Dearevaun Seraun! Dearevaun Seraun!*

* "The end of pleasure is pain!" (Gaelic)

A. First-person narrator

B. Second-person direct address

C. Third-person omniscient

D. First-person omniscient

(Rigorous) (Skill 12.3)

105. For students to prepare for a their roles in a dramatic performance:

A. They should analyze their characters to develop a deeper understanding of the character's attitudes and motivations

B. They should attend local plays to study settings and stage design

C. They should read articles and books on acting methodology

D. They should practice the way other actors have performed in these roles

(Average) (Skill 12.4)

106. Which of the following is the least effective procedure for promoting consciousness of audience?

A. Pairing students during the writing process

B. Reading all rough drafts before the students write the final copies

C. Having students compose stories or articles for publication in school literary magazines or newspapers

D. Having students write letters to friends or relatives

(Average) (Skill 12.6)

107. The new teaching intern is developing a unit on creative writing and is trying to encourage her freshman high school students to write poetry. Which of the following would not be an effective technique?

   A. In groups, students draw pictures to illustrate "The Love Song of J. Alfred Prufrock" by T.S. Eliot

   B. Either individually or in groups, students compose a song, writing lyrics that try to use poetic devices

   C. Students bring to class the lyrics of a popular song and discuss the imagery and figurative language

   D. Students read aloud their favorite poems and share their opinions of and responses to the poems

(Easy) (Skill 13.1)

108. Which of the following is most true of expository writing?

   A. It is mutually exclusive of other forms of discourse

   B. It can incorporate other forms of discourse in the process of providing supporting details

   C. It should never employ informal expression

   D. It should only be scored with a summative evaluation

(Average) (Skill 13.1)

109. Explanatory or informative discourse is):

   A. Exposition

   B. Narration

   C. Persuasion

   D. Description

(Rigorous) (Skill 13.1)

110. Which of the following is an example of the post hoc fallacy?

   A. When the new principal was hired, student reading scores improved; therefore, the principal caused the increase in scores

   B. Why are we spending money on the space program when our students don't have current textbooks?

   C. You can't give your class a 10-minute break. Once you do that, we'll all have to give our students a 10-minute break

   D. You can never believe anything he says because he's not from the same country as we are

(Easy) (Skill 13.3)

111. In the paragraph below, which sentence does not contribute to the overall task of supporting the main idea?

   (1) The Springfield City Council met Friday to discuss new zoning restrictions for the land to be developed south of the city. (2) Residents who opposed the new restrictions were granted 15 minutes to present their case. (3) Their argument focused on the dangers that increased traffic would bring to the area. (4) It seemed to me that the Mayor Simpson listened intently. (5) The council agreed to table the new zoning until studies would be performed.

   A. Sentence 2

   B. Sentence 3

   C. Sentence 4

   D. Sentence 5

(Average) (Skill 13.4)

112. Which transition word would show contrast to these two ideas?

We are confident in our skills to teach English. We welcome new ideas on this subject.

A. We are confident in our skills to teach English, and we welcome new ideas on this subject

B. Because we are confident in our skills to teach English, we welcome new ideas on the subject

C. When we are confident in our skills to teach English, we welcome new ideas on the subject

D. We are confident in our skills to teach English; however, we welcome new ideas on the subject

(Rigorous) (Skill 13.6)

113. What syntactic device is most evident from Abraham Lincoln's "Gettysburg Address"?

It is rather for us to be here dedicated to the great task remaining before us —that from these honored dead we take increased devotion to that cause for which they gave the last full measure of devotion—that we here highly resolve that these dead shall not have died in vain—that this nation, under God, shall have a new birth of freedom—and that government of the people, by the people, for the people, shall not perish from the earth.

A. Affective connotation

B. Informative denotations

C. Allusion

D. Parallelism

(Skill 14.4) (Rigorous)

114. Identify the type of appeal used by Molly Ivins in this excerpt from her essay "Get a Knife, Get a Dog, But Get Rid of Guns."

As a civil libertarian, I, of course, support the Second Amendment. And I believe it means exactly what it says: A well-regulated militia being necessary to the security of a free state, the right of the people to keep and bear arms shall not be infringed.

A. Ethical

B. Emotional

C. Rational

D. Literary

(Rigorous) (Skill 14.5)

115. What type of reasoning does Henry David Thoreau use in the following excerpt from "Civil Disobedience"?

Unjust laws exist; shall we be content to obey them, or shall we endeavor to amend them, and obey them until we have succeeded, or shall we transgress them at once? Men generally, under such a government as this, think that they ought to wait until they have persuaded the majority to alter them. They think that, if they should resist, the remedy would be worse than the evil. But it is the fault of the government itself that the remedy is worse than the evil. … Why does it always crucify Christ, and excommunicate Copernicus and Luther, and pronounce Washington and Franklin rebels?

A. Ethical reasoning

B. Inductive reasoning

C. Deductive reasoning

D. Intellectual reasoning

(Average) (Skill 15.1)

116. Which of the following is a characteristic of blank verse?

A. Meter in iambic pentameter

B. Clearly specified rhyme scheme

C. Lack of figurative language

D. Unspecified rhythm

(Average) (Skill 15.1)

117. Which is an untrue statement about a theme in literature?

A. The theme is always stated directly somewhere in the text

B. The theme is the central idea in a literary work

C. All parts of the work (plot, setting, mood) should contribute to the theme in some way

D. By analyzing the various elements of the work, the reader should be able to arrive at an indirectly stated theme

(Average) (Skill 15.1)

118. In the following quotation, addressing the dead body of Caesar as though he were still a living being is to employ an:

O, pardon me, though
Bleeding piece of earth
That I am meek and gentle with
These butchers.
　　—Marc Antony, *Julius Caesar*

A. Apostrophe.

B. Allusion.

C. Antithesis.

D. Anachronism.

(Rigorous) (Skill 15.1)

119. In the sentence "The Cabinet conferred with the president," "Cabinet" is an example of a/an:

A. Metonym

B. Synecdoche

C. Metaphor

D. Allusion

(Easy) (Skill 15.4)

120. In "inverted triangle" introductory paragraphs, the thesis sentence occurs:

   A. At the beginning of the paragraph

   B. In the middle of the paragraph

   C. At the end of the paragraph

   D. In the second paragraph

(Average) (Skill 15.4)

121. If a student uses slang and expletives, what is the best course of action to take to improve the student's formal communication skills?

   A. Ask the student to paraphrase his writing—that is, to translate it into language appropriate for the school principal to read

   B. Refuse to read the student's papers until he conforms to a more literate style

   C. Ask the student to read his work aloud to the class for peer evaluation

   D. Rewrite the flagrant passages to show the student the right form of expression

(Rigorous) (Skill 15.4)

122. Which sentence below best minimizes the impact of bad news?

   A. We have denied you permission to attend the event

   B. Although permission to attend the event cannot be given, you are encouraged to buy the video

   C. Although you cannot attend the event, we encourage you to buy the video

   D. Although attending the event is not possible, watching the video is an option

(Average) (Skill 16.1)

123. What is the best course of action when a child refuses to complete a reading/literature assignment on the grounds that it is morally objectionable?

   A. Speak with the parents and explain the necessity of studying this work

   B. Encourage the child to sample some of the text before making a judgment

   C. Place the child in another teacher's class where they are studying an acceptable work

   D. Provide the student with alternative selections that cover the same performance standards that the rest of the class is learning

(Average) (Skill 16.1)

124. Oral debate is most closely associated with which form of discourse?

   A. Description

   B. Exposition

   C. Narration

   D. Persuasion

(Rigorous) (Skill 16.1)

125. Which of the following types of question will not stimulate higher-level critical thinking?

   A. A hypothetical question

   B. An open-ended question

   C. A close-ended question

   D. A judgment question

(Rigorous) (Skill 16.1)

126. In preparing a speech for a contest, your student has encountered problems with gender- specific language. Not wishing to offend either women or men, she seeks your guidance. Which of the following is not an effective strategy?

    A. Use the generic "he" and explain that people will understand and accept the male pronoun as all-inclusive

    B. Switch to plural nouns and use "they" as the gender-neutral pronoun

    C. Use passive voice so that the subject is not required

    D. Use male pronouns for one part of the speech, and then use female pronouns for the other part of the speech

(Average) (Skill 16.4)

127. In preparing students for their oral presentations, the instructor provided all of these guidelines, except one. Which is not an effective guideline?

    A. Even if you are using a lectern, feel free to move about; this will connect you to the audience

    B. Your posture should be natural, not stiff; keep your shoulders toward the audience

    C. Gestures can help communicate as long as you don't overuse them or make them distracting

    D. You can avoid eye contact if you focus on your notes; this will make you appear more knowledgeable

(Rigorous) (Skill 16.5)

128. Mr. Ledbetter has instructed his students to prepare a slide presentation that illustrates an event in history. Students are to include pictures, graphics, media clips, and links to resources. What competencies will students exhibit at the completion of this project?

    A. Analyzing the impact of society on media

    B. Recognizing the media's strategies to inform and persuade

    C. Demonstrating strategies and creative techniques to prepare presentations using a variety of media

    D. Identifying the aesthetic effects of a media presentation

(Rigorous) (Skill 16.5)

129. In a class of nonnative speakers of English, which type of activity will help students the most?

    A. Have students make oral presentations so that they can develop a phonological awareness of sounds

    B. Provide students more writing opportunities to develop their written communication skills

    C. Encourage students to listen to the new language on television and radio

    D. Provide a variety of methods to develop speaking, writing, and reading skills

(Rigorous) (Skill 17.1)

130. What is the common advertising technique used by these advertising slogans?

"It's everywhere you want to be."
                    —Visa

"Have it your way."
  —Burger King

"When you care enough to send the very best."   —Hallmark

"Be all you can be."
  —U.S. Army

A. Peer approval

B. Rebel

C. Individuality

D. Escape

(Easy) (Skill 17.2)

131. What is not a characteristic of an effective editorial cartoon?

A. It presents a message or point of view concerning people, events, or situations using caricature and symbolism to convey the cartoonist's ideas

B. It has wit and humor, which is usually obtained by exaggeration that is slick and not used merely for comic effect

C. It has a foundation in truth; that is, the characters must be recognizable to the viewer, and the point of the drawing must have some basis in fact even if it has a philosophical bias

D. It seeks to reflect the editorial opinion of the newspaper that carries it

(Rigorous) (Skill 17.6)

132. In presenting a report to peers about the effects of Hurricane Katrina on New Orleans, the students wanted to use various media in their argument to persuade their peers that more needed to be done. Which of these would be the most effective?

A. A PowerPoint presentation showing the blueprints of the levees before the flood and redesigned now for current construction

B. A collection of music clips made by the street performers in the French Quarter before and after the flood

C. A recent video showing the areas devastated by the floods and the current state of rebuilding

D. A collection of recordings of interviews made by the various government officials and local citizens affected by the flooding

(Rigorous) (Skill 17.7)

133. Which part of a classical argument is illustrated in this excerpt from Caryl River's essay "What Should Be Done About Rock Lyrics?"

But violence against women is greeted by silence. It shouldn't be. This does not mean censorship, or book (or record) burning. In a society that protects free expression, we understand a lot of stuff will float up out of the sewer. Usually, we recognize the ugly stuff that advocates violence against any group as the garbage it is, and we consider its purveyors as moral lepers. We hold our nose and tolerate it, but we speak out against the values it proffers.

A. Narration

B. Confirmation

C. Refutation and concession

D. Summation

ANSWER KEY

1. D	16. C	31. D	46. C	61. C	76. A	91. D	106. B	121. A
2. C	17. C	32.D	47. C	62. A	77. A	92. D	107. A	122. B
3. C	18. D	33. D	48. A	63. A	78. D	93. B	108. B	123. D
4. C	19. A	34. A	49. A	64. B	79. B	94. D	109. A	124. D
5. A	20. A	35. B	50. A	65. C	80. C	95. C	110. A	125. C
6. D	21. C	36. A	51. A	66. D	81. B	96. C	111. C	126. A
7. B	22. A	37. D	52. B	67. A	82. D	97. A	112. D	127. D
8. C	23. C	38. C	53. C	68. A	83. A	98. D	113. D	128. B
9. A	24. C	39. A	54. A	69. A	84. C	99. D	114. A	129. A
10. D	25. B	40. D	55. D	70. B	85. B	100. B	115. C	130. C
11. C	26. A	41. D	56. A	71. A	86. B	101. A	116. A	131. D
12. A	27. B	42. C	57. D	72. C	87. C	102. B	117. A	132. C
13. A	28. D	43. A	58. B	73. D	88. A	103. C	118. A	133. C
14. D	29. A	44. D	59. D	74. D	89. B	104. C	119. B	
15. B	30. D	45. B	60. D	75. D	90. C	105. A	120. C	

RIGOR TABLE

Rigor level	Questions
Easy 20%	1, 8, 17, 18, 21, 27, 28, 39, 44, 49, 57, 68, 74, 78, 82, 88, 89, 91, 93, 99, 104, 108, 111, 120, 131
Average Rigor 40%	2, 3, 4, 9, 11, 19, 20, 22, 23, 24, 25, 29, 30, 31, 32, 33, 34, 35, 37, 45, 48, 52, 53, 54, 55, 58, 62, 64, 65, 69, 70, 71, 75, 76, 79, 80, 81, 83, 84, 85, 87, 90, 94, 95, 97, 102, 103, 106, 107, 109, 112, 116, 117, 118, 121, 123, 124, 127
Rigorous 40%	5, 6, 7, 10, 12, 13, 14, 15, 16, 26, 36, 38, 40, 41, 42, 43, 46, 47, 50, 51, 56, 59, 60, 61, 63, 66, 67, 72, 73, 77, 86, 92, 96, 98, 100, 101, 105, 110, 113, 114, 115, 119, 122, 125, 126, 128, 129, 130, 132, 133